Table of Contents

Dedication 1

Cultural and Healing Acknowledgement 3

Preface 5

Chapter One 7

Chapter Two 9

Chapter Three 13

Chapter Four 27

Chapter Five 47

Chapter Six 63

Chapter Seven 75

Chapter Eight 93

Chapter Nine 111

Chapter Ten 121

Chapter Eleven 143

Chapter Twelve 155

Chapter Thirteen 163

Chapter Fourteen 181

Chapter Fifteen 197

Chapter Sixteen 215

Chapter Seventeen	227
Chapter Eighteen	239
Chapter Nineteen	275
Chapter Twenty	291
Chapter Twenty-One	299
Epilogue: The Laws of HOPE	309
Author's Note	317
Acknowledgements	319
About the Author	321
Final Blessing	323
Resources & Sources	325
APPENDIX	333
WiSH-to-HEAL	341
Somatic Wheel Practices	351
Group Application Guide	353
Quick Start Guide	355
Healing Rhythms	357
Vibrational Nourishment	363
Vibrational Living	369
Energy & Clarity	373
Nourishing The Vessel	377

Supplement Reference Guide 381

Crystals 387

Pineal Clarity 391

Companion Chapter Journal 401

Closing Reflection 433

Closing affirmation 435

The HOPE Method

The Lie About HOPE Uncovered

Reclaim Your Sovereignty

Sharon Lea

Copyright © 2025 by Sharon Lea

All rights reserved. No part of this book may be reproduced in any form or by any means, electronic or mechanical, including photocopying, recording, or by any information storage and retrieval system, without prior written permission from the author, except for brief quotations in reviews or critical articles.

ISBN: 979-8-9991767-4-5 (Paperback, Revised Edition)

Revised Edition: November 21, 2025

This book is a work of nonfiction. The author has made every effort to ensure the accuracy of the information presented. It is intended for educational and inspirational purposes only and should not be considered medical, legal, therapeutic, or financial advice.

For author information, events, and additional resources, please visit:

www.wildsoulhope-authorpage.com

Publisher: Wild Soul HOPE™

HOPE & Honey™ and SoulHOPE™ and The HOPE Method™ are trademarks of Wild Soul HOPE, LLC.

Printed in the United States of America.

Cover & Interior Design: Sharon Lea

Photography: Sharon Lea (Flower Garden)

The cover of The HOPE Method carries its own story. The faded charcoal-to-gray background reflects the passage from heaviness into clarity, the still point between shadow and light. From that quiet ground rises the Prince of Orange heirloom oriental poppy, photographed from my own garden. Orange, the color of vitality and renewal, blooms against gray's neutrality — a reminder that creativity, passion, and hope can emerge even from the most uncertain soil.

Dedication

For the ones healing quietly, fiercely, without applause. For the souls who keep choosing light even in the darkest hours. For my children, who taught me love, grace, and motherhood. For the daughter, whose spirit walks beside mine in every chapter. This work, this light, is for you. For those told they were too sensitive, too much, or not enough. For the souls who carry sorrow in their bones yet still dare to shine.

For My Divine Goddess Within me: the one who waited patiently through years of doing, fixing, striving, surviving. You who whispered beneath the noise, who held the knowing while I walked in sacred masculine strength. You now teach me to walk alongside My Inner Child with a wonder lust wild-hearted, wide-eyed, tender with wonder. Keeper of my light, thank you for never giving up on me, for believing in magic even when I forgot. This is our homecoming. I would be nothing without my spirit team.

And for My Honey Bear King: whose steady kindness and quiet belief keep me grounded. You are the unseen strength behind my steps, the one who makes space for my healing and holds me safe as I walk this path. I am the healer, and you are the protector as a presence both grounded and timeless. Together, we are proof that connection can be both sanctuary and fire.

Cultural and Healing Acknowledgement

Throughout this book, I reference practices such as chakras, breathwork, meditation, and Akashic perspectives. These teachings come from diverse and ancient traditions, each carrying deep cultural roots. I offer them here with respect and gratitude.

While the HOPE Method is a modern framework, it is interwoven with timeless threads of human experience. I encourage you to adopt these practices in ways that honor your own background or belief system.

The heart of HOPE is universal: remembering your own light, reclaiming your energy, and walking a path of healing that honors both individuality and shared humanity. Healing is never linear — it is cyclical, layered, and deeply personal.

The practices and reflections in this book are tools for growth and exploration, not substitutes for professional medical or psychological care. If you are experiencing severe or persistent symptoms of trauma, grief, or mental illness, please seek support from a qualified healthcare provider.

Your story, your body, and your healing deserve compassion and safety. May you move through these pages at a pace that feels right for you, carrying forward only what nourishes your soul.

Preface

There comes a moment when surviving your daily life is no longer enough. When the ache of just making it through another day collides with the longing for the life you really want. When surviving feels like both a victory and a loss. When your soul feels as if it is about to fracture under the weight of its own stories. It was in that fractured moment, in that growing coalescence of ache and longing; where I began to realize survival was not enough. I needed more than borrowed words, more than gratitude lists or affirmation statements, more than vision boards and goal graphs. I needed a structured map.

I spent years searching for answers in other people's words, waiting for the spark that would show me how to climb out of the shadows. Many voices inspired me, many tools brought comfort; but what I whole-heartedly longed for was a compass. A way to move, step by step, from the weight in my chest to the resonance of a life fully lived.

That's where the HOPE Method was actualized. HOPE stands for Harness Optimal Positive Energy which becomes more than a phrase. It is a compass, a way of gathering scattered fragmented energy by unlocking the stuck, hidden parts that hold us back from our true self. It is about choosing what truly serves your soul, embodying positivity that is not fake or forced, and learning to live in alignment with your deepest truth.

And because life is not just about light, the WiSH-to-HEAL cadence grew to become a living practice. This cadence offers practices for wisdom, serenity, and heart; teaching you to hold your shadow with compassion until it can begin its own healing. Through expression, the shadow becomes a doorway to acceptance and ultimately resonates with self-love and sovereignty.

This book is part of that remembering. A weaving of timeless wisdom with real, everyday struggles. It is not about becoming perfect. It is about becoming whole. It is about learning to laugh again, to cry without shame, to find joy in small places, and to trust your own resonance.

So, if you have ever felt "too much" or "not enough," if you have ever wished life came with a manual, or if you have ever wondered whether the light inside you is still alive — this book is for you.

My gift to you is simple: that the pages of this compass of HOPE will be both lantern and map as you take your next step home to yourself.

Chapter One

Everything You Think You Know About HOPE Is Wrong

Most people hear the word hope and think of something soft. A wish. A whisper. A prayer you say when you feel powerless. Hope, in its common use, has been reduced to fragile optimism — something you cling to when you've run out of options.

And in the world of manifestation, it's often treated as unnecessary, even weak, low vibration. You'll hear teachers tell you to focus only on belief, visualization, or vibration. They skip over hope as if it's a steppingstone you can toss aside once you've built enough faith.

But here's the truth: without HOPE, manifestation has no foundation, dreams have no anchor, and life loses meaning.

Try to build your future without it, and it's like standing on quicksand — the structure cannot hold. Belief without hope collapses into delusion. Vision without hope fades into fantasy. Action without hope burns out before it bears fruit.

Everything you think you know about HOPE is wrong. HOPE is not passive. It is not wishful thinking or a beginner's crutch. HOPE is the ground under your feet. The force that steadies you when the storm rages. The current that keeps your energy from scattering before you can ever align it.

HOPE is not fragile. It is ferocious. And it is the foundation every manifestation teacher forgot to mention.

The HOPE Method — Harness Optimal Positive Energy — is not about pretending life is good when it isn't. It is about reclaiming your scattered energy, choosing what aligns with your soul instead of what is merely familiar, redefining positivity as something authentic and embodied, and learning to live in the vibrational truth of your own light.

It is not manifestation in the way you've been taught. It is transformation in the way you've been longing for.

This book is not about lofty concepts. It is about daily rhythms, nervous system awareness, and energy practices that root themselves in both ancient wisdom and modern science. It is about becoming whole — not by skipping your pain, but by transmuting it into strength.

If HOPE is not what you thought, then what is it really? To answer that, we must first expose the hidden problem that no one else is talking about.

And once you see it, you will never see stress, self-help, or healing the same way again.

Chapter Two

The Hidden Problem No One Is Talking About

If the wellness industry has taught you anything, it's this: think positively, manage your stress, manifest your dreams, and you'll be fine. But here's the hidden problem: those approaches ignore the very thing that keeps most people stuck. They don't address fragmentation. We discovered the very same issue in the diet industry. Calories in equals calories out, no longer applies unless – you identify and clear your fragmentation. While you must create a calorie deficit to see change, in order to maintain that constant deficit you must also clear the fragmentations that block you and prevent lasting change.

Fragmentation is what happens when your nervous system experiences more than it can process. It's not just what happened to you — it's what happened inside you. It's the way your body stored the scream you couldn't let out, the flight you couldn't take, the grief you weren't allowed to express.

And statistics confirm this isn't just "in your head":

> According to the CDC, over 60% of adults report experiencing at least one adverse childhood experience (ACE), with many reporting more than one.

> The American Psychological Association reports that 77% of adults regularly experience physical symptoms caused by stress.

The World Health Organization has identified stress as the "health epidemic of the 21st century," linking it to heart disease, diabetes, depression, and premature death.

Studies in polyvagal theory show that chronic stress literally rewires your nervous system to live in survival mode — making it harder to feel safe, joyful, or whole.

What the self-help industry often misses is that you can't just "think positive" when your body is still carrying the imprint of trauma, grief, loss, or burnout. You can't manifest your dream life if your nervous system doesn't yet believe you are safe. You can't meditate your way to peace if your body still flinches at the memory of being silenced.

This is the hidden problem: most self-help models stop at the surface. They address thoughts but not the body. They focus on goals but not on nervous system regulation. They ask you to "raise your vibration" without teaching you how to release the energy that's weighing you down.

Fragmentation is the quiet epidemic beneath stress, burnout, and anxiety. And unless you heal fragmentation, no amount of affirmations, reformed habits, or productivity hacks will bring lasting peace.

The HOPE Method is different because it begins here: at the place where body, mind, and spirit fractured. It gives you a way to call your energy back home, step by step, until wholeness is no longer a concept but a lived experience.

The problem isn't that you've failed. The problem is that you were never taught how to heal that fragmentation. Until now.

And if fragmentation is the hidden wound, what does healing look like? That is where the HOPE Method begins.

Chapter Three

When Energy Becomes Remembering

You've been told that healing takes years of therapy, that trauma leaves permanent scars, and that self-help only works if you try harder. You've been taught to think positive, journal it out, manifest it away. But here is the truth: none of that is enough.

You cannot think your way out of a nervous system stuck in survival. You cannot "just get over it" or manifest peace while your body still trembles from grief. You cannot meditate yourself whole when fragmentation keeps pulling you apart. Healing is not about force. It is about rhythm. And this is where HOPE changes everything.

There comes a moment, often subtle, often quiet, when we realize we are not merely tired but deeply disconnected. Disconnected from joy, from clarity, from vitality, and sometimes, from the self entirely. It's not always caused by catastrophes. Often, it is the slow erosion of our wholeness through small betrayals: the silencing of our voice to keep the peace, the dismissal of our needs to meet others' expectations, the constant override of intuition in exchange for approval.

Over time, these quiet ruptures begin to fragment us. The body tenses. The fascia constricts. The heart dulls. The mind numbs. The spirit flickers. Inflammation ignites. And sometimes life itself stops feeling real as if we're living in a simulation. We scroll, perform, produce day after day, but inside we feel hollow, drifting, as though we've stepped outside our own existence. This, too, is disconnection from our intuition and gut instinct. It makes us forget not only how to feel like ourselves but also prevents us from living in the higher energetic vibration that was always ours.

This book is an invitation to remember. Not through performance or perfection, but through presence. Through a reclamation of energy not just physical stamina, but the deeper, primordial kind. The very spark of light that was given to you at conception. The energy that once flowed freely through your body, your breath, your being. The energy that fuels your creativity, your clarity, your capacity to love and be loved. The energy that grief cannot steal, trauma cannot destroy, and disconnection cannot erase. It may be dimmed, but it is never gone. It waits for you to return.

The HOPE Method™ — Harness Optimal Positive Energy — was realized not from ideology, but from lived experience and sacred inquiry. It is not doctrine or dogma. It is a path of restoration. A way of returning to the self through breath, movement, truth-telling, silence, and sacred action. You will not find here a quick fix or a shallow promise. What you will find are teachings rooted in ancient wisdom, trauma-informed science, and soul-centered living. This book will offer you tools, practices, and perspectives that help you remember what is already within you.

Why HOPE?

I DIDN'T DISCOVER HOPE in a classroom or a seminar. I discovered it in the mess — in the night's grief that took me to the floor, in the burnout that hollowed my body, in the caregiving that drained me dry, in the shame that told me I was too broken to change.

It was in those places, when I had nothing left to hold onto, that a pattern began to emerge. A rhythm. A way of calling my scattered energy back, of choosing what nourished me instead of what drained me, of finding real joy in the middle of pain, of learning to live as energy instead of exhaustion.

I named that rhythm the HOPE Method: Harness Optimal Positive Energy.

We live in a world that rewards productivity but forgets vitality. We are taught to chase goals but rarely taught how to harness our own energy, whether it be to protect it, restore it, or trust it. Most healing methods treat body, mind, and spirit as separate parts. The HOPE Method sees them as partners that are woven together into one path of remembering.

This method was created for those who feel the gap between what they know and what they embody. For those who have "done the work" but still feel disoriented. HOPE is not a map toward perfection, but toward wholeness. Toward home.

Along the way, you will see me name many forms of pain — trauma, grief, loss, abuse, burnout, spiritual repression, self-abandonment. Though the circumstances differ, their impact often feels the same: fragmentation. By fragmentation, I mean that split from yourself — the scattering of thought, the heaviness in your body, the dulling of your spirit. Naming it this way allows us to honor the many shapes pain takes without losing sight of the deeper truth: no matter what caused the break, the path of remembering brings you back to wholeness.

HOPE is practical as well as soulful. It can be used as a daily rhythm, a seasonal realignment, or a deep-dive recovery path. HOPE's four pillars: Harness, Optimal, Positive, Energy are explored through teachings, somatic practices, and reflective tools. Whether you are brand new to healing or have been walking this path for decades, HOPE is designed to meet you in motion. It adapts to you because you are dynamic.

Throughout, you will be invited to pause and write. I call these moments Soul Scribbles, because they are not about polished journaling, but about giving your soul a voice. Your scribbles might be doodles, messy words, random thoughts, raw experiences, or unfiltered truth. Each time you scribble, you step out of performance and back into presence. That is how remembering takes root: not only in thought, but in lived expression.

And let me clear something before we go further: hope is not a weak word. Some have dismissed it as waiting instead of acting, wishing instead of creating. Even in spiritual circles, it has been labeled as "low vibration." That dismissal is its own kind of fragmentation — the same way a parent, teacher, or culture once shamed you into silence.

The truth is this: HOPE is the reason people survive the most deplorable conditions. It is the reason a refugee carries a child across oceans, a grieving mother plants flowers in spring, a patient endures one more round of treatment. **HOPE is not passive. It is grit. It is resilient.** It is the lifeline that whispers: keep going as there is something worth reaching for on the other side.

HOPE is not the opposite of manifestation. It is its foundation. It is the compass that sets direction, the fuel that turns vision into movement. To hope is to begin. To hope is to declare your story is not finished. To hope is to plant the seed of self-awareness, the root of self-love, and the path toward self-actualization.

This is why HOPE is not just a word in this book. It is the Universal Law in the making through a Method itself: Harnessing Optimal Positive Energy. It is the foundation of every practice, every chapter, and every step back to yourself.

How HOPE Is Used Today

HOPE IS NOT JUST FOR meditation cushions and moon circles (though you're welcome to use it there too). It's used in the car when you're gripping the steering wheel trying not to scream. It is used in the grocery store aisle when the overstimulation hits and your body starts buzzing. It is used on the bathroom floor when grief knocks you sideways, it is used when you overcome yet another trigger of your abuse, as well as in the garden when the light hits exactly right and you remember what joy feels like again. HOPE is used by trauma survivors to reclaim their breath, by parents resetting after being touched out, by former perfectionists learning to rest, and by everyday people remembering how to feel alive.

One teacher used HOPE brushing techniques in the morning not because she was trying to be "spiritual," but because she needed something more effective than caffeine. A business leader discovered that tapping on his collarbone before meetings steadied his nerves better than any podcast ever did. A nurse kept a stone in her pocket and traced its edges whenever the hospital hallways grew too heavy, reminding her to breathe. Sometimes HOPE looks mystical. Other times, it looks like swearing softly, lighting a candle, and choosing not to text your ex. That counts too.

Think of HOPE as a kind of daily energy hygiene and not just for the body, but for the mind and soul as well. Just as we brush our teeth or wash our hands to stay well, we can also tend to our energy, emotions, and spirit. HOPE becomes a rhythm of inner care that keeps you from drifting back into fragmentation. It is practical enough to use in the car on a stressful morning, yet profound enough to restore the light in your soul. Over time, HOPE feels less like a practice you have to remember and more like a way of living: a mind, body, and soul hygiene that keeps you connected, resilient, and whole.

Beneath this simple hygiene is a deeper music, I call the Law of HOPE that evolved into a song the universe hums when we align with healing. In this law, what you Harness gathers and coheres; what is Optimal aligns and multiplies; the Positive you allow opens flow; the Energy you embody radiates and returns. Practice becomes principle. Rhythm becomes resonance. Private choices tune your field, and your field quietly blesses the world.

In order to shape this living law into something walkable, the letters arrange themselves into a framework that you can hold in your hands and in your heart. They are simple enough for hard mornings, sturdy enough for holy ones, and soft enough for healing hearts.

The Compass and the Rhythm of HOPE

HOPE ITSELF — HARNESS, Optimal, Positive, Energy — is the compass. It orients you to the truth that your energy can be reclaimed, aligned, and elevated. It shows you what direction wholeness lives in.

WiSH-to-HEAL is the rhythm under your feet. Wisdom, Serenity, Heart, Healing, Expression, Acceptance, Love. It is the daily cadence that carries you forward.

Together, they work like maps and footsteps — one shows you where to go, the other makes sure you actually get there.

Maybe you've tried positive affirmations, but they collapsed under the weight of your anxiety.

Maybe you've journaled, but the same old patterns still keep circling back.

Maybe you've meditated, but your body still jolts awake at 3:00 a.m., bracing for danger that never comes.

It's not because you failed. It's because those methods skipped the root: your energy, your nervous system, your soul's alignment.

The four letters of HOPE are more than concepts as they form a compass that shapes itself into a living universal Law of HOPE, guiding you step by step from fragmentation into wholeness, from stagnation into higher vibration.

Harness — reclaim your scattered energy and awaken awareness. Helping you align with the Law of Attraction, because what you reclaim within becomes the magnet that draws life back into harmony.

Optimal — choose what is aligned for your soul, not just what feels familiar. Helping you embody the Law of Cause & Effect, because every soul-aligned choice set ripples in motion that create lasting change.

Positive — embody forgiveness, creativity, and joy as authentic energy. Helping you flow with the Law of Detachment, because positivity blooms not from control but from surrender, allowing joy to coexist with pain.

Energy — refine your frequency as your signature and superpower. Helping you mirror the Law of Polarity, because honoring both shadow and light strengthens the vibration you radiate.

Embody HOPE — where HOPE becomes not something you practice, but who you are. Helping you to live in the Law of Vibration, becoming a living frequency as your resonance in self becomes your offering to the world, carried through love and sovereignty.

These definitions are more than words on a page as they are the living pulse of the HOPE Method. Each one invites you not only to understand, but to embody. Together, you will find they shape a path that is both cosmic in truth and practical in daily life.

Each letter of HOPE becomes a pillar, giving you stability. The pillars then shape into a compass, offering direction. And as you move through this book, you will also encounter the proactive WiSH-to-HEAL cadence. Strategically designed as a simple seven-minute daily rhythm that turns both stability and direction into lived practice. WiSH-to-HEAL through HOPE establishes the foundation, the guidance, and the practice that will help you live whole again.

As a friend once told me, "HOPE is like a permission slip from the Universe. It tells you that you don't have to perform, pretend, or settle. You are allowed to simply "BE" — to breathe, to feel, to live each moment as it arrives, fully and honestly."

HOPE is many things because healing is many things. It is a Method — a practical rhythm of steps you can use every day. It is a Law — a universal truth that whatever you harness, choose, embody, and radiate will always return. And it is a Compass — pointing you from fragmentation back into wholeness.

Taken together, these images form a Map — a guide you can carry with you when life feels disoriented. However you name it, the four steps of the HOPE Method are designed to bring you home: gathering your scattered pieces, reclaiming authenticity, and remembering that sovereignty and self-love are already yours.

This is not a memoir, though its roots are personal (my memoir and the roots of the HOPE Method can be found in When the Soul Remembers HOPE). The HOPE Method is a guide for those who have grown weary of pretending. For those who feel the weight of spiritual repression, self-abandonment, or burnout. For those who carry invisible wounds that can be defined as emotional, mental, physical, or religious and long for a way to heal without bypassing the truth. It is for the overachiever whose nervous system is tired. The sensitive soul who was never taught how to protect their light. The parent, the partner, the provider who forgot themselves in service to others. The seeker who wants to ground their practices in truth, not trend.

I believe in the power of destiny, soul contracts, and soul paths. I believe in the Divine, Source, Creator, God, One True Light, whichever you choose. The name is not the point because it does not matter what language we use. What matters is the recognition: that there is a power greater than ourselves, one that breathes life into us and sets souls on missions to grow in self-awareness, to remember who we are, and to return more whole than we began.

I believe in the wisdom of those who came before us, the teachers and traditions that remind us how to walk in balance. And I believe in the value of modern science and technology, the tools that help us understand the mind, body, and nervous system with greater clarity. In this book, I have tried to weave a level of all of these to include ancient wisdom, sacred insight, trauma-informed science, and practical application. I share this not as an expert from a pulpit, but as an intuitive, claircognizant, empathic healer who has chosen to step out of the safety of silence and speak my truth.

This method is not the only way to heal. It is simply one way or perhaps one language among many. You are encouraged to explore what resonates, to question freely, and to integrate only what feels true for you. HOPE is not a rigid formula, but a living cadence that adapts, breathes, and evolves with your lived experience. You do not need to be spiritual, flexible, wealthy, or free of scars to begin. You need only the willingness to come home to yourself; gently, honestly, and with compassion. Bring your journals, your contradictions, your breath, your longing, and your doubt. HOPE will meet you exactly where you are. Not to judge, but to hold. Not to fix, but to illuminate. Not to erase your story, but to help you remember the light within it.

You will repeatedly read that HOPE is the backbone of grit as it is the steady strength that helps you rise again when life has knocked you down. It is also the first step to manifesting becoming the grounding of energy that makes your visions possible. Too often, manifestation experts speak of abundance and attraction while skipping the foundation. Without HOPE, manifestation is a hollow chant. With HOPE, manifestation becomes self-love in motion acting as the bridge between your prayers and their answers, the soil where the seeds of your becoming take root.

This may not be where your healing begins, but it may be where your remembering begins. And that remembering of your light, your strength, and your wholeness is where this journey starts.

Immediate Embodiment

I WANT YOU TO EXPERIENCE HOPE now, not later. Take seven minutes today.

One minute to **journal** a thought dump.

One minute to **sit in stillness**, just following your breath.

One minute to stand in front of a mirror, place your hands on your heart, **look yourself** in the eye and whisper: "I love you. I forgive you."

One minute to **stand, stretch, and shake your arms and legs**, letting stagnant energy fall away.

One minute to take a **slow breath and hum softly**, letting your throat open.

One minute to **whisper**: "I allow life to flow through me."

One minute to **plant your feet on the ground** and say: "I am rooted in love. I am safe to shine."

Seven minutes. Seven steps. A complete cycle.

Notice your breath. Notice your chest. Notice the subtle shift. That is HOPE in action.

How to Move Through This Book

YOU MAY FIND PROMPTS here that feel new, practices that feel unusual, or invitations that stretch you into unfamiliar territory. That's the point. Healing asks us to step beyond what we've always done, and it may feel a little odd at first, much like speaking a language you've always known but never practiced out loud.

There is no "right" way to move through the HOPE Method. Some days you may dive fully into a practice, other days you may simply read and let the words settle. Both are valid. The reflections, affirmations, HOPE in Practice moments, Soul Scribbles journal prompts, HOPEfully Human stories, and Soul Seeds are not tests to pass — they are invitations. You can engage them in the moment, or you can return to them later when the moment feels right.

My aspiration is that you approach them with gentleness, curiosity, and compassion. Let this book be less about getting it right, and more about coming home to yourself.

Note Before You Begin

THE TRUTH IS, HOPE doesn't work because of me. It works because of you. Because you've already survived what should have broken you. You've already carried more than most people can imagine.

All HOPE does is give your survival a rhythm. A way home. But a cadence framework is only theory until you live it. And the reason HOPE works so quickly, so tangibly, is because it begins where other methods end — at the root of your stuck energy.

In the next chapter, you'll discover why this method succeeds where so many others fall short — and why, once you embody it, you'll never see yourself or your healing the same way again. You are not being asked to dig up every carefully packaged fragment of your past. Instead, the HOPE Method shows you how to walk beside what you carry — with compassion, steadiness, and light.

What you will find in these pages is not a substitute for professional medical or psychological care, but a companion for your journey. I am not a therapist, physician, or licensed medical practitioner. I am simply a woman who has walked beside her own fragmentation and gathered tools along the way — tools that helped me come back to myself.

I am just a country girl at heart living in the city, still wishing on dandelion dreams and carrying hope in my pocket, offering what I've learned in case it lights your way, too. Because that's the truth of this book: hope doesn't belong only to the polished, the perfect, or the credentialed. It belongs to all of us — the dreamers, the weary, the ones who have been cracked open and are still searching for light.

This work may stir tender places in you. Old wounds may surface. If they do, I encourage you to seek the support of your tribe (family and friends), a trained mental health specialist, counselor, or holistic care provider who can walk with you through the deeper layers.

And please — take your time. Be kind to yourself. This is not a race. Healing is not built on drastic leaps but on small, steady steps. Each tiny adjustment — a pause, a breath, a boundary, a new choice — creates a ripple that changes the energy you carry and the way you experience your life. Over time, these little shifts become transformational.

As part of my commitment to integrity and to supporting the HOPE Method, I have drawn from many sources of wisdom — the ancient teachings of healers, prophets, and philosophers, as well as modern science and soul-centered practices. I also hold a deep belief in the power of knowledge and independent study, which is why I have included a list of inspiring works and resources in the back of this book. You will quickly notice that the philosophy of Stoicism is one of my favorites, but it is not the only one. If a practice or idea here resonates with you, these resources will offer pathways to explore further and expand beyond my perspective. HOPE is just one language of healing, and you are always free to follow what feels true for you.

In these pages, I share both my own journey and the experiences of clients who have walked with the HOPE Method. While details have been changed to protect privacy, their stories reveal what becomes possible when energy begins to flow again.

And so, we begin.

Before we dive into practices and cadences, we first pause with what I call the Quiet Currency of Being. This is the subtle but steady energy that underlies everything else — the hum beneath your breath, the presence beneath your performance, the quiet strength that remains even in fragmentation. It is here, in this current of being, that HOPE takes root.

Chapter Four

The Quiet Currency of Being

Most self-help books start with goals, metrics, or mindset hacks. They tell you to push harder, journal more, or manifest with greater clarity. But here's the truth: you cannot affirm your way out of fragmentation. You cannot manifest peace when your nervous system is still wired for survival.

This is where the HOPE Method separates itself. We do not begin with your goals. We begin with your energy.

Not the kind tracked on a screen, but the quiet pulse under your skin. The breath that rises when you pause. The ache that lingers when joy feels far away. Energy is not mystical — it is measurable, thermal, and honest. It tells the truth even when your mouth cannot.

Science now confirms what ancient wisdom always whispered: the heart is not only a muscle that pumps blood — it is an electrical beacon. Studies from the HeartMath Institute show that the heart generates an electromagnetic field measurable up to four feet beyond the body, with a signal sixty times stronger than the brain's signal. This means your presence is not confined to your skin. Every heartbeat sends a frequency into the room, announcing whether you are at peace, in panic, or resting in love.

The problem is most of us were taught to override that truth. To smile through it. To "fake it till we make it." Our culture rewards exhaustion and numbs intuition, leaving us fluent in performance but illiterate in our own signals. That is when our energy leaks begin.

Energy is your first language. Before you had words, you felt vibration. You danced when the music was safe, froze when the room grew tense, lit up like a sunflower in the presence of love. Your body remembers this. And it is still speaking.

The invitation is simple: listen. Place your hand over your heart. Feel the breath, the pulse, the ache. That is your energy saying, I'm still here.

HOPE begins at that pause. Not with a perfect plan, but with presence. Not in performance, but in honesty. Because energy is the quiet currency of being — and once you reclaim it, you no longer need to outsource your power.

HOPE is not about becoming someone new. It is about remembering who you were before the noise. It is choosing what is optimal, not just what is habitual. It is letting your nervous system whisper the truth and honoring it.

This method doesn't hand you a shortcut. It gives you something better — a compass lit with honesty — guiding you back to yourself.

Why Other Approaches Fail

MOST METHODS OF "HEALING" only skim the surface. Positive thinking asks the mind to glow while the body still trembles in silence. Productivity tricks keep us busy but never restore our strength. Even in wellness spaces, we learn to perform presence — smiling through the pain, holding it all together — while inside, the fracture remains.

And so, the cycle repeats. Burnout returns. Grief resurfaces. Shame creeps back in. Not because you failed, but because no quick fix can reach the root. The body whispers, the soul aches, and still, we push forward — until the weight becomes unbearable.

Why HOPE Succeeds

TRUE HEALING BEGINS when you reclaim your energy — the quiet currency you've scattered through exhaustion, old wounds, and silent agreements you never knew you made. Where other approaches demand hustle, this one calls you to pause. Where others give you borrowed mantras, it teaches you to hear your own truth. Where others promise perfection, it invites you into presence.

You do not need to perform healing — you need to embody it. And that begins by recognizing where your energy is leaking away. These hidden drainers are subtle, but once they are revealed, they change everything. As you keep reading, you'll discover how to name them, stop them, and finally free the power that was always yours to claim.

The Frequency of Imposter Syndrome

TAKE IMPOSTER SYNDROME. Conventional wisdom frames it as a mindset issue. "Just think more confidently." But science and lived experience tell us otherwise: it's a nervous system disruption, a frequency misalignment.

Your soul wants to expand; your conditioning tells you to shrink. That friction isn't failure — it's energy trying to find its rightful alignment.

Where others call it insecurity, HOPE recognizes it as signal. And when you learn to realign frequency, the falsehood of being "a fraud" dissolves.

Imposter syndrome is not just a mindset issue; it has steadily become a frequency disruption.

When we feel like we do not belong, when we second-guess our success or quietly fear we will be "found out," what we are really experiencing is energetic misalignment. The sensation of being fake, unworthy, or not ready is not a moral failing or a lack of talent. It's stuck energy that shows up as the emotional residue that accumulates when we resist our own truth.

You are not an imposter. You are someone who learned to shrink, to shape-shift, to stay silent in order to stay safe. And now, when your soul is ready to be seen, your nervous system panics because it no longer recognizes what it feels like to stand fully in your light.

Imposter syndrome is not random. It often lives inside people who have been told they are too much, or not enough. It takes root in the minds of those who have been praised for pleasing others and punished for being authentic. It hides in the crevices of codependency and people-pleasing, those exhausting patterns where your worth is measured by how well you manage everyone else's needs.

And then there is the new addiction most of us do not even notice, "validation syndrome." We scroll, we post, we perform. We craft captions and selfies and small bites of curated life, hoping someone will affirm that we matter. But social media, though it offers connection, often feeds the illusion that we must be more: shinier, louder, better in order to just be accepted for who we are.

The HOPE Method teaches that what we are really seeking is vibrational alignment. Imposter syndrome is what happens when your soul wants to expand, and your conditioning tells you to shrink. It is the friction between who you truly are and who you have been trained to be.

To Harness Optimal Positive Energy, you must return to the frequency of your own authenticity.

That means learning to say what you mean, even when it feels uncomfortable. It means choosing what supports your soul's truth, not just what feels familiar or wins applause. It means living with a little bit of nervousness, you know the good kind of butterflies that scream as excitement. The kind that emerges as you begin to show up more fully as yourself.

There will be a pivotal moment when your old patterns whisper, "Who do you think you are?" But your healing will answer, "I'm someone who finally remembers."

You were never a fraud. You were simply out of alignment. And now, you are coming home.

This understanding isn't just intuitive, but it is strongly supported by research. Psychology and neuroscience both show that imposter syndrome is deeply connected to nervous system dysregulation, people-pleasing behaviors, and early emotional conditioning. Social media and external validation loops often intensify these patterns. When we resist our own truth, our energy contracts. But as we begin to live in alignment with who we truly are, that imposter feeling starts to fade. What science calls regulation, the HOPE Method calls frequency realignment, and both speak to the same truth: *your authenticity is healing.*

Relevant studies and sources are listed in the "Sources & Inspirations" section for those who wish to explore further.

Validation Syndrome: Reclaiming Your Inner Authority

THE DOPAMINE LOOP OF external validation — likes, scores, applause — is not a "discipline problem." It's your nervous system trapped in unpredictable reward cycles, mirroring addiction. One notification can lift you up or leave you restless, waiting for more. That's not just psychology; it's neurology.

We live in a world obsessed with mirrors, but not the kind that reflects your truth. These mirrors measure performance, not presence. Social media metrics. Corporate dashboards. Satisfaction surveys. All of them turning human worth into a number. Over time, the nervous system adapts to this unpredictability like a gambler at the slots: check, anticipate, reward, repeat. Exhaustion follows, not because we are incapable, but because no human can thrive when identity is reduced to a score.

This is Validation Syndrome. Whether it comes as a heart on social media or a dip in workplace ratings, the result is the same: worth outsourced, joy entangled with algorithms, identity fractured by external mirrors.

HOPE reframes this. Instead of outsourcing worth, HOPE teaches you to self-validate through its four steps — Harness, Optimal, Positive, Energy — a framework that restores authenticity, sovereignty, and self-love. Alongside HOPE, the WiSH-to-HEAL rhythm offers seven daily practices that retrain your nervous system to return to safety, belonging, and love. Together, they form both compass and cadence — one giving you direction, the other teaching you how to walk it.

This is why HOPE succeeds where other methods fail: it doesn't bypass the body or shame the nervous system. It doesn't confuse performance with healing. It meets you in the quiet ache, the restless night, the unfinished tears. And instead of demanding you "fix it," it gives you rhythm, resonance, and return.

Reclaiming your authority begins when you step out of the loop. Authority is not about control over others — it's about taking back what already belongs to you: your focus, your peace, your worth, your voice. Each time you resist the urge to measure yourself against a screen, you restore power to your nervous system and strength to your soul's voice.

That is the work of HOPE. By teaching you to harness awareness, choose what is optimal, redefine positivity, and reclaim your energy, HOPE invites you to step off the dopamine carousel and root yourself in truth. Not in comparison. Not in applause, but in the steady authority of who you really are.

Reclaiming your authority is not a single dramatic act. It's a quiet return. Moment by moment. Choice by choice. Each time you choose to listen inward instead of outward, your soul's voice grows louder than the noise.

Take a moment to contemplate: Where in your life have you given away your authority to external validation and what would it look like to call it back, one breath, one choice, one moment at a time?

HOPE in Practice: Validate Yourself First

THROUGHOUT THIS BOOK, you will find HOPE in Practice sections. These are designed to invite you into individual thought and self-discovery. They are not just for reading but they are for doing. Whenever you see this section, pause and get yourself ready for action.

This may mean you are doing a breathing exercise or taking out your journal to scribe some soul scribbles. Take time to slow your breathing and give yourself space to reflect honestly. Your healing deepens when you bring awareness out of your head and onto the page.

This practice is about self-validation. Validation from others is not wrong, because we all need encouragement and connection. But self-validation is foundational. It is saying: "I see me. I know what I need. I trust what I feel."

To begin, write freely in response to these questions: Am I functioning as my highest self or am I just trying to look like them? What truth have I been avoiding? What emotion needs space to breathe? Where am I leaking my energy for validation I could be giving myself?

Let this be a private, honest conversation with yourself. No performance. No mirror. Just you, listening to you.

Why Stress Management Techniques Fail

MOST STRESS-MANAGEMENT advice focuses on symptoms — breathing tricks, productivity hacks, or mindset shifts. Helpful for a moment, yes, but they rarely touch the deeper imprint that keeps the nervous system on high alert. That's why so many people relapse into burnout or anxiety even after "doing all the right things."

Stress doesn't live only in the mind; it's etched into the body, the breath, and the nervous system. Without addressing those imprints, no technique can create lasting peace.

The Stoics understood this long before neuroscience gave us language for it. Epictetus taught that freedom begins not in controlling circumstances but in mastering your response to them. Marcus Aurelius wrote about returning to the inner citadel — that unshakable core no storm could breach. Their wisdom mirrors what modern somatic now affirms: the body holds both the tension and the key to release.

This is where WiSH-to-HEAL shifts the ground. Instead of patching over symptoms, it offers a rhythm — seven practices that retrain your system toward safety, belonging, and love. Each step helps you reclaim authority over your energy, not through suppression, but through presence.

A Path Back to Calm

STRESS WILL NEVER DISAPPEAR — but how you respond to it will decide whether it steals your vitality or strengthens your resilience. Most coping strategies offer temporary relief: a candy bar, a dopamine hit from scrolling, or the popular "just change your mindset" advice. But these don't touch the roots. They bypass the nervous system, leaving the body still flooded with cortisol and the mind still wired for survival.

WiSH-to-HEAL is different. It's a 7-minute daily rhythm designed to unlock stuck energy and re-train your nervous system toward safety, authenticity, and sovereignty. Backed by both clinical research and ancient wisdom, it works because:

Science confirms that consistent micro-practices lower cortisol, balance heart rate variability, calm inflammation, and strengthen neuroplasticity — literally rewiring stress into resilience.

Ancient traditions confirm that healing happens in rhythm — through breath, presence, and small daily rituals that keep energy flowing. The yogis called it prana; the Stoics called it governing the inner life; today we call it nervous system regulation.

Your lived reality confirms that willpower and quick fixes fail. But gentle, repeated practices change the baseline of your being — making peace a habit, not just a moment.

Think of these seven touchpoints as anchors you can carry anywhere: a single line in your journal, three breaths in stillness, a hand over your heart, a whispered truth of accountability, an exhale or movement to release, a walk of acceptance, and a return to love.

Over time, these tiny acts build something radical: A nervous system that feels safe. A mind that feels clear. A heart that remembers HOPE.

This is why WiSH-to-HEAL through HOPE matters. Not because it makes life stress-free, but because it teaches you to meet stress differently — and in doing so, it gives you back your freedom.

Wisdom — I connect: the crown of knowing, remembering who you are.

Somatic signal: Headaches, mental fog, or racing thoughts often point to scattered energy and overwhelm.

Somatic activity: Lightly tap or massage the crown of your head with your fingertips while taking slow breaths. This practice grounds scattered energy and re-centers awareness.

Practice: Journal it: Pause for two minutes to write down what you are feeling. Getting it out of your head and onto paper clears space for calm and clarity.

Chakra resonance: Crown (Sahasrara), mantra: OM or Silence.

Serenity — I see: the calm of mind, surrender, where clarity restores peace.

Somatic signal: Tension in the temples, eye strain, or insomnia often reveal overstimulation or stress.

Somatic activity: Place your palms gently over your eyes in darkness for 30 seconds; this soothes overstimulated nerves and resets your parasympathetic system.

Practice: Meditate on it: Close your eyes, breathe deeply through your nose and out through your mouth, for a count of three to eight slow breaths. Even thirty seconds of stillness resets your stress response.

Chakra resonance: Third Eye (Ajna), mantra: OM.

Heart
— **I love:** the center of compassion, forgiveness, and connection.

Somatic signal: Tightness or heaviness in the chest, shallow breathing, or aching lungs may carry grief, sadness, or unspoken love.

Somatic activity: Stretch your arms wide or gently pat the center of your chest to open circulation. Movement here loosens grief's grip.

Practice: Feel it: Place your hand over your heart and name the emotion you're carrying. Acknowledging it releases the grip of denial.

Chakra resonance: Heart (Anahata), mantra: YAM.

Healing
— **I act:** the space of restoration, empowerment, and renewal.

Somatic signal: Stomach knots, nausea, or digestive upset can signal fear, power struggles, or disempowerment.

Somatic activity: Rub small circles around your navel or practice a gentle forward bend; both stimulate release and calm digestive stress.

Practice: Account for it: Whisper to yourself, "This is mine, but it does not define me." Healing begins with accountability, choosing to own your story instead of letting stress own you.

Chakra resonance: Solar Plexus (Manipura), mantra: RAM.

Expression
— **I speak:** the release of truth, creativity, and authentic voice.

Somatic signal: Jaw clenching, throat tightness, or voice strain often point to unspoken truth or withheld creativity.

Somatic activity: Massage your jaw hinge or hum gently on the exhale; vibration loosens throat tension and restores voice flow.

Practice: Breathe it out: Inhale deeply and sigh it out. Exhale through sound, movement, or even a gentle shake of your shoulders. Release is the body's natural reset.

Chakra resonance: Throat (Vishuddha), mantra: HAM.

Acceptance — I feel: the grounding of safety, belonging, and worth.

Somatic signal: Low back pain, hip stiffness, or reproductive discomfort can reflect survival stress, blocked creativity, or disconnection from belonging.

Somatic activity: Do gentle hip circles or a forward fold; both signal safety to the body and reconnect you with grounding.

Practice: Walk with it: Take a short mindful walk. Let your steps match your breath. Acceptance is movement with gentleness, not stagnation.

Chakra resonance: Sacral (Svadhisthana), mantra: VAM.

Love — I am: the root of life force, stability, and unconditional presence.

Somatic signal: Leg heaviness, foot pain, or overall fatigue often reveal instability or lack of grounding.

Somatic activity: Stomp your feet gently on the ground or stand barefoot on the earth; both re-anchor your energy into stability.

Practice HOPE it: Repeat a love-based mantra: "I choose love over fear. HOPE begins with me." This is where you Harness Optimal Positive Energy—turning stress into strength, fear into faith, and heaviness into healing. Love is the energy that makes HOPE more than an idea; it is a way of life.

Chakra resonance: Root (Muladhara), mantra: LAM.

Why It Matters?

MANAGING STRESS IS not just about feeling better in the moment, it is about transforming the course of your health and your life.

WiSH-to-HEAL isn't just another stress-management tool. It's a seven-minute seven-step daily practice designed to unlock stuck energy, regulate your nervous system, and guide you back into authenticity, sovereignty, and wholeness.

Emotional intelligence is more than just being "aware" of feelings — it's the ability to pause, discern, and choose what is optimal in the moment instead of what is reactive, habitual, or externally conditioned. And that's where WiSH-to-HEAL through HOPE shine:

Harness → noticing your energy honestly, instead of ignoring or overriding it.

Optimal → choosing what truly serves your wholeness, not just what's familiar or easy.

Positive → redefining positivity as emotional integrity, joy, and expression (not faking it but aligning with truth).

Energy → cultivating presence and frequency so your inner state fuels your outer choices.

In practice, this is emotional intelligence at its deepest level. You're not just managing stress — you're becoming fluent in your own energy. Once you can read those signals, you can choose what is optimal and sustain positivity that is rooted, not performative.

Science confirms the stakes: unmanaged stress raises cortisol, weakens immunity, disrupts sleep, increases inflammation, and accelerates aging. But consistent practices — even small ones — reshape the nervous system. Research in psychoneuroimmunology shows that breathwork, journaling, and compassionate self-talk lower stress hormones and boost resilience. Neuroscience calls it neuroplasticity: the brain rewiring itself through repetition.

Ancient traditions taught this long before science named it. Yogis mapped energy through chakras, the Stoics through self-mastery of perception, the Chinese through meridians and qi. Across cultures, the message is the same: regulate your inner life, and your outer life transforms.

WiSH-to-HEAL brings this wisdom into modern rhythm. Seven steps. Seven minutes. Each one reclaims a piece of you: Wisdom clears the mental fog. Serenity calms the body. Heart softens grief and reconnects you to feeling. Healing restores vitality. Expression gives your voice back. Acceptance ends resistance to what is. Love anchors everything in wholeness.

But here's the deeper truth: healing was never meant to be carried alone. For centuries, families, elders, and neighbors formed webs of care where no one held every burden in isolation. Today, much of that village mentality has been lost. Yet your nervous system still longs for it — not just self-regulation, but co-regulation.

When you practice WiSH-to-HEAL, you strengthen your own rhythm. And when you bring that rhythm into relationships, you ripple calm, compassion, and coherence into the collective. In this way, your healing multiplies — not only restoring you but reminding others of their own inner compass.

This is why WiSH-to-HEAL matters: because it is not theory, but practice. Not a "someday" healing plan, but a rhythm you can live today. It is the bridge between survival patterns and sovereign presence. And the more you return to it, the more your nervous system learns a new truth: safety is possible, joy is allowed, and wholeness is your birthright.

HOPE in Practice: The First Sacred Yes

THROUGHOUT THIS BOOK, you'll find HOPE in Practice invitations. These are not for rushing past. They are moments designed for you to pause, step out of reading, and step into doing — to embody the HOPE Method one breath, one choice, one page at a time.

In this first breath practice, we will help you discover your First Yes. Healing does not begin with perfection or with a plan. It begins with willingness. A single honest yes to yourself creates the opening for everything that follows.

Here's how to begin: Take a slow, steady breath through your nose. Place your hand gently over your Heart — the center of compassion, connection, and forgiveness in the WiSH-to-Heal flow. Speak aloud, even if it feels uncomfortable: "I am willing to begin. I am willing to remember."

That's it. That's your first yes. By saying yes to your own heart, you open the path for healing to follow — through expression, acceptance, and love. You've already begun.

HOPE in Practice: Belly Breath to Self-Validate

THIS PRACTICE is designed to guide you inward and to rebuild self-trust and discover what your energy is telling you. Think of it as holding up a mirror, not to your face, but to your soul. You don't need permission to know your truth. You are already allowed.

Start Here: Take a slow breath. Breathing in through your nose, out through your mouth. This pattern gently resets your vagus nerve, helping calm your nervous system and bring your body back into balance. Let your belly rise as you inhale and fall as you exhale; belly breathing invites more oxygen into the body and signals safety.

If this feels awkward or unnatural at first, that's okay. Many of us were never taught how to breathe this way. With practice, it becomes easier and eventually, it begins to feel like a reset button your body knows how to press on its own.

Place your hand gently over your heart. Whisper, even if it feels new or uncomfortable: "I am allowed to know what I need."

Notice how your body responds. You may feel warmth in your chest, tightness in your throat, or a flutter in your belly. Every sensation is valid. It's your energy speaking.

If Belly Breathing Feels Hard: For many people, belly breathing doesn't always feel natural, especially if your body is used to holding tension. If you can't seem to do it, or if it doesn't feel safe, that's okay.

Instead, simply breathe in through your nose and out through your mouth at a comfortable rhythm. Let the breath be easy, without forcing it. With time and practice, your body may begin to relax into deeper belly breathing on its own.

The point isn't to get it "perfect." The point is to give your nervous system a moment of calm and reset in whatever way it feels safe for you.

Affirmation Reflection

THROUGHOUT THIS BOOK, you'll find Affirmation Reflections. These are not just words on a page; they are invitations to speak directly to yourself in a new way. If you've never practiced affirmations before, here's what to know: Read the affirmation slowly, either aloud or silently. If the exact words don't feel like you, rewrite them in your own voice. Repeat the words a few times, letting them sink in. You might feel resistance at first and that's normal. The point is not to fake it, but to practice planting seeds of self-trust. Here's your affirmation for this moment:

> "Even if no one sees me, I see me. Even if no one applauds, I approve. Even if no one agrees, I honor my truth."

You can copy these lines into your journal or rewrite them in a way that feels more natural. For example: "I don't need outside approval to feel valid. I know my own truth, and that is enough."

Why We Do This: Affirmations retrain the nervous system and the mind. Every time you speak or write them, you are interrupting old patterns of self-doubt and creating new pathways of self-validation. Over time, these small repetitions help you embody the HOPE Method, not just as an idea, but as lived truth.

Most frameworks stop at theory. But the HOPE Method doesn't just tell you that energy matters — it shows you how to hold it, reshape it, and live it.

And when you begin to live this rhythm, you'll discover something even deeper: your energy doesn't just heal you — it begins to change everything around you.

Chapter Five

Where the Fracture Begins

Most books on healing tell you the same story: manage your thoughts, stay positive, repeat affirmations. But here's the truth no one is saying out loud: your pain does not live in your mindset — it lives in your body.

The hidden problem is not lack of discipline. It's not laziness. It's not even "negative thinking." The real issue is fragmentation: the way trauma and stress scatter your energy, leaving echoes in your nervous system that no affirmation alone can erase.

This is the part almost every self-help book misses. And it's why so many people feel like they've failed when the old patterns return. If your energy feels chaotic, frozen, heavy, or constantly hijacked — that is not weakness. That is a signal.

The Many Faces of Fragmentation

FRAGMENTATION IS NOT failure. It is adaptation. It is what happens when the nervous system whispers, "This is too much," and carries what could not be expressed: the unscreamed cry, the unwitnessed grief, the unspoken rage. The body does not erase what it cannot release; it holds it, faithfully, waiting for the day safety returns.

This is sovereignty of the mind — reclaiming the power to choose thoughts aligned with truth instead of trauma. Carl Jung reminded us that healing is not perfection but wholeness. To recognize fragmentation is the first step toward that wholeness.

Your body did not betray you. When you could not run, your Heart center stored the urge in your legs. When you could not scream, your Expression center held it in your throat. When you could not fight back, your Healing center dimmed its flame to keep you safe.

Fragmentation is energy lodged in time, echoing like an unfinished song. And the miracle is this: what was paused can also be resumed.

The Body Remembers

BEFORE YOU HAD WORDS for fear or abandonment, your body was already memorizing the world. Every clenched jaw, every shallow breath, every racing heart became a stored imprint.

This is the nervous system's brilliance — not weakness. But conventional healing approaches often frame these imprints as flaws to be conquered, rather than signals to be honored.

This is the hidden failure of other methods. They ask you to change your thoughts while your body is still carrying the weight of unfinished survival.

Even if you cannot recall the story, your body remembers. It remembers in the silence of your gut. It remembers in the buzzing under your skin. It remembers in the numbness that drapes itself over joy like a wet towel.

Before you had words for fear, abandonment, or love, your body was memorizing the world. It is more than a vessel; it is a record keeper. It carries not only your genetics and your smile, but also your emotional history: the flinch no one noticed, the silence you swallowed to stay safe, the racing of your heart when a door slammed just a little too loud.

The nervous system is not your enemy. It is not a broken fuse box or a weak design flaw. It is the most intelligent part of you. It scans for danger before your mind can form a thought. It remembers who did not hold you, who gaslit you, who demanded stillness when you needed to scream.

It does not do this to punish you. On the contrary, it does this to protect you. But protection, when repeated too long, becomes pattern. And patterns, lived without awareness, become prisons.

HOPE as a New Pattern

WHERE OTHERS URGE YOU to "fix" fragmentation, HOPE offers something different: a rhythm for rewriting it.

Fragmentation says: Stay small to stay safe.

HOPE says: You are allowed to take up space again.

This is not about force or perfection. It is about creating the conditions where safety can return — where breath flows without effort, where presence no longer feels like a trap, where your energy serves restoration instead of survival.

You are not broken. You are patterned. And the beauty of patterns is that they can be rewritten — not through shame or striving, but through gentleness, curiosity, and repetition.

My Story of Fragmentation

I KNOW THIS BECAUSE I lived it. For years, I told myself I was fine. I worked, I cared for others, I accomplished. But inside, I was exhausted, scattered, and quietly unraveling. Some nights I drowned my bad days in a bag of wavy potato chips and a can of cheddar cheese sauce. Other times, I threw myself into yet another diet, self-help class, or exercise plan — convinced the next one would finally fix me. But I wasn't lazy. I wasn't weak. I was fragmented. I was existing instead of living.

The truth is, many of us describe it as living in a kind of matrix — the motions continue, but the meaning disappears. Days blur into one another. You wake, work, sleep, repeat. And before you know it, ten years have passed, and you wonder if you've truly lived at all.

It wasn't until I stopped breaking vows to myself and started keeping small promises that things began to shift. Through the HOPE Method, I began to breathe when I wanted to shut down. I wrote when I wanted to hide. I practiced presence when my instinct was to abandon myself.

Over time, shame softened. Self-betrayal lifted. My body responded. I released not just 85 pounds of physical weight, but the heavier burden of self-rejection.

HOPE didn't just change my body. It changed my relationship with myself.

Stories of Transformation

I'VE SEEN THIS IN OTHERS too. Maria came to me feeling numb, drained, and disconnected. She described her days as "autopilot" — a Groundhog Day of exhaustion and emotional eating.

Her journey didn't begin with a dramatic overhaul. It began with a pause. A breath. A messy journal scribble. These small acts-built integrity: little vows she could keep. And over time, her energy shifted. Her choices aligned. She shed not only physical pounds but also the heaviness of carrying herself half-alive.

Her story, like mine, is not about weight. It is about energy. Because when energy flows, life begins to change.

But before flow can return, we must notice where it has been held. This is where practice begins for all of us: with the imprints.

Spirit Stealers & Sovereignty

HERE'S the paradox: most of us try to escape fragmentation with quick fixes — smoking, drinking, scrolling, even over-giving in relationships. These "spirit stealers" feel like comfort in the moment, but they're really sovereignty thieves, pulling your energy further out of alignment.

The hidden cost? Relief that numbs is always borrowed from your future. HOPE reframes sovereignty as awareness, not abstinence. It's not about shame or perfection. It's about pausing before you reach for escape and asking: Am I choosing in alignment with love — or am I just escaping? This is the kind of sovereignty most frameworks never touch.

When life feels heavy, it is human to want relief. Many turn to smoking, alcohol, substances, or even relationships as quick escapes from stress, grief, or trauma. What begins as a moment of comfort or distraction can become a thief — slowly stealing sovereignty over your body, your mind, and your spirit.

Tobacco: Nicotine creates the illusion of calm by releasing dopamine — but at a cost. It constricts blood flow, damages the lungs, and clouds the breath that your nervous system relies on to find true regulation. Smoking may soothe nerves for a moment, but research shows it narrows breath and restricts the very life force that fuels healing. Smoking becomes less about choice and more about craving, binding energy to dependency.

Alcohol: Alcohol numbs pain and loosens tension, but overuse drains life force and disconnects you from your inner compass. A useful guide is the rule of three drinks: more than this in one sitting tips your body into harm instead of release. Today, many non-alcoholic spirits and mocktails exist — consider alternating them with your drink of choice if you want to enjoy the celebration without sacrificing clarity.

Substances & Medications: Every substance that enters your body carries vibration, whether illicit, prescription, or nutritional supplementation can often carry a cost. Some are necessary for survival and healing, yet even then, sovereignty means understanding why they are needed, seeking balance, and exploring alternatives where possible. Illicit drugs can hijack the nervous system, stealing presence and sovereignty. Even prescriptions and supplements — though often necessary — shift homeostasis. Sovereignty means knowing why you take them, understanding their impact, and seeking complementary support whenever possible (nutrition, movement, somatic practices, energy hygiene). Too much of anything disrupts the homeostasis your body depends on.

Codependency — Spirit stealers are not always chemical. Over-giving, living in someone else's chaos, or confusing devotion with self-erasure drains energy jut as surely as any drug. What looks like devotion often hides an escape from your own healing.

The Cost of Escape: All of these share one thread: The temptation of escape. Relief that numbs may look like love or safety in the moment, but it is borrowed from your future. Each time you outsource peace to a substance, you weaken your inner reservoir of resilience.

True sovereignty is not about perfection. It is about awareness. It is the pause before you light, pour, or give yourself away, asking: Am I just escaping? Am I choosing to align with love?

The HOPE Perspective: Sovereignty does not mean perfection or abstinence. It means awareness. It means pausing before you light, pour, or swallow and asking: Am I escaping, or am I choosing in alignment with love?

Because healing is not found in numbing what you feel — it is found in reclaiming your energy, one sovereign choice at a time.

Procrastination as a Pattern

EVEN PROCRASTINATION carries a hidden truth. It's not laziness — it's fear wrapped in longing. It's the nervous system hesitating because safety doesn't feel certain yet.

Conventional wisdom calls procrastination a willpower issue. But HOPE teaches that procrastination is just another imprint of fragmentation. Once you see that, you can stop shaming yourself and start asking: What feels unsafe about beginning?

There is another thief of energy — quieter, but just as heavy. Procrastination. On the surface, it looks like avoidance, delay, or lack of willpower. But beneath it lives something tender: a nervous system caught between fear and longing.

Sometimes procrastination is your body whispering, "I don't feel safe enough to begin." Other times, it is perfectionism in disguise — the belief that unless it can be flawless, it cannot be started at all. What feels like laziness is often just fragmentation: energy stuck in hesitation, looping between the urge to act and the fear of what action might awaken.

The invitation is not to shame yourself into productivity, but to notice what your procrastination is protecting. Ask softly: "What feels unsafe about beginning? What small step could I take with kindness?" In this way, even procrastination becomes a doorway back to sovereignty.

HOPE in Practice: Noticing the Imprint

CLOSE YOUR EYES. TAKE a deep breath in through the nose. Ask your body gently: "Where do you hold the oldest pain?"

Notice without judgment — a tight chest, a clenched jaw, a heavy gut. Then ask: "What does this part of me need to feel safe?"

Do not rush. Begin a dialogue. Your body has waited a long time for this.

The inner child is not just a metaphor; it is an imprint. They live in the subconscious, holding memories of your formative years. They show up in your reactions, your fears, your longings. Especially when you feel unseen. Many of us learned to survive by muting these tender parts. But healing is the return. Now, you get to go back and retrieve them.

Soul Scribbles Prompt: After this pause, write down what you noticed. A word. A sensation. A memory. Let it be messy and raw. This is not about performance. It is about presence.

The Science Behind the Inner Child

NEUROSCIENCE AND PSYCHOLOGY confirm what the mystics always knew: our inner child never leaves us. Before age seven, most of our core beliefs are imprinted — not as logic, but as felt experiences. This is why self-talk matters. Not because words alone heal, but because every new act of compassion creates a fresh imprint of safety.

Carl Jung called this the "eternal child" — always becoming, never complete. HOPE helps you reparent this eternal child, not with blame, but with presence. Every small act of compassion becomes cognitive self-change, rewriting the inner script of fragmentation.

Neuroscience tells us that most of our core beliefs are formed before age seven. They are not stored as facts but as felt experiences: I'm not safe. I'm too much. I have to earn love.

Your nervous system runs these silent scripts until they are replaced — not with logic, but with new experiences of safety and compassion. This is why reconnecting with your inner child is so powerful. Each act of self-compassion becomes a new imprint: It's safe to be me now.

In WiSH-to-HEAL, these imprints show themselves as signals: Wisdom fragments into self-doubt. Serenity unravels into racing thoughts. Heart carries grief and unworthiness. Healing dims into powerlessness. Expression chokes on unsaid words. Acceptance feels unsafe in joy or intimacy. Love falters when grounding and trust are shaken.

Each time you tend to these centers with breath, truth, or compassion, you rewrite the story your body has carried. This is the work of HOPE: restoring sovereignty where fragmentation once ruled.

Cognitive Self-Change: Rewriting the Inner Script

MY FIRST ENCOUNTER with cognitive self-change was not in a classroom or textbook, but in my own home. As a mother, I walked beside a child whose early challenges were often misunderstood — labeled by others as something they were not. What we discovered together was that growth was never just about physical milestones; it was about learning new ways of seeing oneself and the world. With patience, support, and steady practice, those struggles gradually gave way to strength. Today that child has grown into an upstanding, responsible, and deeply thoughtful human being.

The second time I met this concept was in the courtroom. As the Drug Court Coordinator for the District Court Program, I witnessed firsthand how cycles of trauma, addiction, and survival thinking could keep people trapped. The program's success often depended on more than rules and accountability; it required participants to learn a new way of thinking. They had to recognize the thoughts that fueled their old patterns and practice choosing new ones. Without changing the inner script, the outer life could not hold.

This is the heart of cognitive self-change. It is the practice of noticing the beliefs that drive us — often shaped by trauma, shame, or survival — and gently rewriting them. The thoughts we repeat become the maps we live by. To heal, we must learn to ask: Is this thought true? Is it kind? Is it useful for the person I am becoming?

HOPE and cognitive self-change work hand in hand. In HOPE, we choose the Optimal — what is aligned with healing, not just what is familiar. Cognitive self-change gives us the daily tool for that choice: replacing self-defeating thoughts with truthful, life-giving ones. Over time, this reshapes not just the mind but the nervous system, the heart, and the body itself.

HOPE in Practice:

WHEN YOU NOTICE A SELF-defeating thought today, pause and write it down. Then reframe it into a statement of strength:

"I can't handle this" → "I can take one step at a time."

"I'm broken" → "I am healing."

"Nothing ever changes" → "Small choices create new patterns."

This is sovereignty of the mind — reclaiming your power to choose thought aligned with truth instead of trauma. And it is the natural bridge into the wisdom of Carl Jung, who reminded us that healing is less about perfection and more about wholeness.

Wisdom Through the Ages

CARL JUNG ONCE SAID, "In every adult, there lurks a child, your eternal child, something that is always becoming, is never completed."

Ancient wisdom, neuroscience, and energy practice all point to the same truth: wholeness doesn't come from erasing your past. It comes from tending to the eternal child who still asks, Am I safe? Am I loved? Do I matter? This is what most frameworks miss. They focus on outcomes, while HOPE focuses on the root.

Carl Jung once said, "In every adult, there lurks a child, your eternal child, something that is always becoming, is never completed."

Jung understood what neuroscience and energy work affirm today: the child within us is not left behind with age. They live within our stories, our bodies, our reactions, our longings. This eternal child carries both the wounds of what was unmet and the wonder of what is still possible.

Healing, then, does not mean erasing your past or silencing the child within. It means learning how to tend to them differently: with compassion, sovereignty, and truth. It means offering that inner child the safety and guidance they did not always receive and allowing their wonder to reawaken in your present life.

When we speak of reparenting, it is not about blaming those who raised us or endlessly revisiting what they lacked. It is about becoming the parent, protector, and presence our soul has always needed. Reparenting your future means giving yourself new experiences of safety, acceptance, and love — the very experiences that begin to replace old imprints with new truth.

This is why the HOPE Method places such emphasis on the inner child. Because no matter how many years pass, that child is still alive in you. They are still asking: Am I safe? Am I loved? Do I matter? And each time you pause, breathe, and choose self-compassion, you answer back: Yes.

Healing does not mean erasing your past. It means reparenting your future — moment by moment, choice by choice, until the eternal child within you feels whole again.

HOPEfully Human Moment

ONE MORNING, I SPILLED coffee on my shirt and, without thinking, muttered: "You're so stupid." I froze. That voice deep inside but it was not mine. It was inherited, echoing from years of being told mistakes made me unworthy or careless.

So, I tried again. I stood in the kitchen and said softly: "That is not a very kind thing to say to yourself. You are better than that. Let's try again."

And then I did. I smiled a little, took a breath, and said: "Oops... wasted coffee. It's alright, sweetheart, accidents happen. Slow down. You have time. You didn't even want to wear this shirt anyway. I told myself with confidence, let's change it and move on with our morning."

I wasn't just talking to the adult standing in the kitchen. I was talking to the younger version of me who used to get a humiliating spanking and would cry when she made a mess. And in that moment, the shame dissolved into softness.

That is healing. Not in grand, dramatic gestures, but in the ordinary choice to meet yourself with kindness instead of criticism. HOPE reminds us that every small moment of compassion is a step toward wholeness.

HOPE in Practice: Inner Child Letter

THIS IS YOUR MOMENT to pause and take action. Do not just read it, I encourage you to experience it.

Write a short letter to your inner child. Begin with, "I'm so sorry you had to…" and let it flow. Then write, "But I promise you now…"

You do not have to know all the answers. You just have to show up. Every time you write, you prove to your younger self that they are no longer alone.

Soul Seed to Take With You

YOUR INNER CHILD IS waiting to be held. And sometimes, holding begins with something as simple as a sentence — a truth small enough to carry, but strong enough to grow inside you. This is what I call a Soul Seed.

A Soul Seed is not a mantra to force or a slogan to memorize. It is a whisper you can return to in ordinary moments — in the car, at the grocery store, in the quiet before sleep. It is a seed planted in your heart that, over time, begins to grow new roots of safety, self-compassion, and truth.

This is only the second Soul Seed you've encountered in these pages, so take your time with it. Let yourself get used to the rhythm of carrying a seed. Each time you pause and repeat it, you are teaching your nervous system a new story: that you are safe, that you are seen, that you are allowed to exist in wholeness.

Examples

MY ENERGY BELONGS TO me. I cannot always choose what happens, but I can choose how I tend, respond, and align.

I do not have to earn my place. I was born enough. Acceptance is already mine.

Wholeness is not the absence of pain. It is the courage to keep returning, again and again, to my light.

Carry one of these with you today. Write it on a sticky note. Whisper it to yourself in the mirror. Breathe it into your chest when the old patterns rise again. The more you return to it, the deeper it roots, until one day you find the seed has grown into something steady and alive inside you.

Remember

THE BODY REMEMBERS what the mind forgets. And the child within is not waiting to be fixed — they are waiting to be held.

Fragmentation is not your fault. It is your body's devotion to survival. But survival is not the same as living. The real transformation begins when you stop outsourcing sovereignty — to substances, to procrastination, to old patterns — and begin reclaiming it breath by breath. In the next chapter, I'll show you how HOPE does this in minutes, where other frameworks take months.

Chapter Six

The Four Directions of HOPE

If you have made it this far, you might be asking, "Okay... so what do I actually do with all this?"

The world has no shortage of feel-good quotes and healing hashtags. You can buy a crystal water bottle, scream into a pillow, and still feel like your energy is being siphoned by life itself. Because healing is not about the tools but about the framework behind them. Without a compass, even the most sacred practices can feel like spiritual guesswork.

The HOPE Method was born from that longing of always wishing for something simple, sacred, and structured. Something that speaks both to the part of you that wants a convenient daily practice and the part of you that just wants to function without burning out or disappearing.

Soul Seed to Take With You

YOUR BODY IS NOT A battlefield to fight against. It is an altar — a sacred place where healing takes root. Each time you return to your breath, you are making a choice: peace instead of panic. In that moment, you are tuning yourself back to HOPE, remembering that your body was always meant to be a place of presence, safety, and renewal.

At its heart, HOPE is a map. Four directions. Four invitations. Four ways of coming home.

Each letter holds a principle, not a rule, but a rhythm. Let's begin.

H — Harness – The Power of Gathering

TO HARNESS IS TO GATHER. To pull your energy back from all the places it has been scattered or left behind. This is not just physically, but emotionally, mentally, and spiritually.

When you harness, you reclaim your awareness from the past that haunted you, the future that panicked you, and the people who never returned what they borrowed. You come back into the now. You come back into your body. Harnessing is not a power move. It's a prayer. A quiet act of sovereignty that says: "I belong to myself again."

You'll know you need to harness when you feel unanchored, hyper-vigilant, hyper-focused, dissociated, or like everyone else's energy lives in your nervous system rent-free. Procrastination is also a signal that often it is not laziness, but scattered energy that has not yet been gathered back into focus. Harnessing gathers the fragments and makes space for movement. At its heart, Harness is about awareness, gathering, and presence. It reminds you that healing cannot begin until you have called yourself back. In simple terms, Harness means learning how to gather your energy.

Harnessing is the first step in the rhythm of HOPE, because without gathering your scattered pieces, there is nothing steady to build upon. Each return teaches your body and soul what safety feels like — the foundation for wisdom, healing, and love to come.

O — Optimal – The Courage of Choosing

THIS PILLAR MAY SURPRISE you. It is not about being the best version of yourself, but it is about choosing what is most aligned.

Fragmentation and survival often teach us to choose what is familiar, not what is healthy. Familiar can be chaos. Familiar can be over-functioning. Familiar can be self-abandonment dressed up as loyalty.

To choose what's optimal means asking: "What serves my energy, not just my ego?" "What helps me expand, not contract?" "What actually feels true in my body?"

This is not about perfection or productivity. It is about recognizing the difference between survival patterns and soul patterns. That way you can choose the one that keeps you whole.

At its heart, Optimal is about choice, alignment, and honesty. It is the invitation to stop defaulting to old patterns and begin choosing what is best for your soul.

When you choose what is optimal, you begin the lifelong practice of self-love — not as a feeling, but as a daily act of alignment. Each choice becomes a declaration: I am worthy of what supports my wholeness.

This is why the HOPE Method begins here. It starts with you. With the courage to choose what is optimal, so you can reclaim authenticity, self-love, and the sovereignty of living in harmony with your true self.

P — Positive – Redefining Joy

LET US BE CLEAR: HOPE does not ask you to slap a smile on your grief or chant affirmations over your suppressed rage. This pillar is about authentic positivity. It is the kind of positivity that grows from truth, not performance. Being "positive" in the HOPE Method means choosing to work with your emotions, not against them. It means embracing the kind of joy that can coexist with tears. It means knowing that laughter is not a betrayal of your pain, but it is alchemy.

Here, positive is not the absence of shadow. It is the presence of light in the middle of it. To live in this kind of positivity is to honor your whole spectrum of feeling. It is to say: I can carry grief and still open to beauty. I can name my anger and still choose peace. I can feel sorrow and still allow myself to dance.

This positivity does not erase the wound because it teaches you that you are more than the wound. It transforms survival into creativity, heaviness into expression, and silence into song. At its heart, Positive is about joy, forgiveness, and creativity. It redefines positivity as a practice of truth-telling that makes space for both sorrow and light. And when you practice this kind of positivity, you discover that hope is not fragile, it is regenerative, multiplying each time you choose to meet life with honesty and wonder.

E — Energy – The Thread that Connects It All

ENERGY IS THE THREAD that runs through it all. It is both the result and the resource. To honor energy is to protect your field, cleanse your inputs, and learn how to raise your vibration without bypassing the human experience. This is where we work with your frequency. Your rhythms. Your environment. Your sensory landscape.

It is not about doing more; it is about doing what actually replenishes you. When you understand energy, you no longer spend your life trying to be "more." You begin choosing to be well. Energy is felt in the smallest details — the foods you eat, the colors that surround you, the conversations you keep. It is drained when you stay in places or patterns that no longer fit, and it expands when you align with truth.

Scattered energy feels like noise in your system, while stagnant energy feels like heaviness in your body. Both are invitations — not to push harder, but to return to practices that clear, ground, and restore. At its heart, Energy is about reclaiming, refining, and raising. It teaches you to protect your frequency, restore what feels heavy, and rises into the vitality that makes you fully alive. And when you tend to your energy with intention, you discover that wellness is not a task to achieve — it is a state of resonance you can return to, again and again.

These four directions or pillars of HOPE defined through Harness, Optimal, Positive, Energy that are not steps on a ladder. They are more like seasons, waves, or sacred breaths. You will move through them cyclically. Sometimes all in a day. Sometimes all in a moment.

HOPE does not ask for perfection. It asks for practice. And now that you have met the pillars, you are ready to begin the work of living inside them.

To live inside them, you must first understand the instrument they are designed to steady: your nervous system. Your nervous system is your internal tuning fork. It sings to the key of safety through the dissonance of survival. It does not speak in words or logic. It speaks in sensations: the tightness in your chest, the urge to flee a room, the tear that comes out of nowhere when someone finally looks you in the eye.

The truth is, we do not rise to our goals, but we return to our regulation. And if the world taught you early on to scan for danger, to brace for impact, to hold your breath and wait for the blow. Then it is not your fault that relaxation feels foreign.

But healing means creating a new rhythm inside your body. Not just thinking differently but also feeling differently. Regulation becomes the ground on which sovereignty and wholeness are rebuilt.

The HOPE Method holds regulation as sacred. Because when you are regulated, you can reconnect. To your breath. To your truth. To your joy. To your higher self. And to others, primarily not through performance, but through presence.

And presence is where your healing begins to take root.

Sound as the Universal Language of Energy

SOUND IS ONE OF THE oldest languages of HOPE. Every culture has turned to rhythm, song, or chant to carry them through suffering and into celebration. Drums steady the heartbeat. Lullabies soothe the anxious child. Bells remind us of the sacred. These sounds are more than traditions — they are frequencies that align us with something greater.

To understand HOPE is to understand that you are not separate from vibration. The very atoms in your body move in resonance. Your voice, your breath, your heartbeat — they are all frequencies, carrying messages of alignment or dissonance. When you choose sound intentionally, you choose to remember your connection to the whole.

The HOPE Method begins within you, yet its impact ripples far beyond — because healing is never only personal; it resonates through the collective field we all share. Sound reveals that healing is both individual and collective, vibrating through the shared human field. To harness HOPE is to listen for resonance — in music, in silence, in the rhythm of your own breath — and let that resonance call you home.

HOPE in Practice: Rhythm Reset

PAUSE HERE. Let's reset your rhythm together. Right now, drop your shoulders. Unclench your jaw. Breathe in through your nose for four counts, hold for four, exhale out your mouth for six. Let the exhale be longer than the inhale — this is how you signal safety to your body. Repeat three times.

Notice: the world didn't change, but something inside you did. You've likely heard of fight, flight, freeze, or fawn — these are not personality flaws. They're survival states. Your nervous system developed them to protect you. When something felt too big, too fast, too much — your body said, I've got you.

Even now, that same system is trying to help you. But you no longer live in that same danger. You are safe to recalibrate.

Regulation is your birthright. It doesn't mean you're always calm. It means you know how to return to calm. It means you can feel without flooding. Hold space without collapsing. Speak your truth without shaking.

This is nervous system alchemy. This is turning survival into sovereignty.

Soul Seed to Take With You

I CAN RETURN TO CALM. My body knows the way.

The Science of Safety

THE VAGUS NERVE IS the body's superhighway of safety.

It runs from the brainstem through your throat, heart, lungs, and gut — carrying signals that tell your system: fight or rest.

When you hum, breathe deeply, cry, laugh, sing, or even gargle — you are toning this nerve. You are not just coping. You are reprogramming. Through daily, simple rituals — breathing, shaking, walking barefoot, placing a hand on your chest — you are literally creating new neural pathways. This is how fragmentation begins to be repaired. This is how we harness optimal positive energy — one moment, one breath at a time.

And this is also the science of safety: your nervous system learns through rhythm, repetition, and relationship. Each small signal of safety builds on the last, reminding your body that it does not have to live braced for danger. Over time, those tiny rituals of breath, laughter, and presence create a new baseline.

Fragmentation heals not through one dramatic breakthrough, but through steady reminders that you are safe enough to soften. This is how we begin to Harness Optimal Positive Energy — not just as an idea, but as lived truth in your body.

For those who want to explore the research more deeply, Stephen Porges' Polyvagal Theory offers a clear explanation of how the vagus nerve shapes safety and connection.

Soul Seed to Take With You

SAFETY IS NOT A DESTINATION. It is a rhythm my body can return to, one breath at a time.

Why HOPE Works When Others Fail

OTHER METHODS ARE LINEAR — step one, step two, step three. They expect healing to move like a straight road. But trauma does not move in straight lines. Neither does life.

HOPE succeeds because it is cyclical. Like seasons, like breath, like tides. You don't climb HOPE like a ladder — you live inside it like a rhythm. That's why HOPE works where other methods fail: it meets you in the middle of real life, in real time, with real energy.

Wisdom Through the Ages

THE TAO TE CHING SAYS, "Nature does not hurry, yet everything is accomplished."

Taoist wisdom reminds us that life unfolds in rhythms — sunrise and sunset, tides rising and falling, seasons shifting in their time. Nothing in nature forces itself forward, yet everything finds its place.

Your nervous system is not a machine to fix — it is nature to tend. Like a river, it knows how to flow when the debris is cleared. Like a tree, it knows how to grow when rooted in safety. Healing does not happen on a stopwatch. It happens in cycles, at the speed of trust. So, you are not behind. You are remembering. Each pause, each exhale, each moment of softening is a way of returning to the rhythm your body has always known. This is what it means to move at the speed of safety.

Soul Scribbles Prompt: Where in my life am I hurrying when I could let safety set the pace?

HOPEfully Human Moment

ONCE, DURING A HIGH stakes work meeting, my hands began to shake. Old trauma, old programming. My body went into survival mode even though I was not in danger.

At first, shame tried to take over — Not here, not now, hold it together. But instead of pushing through, I listened. I excused myself and walked to the restroom. Under the fluorescent lights, with the hum of the fan above me, I placed one hand on my heart and the other on my belly.

"I'm safe now," I whispered. Again, and again, until my breath caught the rhythm. In through the nose, out through the mouth. Slowly, my shoulders dropped. The trembling softened. It only took ninety seconds.

When I returned to the meeting, I did not just speak. I spoke from center. My words were not rushed. My tone wasn't defensive. I felt grounded, steady, and present — like I was finally leading the conversation instead of being led by my fear.

That moment taught me something I will never forget: regulation does not always require a retreat, a ritual, or an hour of meditation. Sometimes it is as simple as one pause, one breath, one whispered reminder: You are safe enough now.

Soul Scribbles Prompt: When was the last time my body reacted as if I were in danger, even though I was not? What simple reminder could I use next time to bring myself back to safety?

HOPE in Practice: Build Your Regulation Menu

TAKE A MOMENT TO CREATE a short list of practices that help you return to yourself. These might include simple, body-based resets like breathwork, tapping, humming, gently rocking, laying flat on the ground, or even speaking aloud: "I am safe. I am here."

Keep this list somewhere visible — on your desk, by your bed, or in your journal. On the harder days, do not force yourself to remember what works. Simply glance at your list and choose one practice from the menu.

This is how rewiring happens: not through force or perfection, but through small, consistent, compassionate action.

Soul Seed Affirmation

I DO NOT HAVE TO REMEMBER everything. I just have to choose one thing that brings me back.

HOPE is more than a framework — it is a rhythm your soul already knows.

Harness teaches you to gather what was scattered.

Optimal teaches you to choose what keeps you whole.

Positive reminds you that joy is not fragile but regenerative.

Energy shows you that vibration is the thread holding it all together.

But a framework, no matter how powerful, must begin somewhere. And every journey of HOPE begins the same way: with Harness — the sacred art of calling your energy back home. The question is: how do you gather what life has scattered, so you can finally feel whole again? That is where we turn next.

Chapter Seven

Harness – Gathering & Reclaiming Your Energy

You can't heal what you are not present for.
That is why the first pillar of the HOPE Method is not about fixing anything, rather it is about coming home. Before you can recalibrate, before you can rewire or reimagine, you must first return to yourself. And that begins by harnessing your energy.

To harness is not to control. It is to gather. To bring your energy — your attention, your breath, your essence — back from all the places it has been leaked, looped, or lost. To call your spirit out of the past, out of the panic, out of the people and places who never gave you safe passage. It is the energetic version of whispering to yourself, "Come back. I'm here. It's safe now."

Most of us are not aware of how dispersed our energy really is. It is in the unfinished conversation from three days ago. The story looping in your mind that never got closure. The unresolved tension in your chest from trying not to cry at work. The imaginary argument you had in the shower this morning. The energy it takes to keep all that held — that is what keeps you tired.

It is exhausting to live a life you are not fully inhabiting. And so, the invitation is this: Come back to the body. Come back to the breath. Come back to the now.

Not because the past did not matter. But because this is where the power lives.

Signs you need to harness your energy:

You feel "on edge" but cannot name why.

Your body is present, but your mind is three weeks, three years, or three lifetimes away.

You are absorbing everyone else's emotions and calling it empathy.

You have been doom-scrolling, people-pleasing, or over-explaining yourself into energetic bankruptcy.

You start and end the day with a sense of depletion — even when "nothing happened."

These are not failures. These are flags. And your body is waving them for a reason.

How We Begin to Harness

We do not need to build anything new here. We need to gather what was scattered.

Harnessing happens in moments — not monuments. A hand on the heart. A deep sigh. A whispered "I am here." It is brushing your arms with oil or warm water and telling your skin, "This is mine. I belong to me." It is sitting in silence until the noise recedes enough for your soul to speak again.

You can do this with ritual. You can do this in the car. You can do this at the kitchen sink, in the middle of a messy life.

Harnessing means reclaiming your center — not when life is calm, but especially when it is not.

And sometimes, the most powerful act of self-healing is not an hour of yoga or a perfect meditation. It is turning off your phone, drinking water, and saying no to the version of you that needs to earn love through exhaustion.

Wisdom Through the Ages

THE BUDDHA ONCE SAID, "With our thoughts, we make the world." To harness your awareness is to reclaim the pen. You become the author of your response instead of a character in someone else's chaos.

when you begin to harness, you will notice where your energy leaks. You might realize you have been giving it all away to people who do not honor it — or burning it at the altar of productivity. You may also discover that much of your energy was frozen in trauma, quietly stored in your nervous system, waiting for you to remember it existed.

Harnessing does not mean forcing yourself into stillness or perfection. It means making a commitment to notice, be mindful and redirect again and again. It is a sacred form of self-parenting. Of saying: "Hey, I see you. You matter. Let's move toward what feels like home."

You do not have to do it right. You just have to show up. And showing up for your energy is one of the most revolutionary things you can do in a world that profits off your depletion.

The Energetic Practice of Recalling Yourself

TRY THIS:

Close your eyes.

Breathe in slowly, softly.

And in your mind, say:

"Where is my energy right now?"

Wait. Feel. Listen.

Is it in a memory? A regret? A relationship? A conversation?

With compassion, say gently:

"I call myself back."

Breathe out.

Again:

"I call myself back."

Do this until you feel the whisper of presence returning.

Even if just for a moment. That's enough.

You do not need to harness perfectly.

You only need to begin.

HOPE starts by honoring that you can't raise your energy if you have never first claimed it as your own.

You might think healing begins with a bang, a breakthrough, a bolt of lightning, or a bottoming out. But more often, it starts as a whisper. A question. A tremble of truth. It begins when you harness the smallest sliver of willingness.

Harnessing is the first step of the HOPE Method because it calls you back into relationship with your own energy. It does not require perfection. Just participation. To harness something means to gather it in, to hold it close to partner with it. You begin to gather your breath, your courage, your curiosity and all the scattered parts of you and you gently begin the work of coming home.

There was a time I thought I had to "get it together" to be worthy of healing. But the truth is, I had to fall apart to see which pieces I wanted to keep. Harnessing taught me that the most important energy to start with is not motivation or joy. Truthfully, it is simply the awareness of noticing. Noticing what drains you. Noticing what feeds you. Noticing who you become around certain people or in certain places.

Belonging at a Cost

I WAS ONCE THE PERSON who showed up before anyone else. I unlocked the doors, stacked the chairs, taught the lessons, and led the lectures. I believed devotion meant more serving, more giving, more proving. And for a while, it looked like belonging.

But belonging built on performance always takes its toll. Exhaustion became my companion. My family life faded into the background. Assumptions were made, labels were whispered, and still I kept saying yes. Yes, even when my soul begged me to stop. Yes, even as my body began to break down. Yes, because I thought belonging depended on it.

In the end, my loyalty did not earn me love. It left me depleted and alone — carrying the weight of a community that only valued me when I was useful. What felt like rejection was, in truth, redirection.

Stepping away did not strip me of faith; it deepened it. I began to notice the sacred in places I had never been taught to look — in the warmth of sunlight, the silence of trees, the rhythm of the land. Out there, I could be myself without judgment, labels, or someone else's story defining me.

This is where the truth revealed itself: awareness is a reclaiming. And that reclaiming is simple, almost ordinary, yet profoundly powerful. It sounds like pausing long enough to listen for Wisdom. It feels like taking three conscious breaths to anchor Serenity. It looks like letting your Heart be honest about what it feels instead of burying it. It begins to Heal when you give your body what it has been crying for. It gains strength when you Express your truth, even if your voice shakes. It softens when you Accept what cannot be controlled. And it blooms when you choose Love — not the kind you have to earn, but the frequency you carry within.

These are the WiSH-to-HEAL practices. They are not lofty ideals, but daily anchors — gentle ways of gathering your scattered energy back to yourself. Each one invites you out of performance and back into presence. Each one offers a way to say, "I can carry what I've lived through and still choose joy in the present."

Embodied HOPE: Everyday Alignment

THIS SECTION is designed to support daily life through energetic alignment, frequency awareness, and soul-nourishing habits. These tools are not abstract ideas, they are anchors. They exist to help you live the HOPE Method not just in theory, but in your body, your space, and your rhythm.

Because here is the truth: fragmentation does not always show up in dramatic ways. Sometimes it looks like saying yes when you want to say no, wearing clothes that make you feel drained, scrolling past midnight, or running on caffeine instead of breath. These small, daily fractures in alignment add up until you feel scattered, heavy, or unrecognizable to yourself.

That is why everyday practices matter. They are how you reclaim your authority in real time. This is accomplished not by erasing your grief, loss, or burnout, but by walking beside those fragments with presence and joy. Each choice becomes a way of saying: "I see myself. I choose differently."

Embodied HOPE is where theory becomes rhythm. It is where sovereignty is built not in grand gestures, but in ordinary acts of care. When you learn to tend your body, your space, and your energy with intention, you stop leaking yourself into everything and everyone else. You begin to carry your energy gathered, grounded, and whole.

Sometimes when your energy feels low — when you are tired, foggy, heavy, or weighed down by a mood you cannot quite name — the cause is not always inside you. It may be around you. Your environment carries frequency, and so does everything in it. Where your phone is charging, what you've been eating, the sounds and lights surrounding you, even the products you put on your skin — these are not small details. They are signals, and they quietly shape how you feel about your body, your worth, and your energy.

Harnessing is not only about pulling your energy back from the past; it is also about noticing the everyday leaks in the present. Small adjustments in your environment — clearing clutter, dimming harsh lights, eating foods that feel clean, or choosing natural textures — create a field that supports you instead of scattering you. As you read earlier, HOPE is as much about alignment in the moment as it is about long-term healing.

HOPE in Practice: Soul-Aligned Fabric Field Guide

YOUR SKIN IS YOUR LARGEST organ, and the fabrics you wear touch your energy field all day long. Natural fibers like cotton, wool, hemp, linen, and silk allow your energy to breathe and realign. They feel alive because they come from life. Synthetics, by contrast, are petroleum-based and can block energetic flow, leaving you heavy or restless. If you've ever put on an outfit and felt drained before you even left the house, it may not have been the fit — it may have been the frequency of the fabric.

This is not about perfection or throwing out your closet. It is about awareness. Ask yourself: Does this fabric bring me home to myself? If the answer is yes, you are harnessing your energy in one of the simplest ways possible, by choosing to be wrapped in support instead of depletion.

Soul Scribbles Prompt

THINK OF AN OUTFIT that makes you feel alive, confident, or safe. What fabric is it made from? What does that teach you about the frequency your body prefers?

What you just noticed with fabrics is only one example of how energy awareness can shift your daily life. The same invitation applies to how you nourish yourself, how you rest, how you speak, and how you create space for joy. Each choice is a quiet commitment to a way of saying yes to yourself.

My HOPE Commitments

THIS IS YOUR PLACE to pause and make gentle promises to yourself not from pressure, but from presence. Think of these commitments as touchstones you can return to daily or weekly. They do not have to be perfect or permanent. They are reminders that your energy, your body, and your truth are worth honoring.

Begin with what feels simple and true. You might write:

I commit to speak to myself with…

I commit to nourish my body with…

I commit to honor my energy by…

I commit to release…

I commit to remember…

Return here often. Reflect. Refine. Rewrite if needed. These are not vows to trap you, they are living promises, small acts of alignment that grow with you as you grow.

Wisdom Through the Ages: The Beatitudes & HOPE Commitments

IT WAS NOT UNTIL I sat with these HOPE Commitments that I realized how closely they echo the Beatitudes from Jesus' Sermon on the Mount. The Beatitudes begin with "Blessed are…" and invite us into ways of being that open the heart to divine blessing through humility, compassion, purity of heart, and mercy.

The HOPE Commitments, though written in modern language, carry a similar rhythm. Each one is a vow to orient yourself toward alignment, compassion, and remembrance:

"I commit to speak to myself with…" echoes "Blessed are the pure in heart."

"I commit to nourish my body with…" reflects "Blessed are those who hunger and thirst for righteousness."

"I commit to honor my energy by…" mirrors "Blessed are the meek," choosing gentleness and respect for limits.

"I commit to release…" resonates with "Blessed are the merciful," letting go to make room for healing.

"I commit to remember…" calls to mind "Blessed are those who mourn, for they shall be comforted."

Both the Beatitudes and the HOPE Commitments remind us: transformation is not about perfection, but about orientation. They are invitations into a way of being that restores wholeness, compassion, and presence for yourself and for others.

And perhaps it is no coincidence that when the Bible was translated, the Beatitudes were preserved almost exactly as they were first spoken, not rephrased, just rendered in English. Their truth was already simple enough to carry across time and culture. In the same way, the HOPE Commitments stand as they are: simple truths, unpolished vows, strong enough to hold their own without needing to be dressed up.

These commitments are about orienting yourself toward presence through simple, intentional choices. And those choices don't just live in your thoughts or habits — they surround you every day, in the textures you touch and the colors you see. Fabrics carry frequency and so does space itself. Ancient wisdom has long affirmed this: in Chinese tradition, feng shui teaches that the way light enters a room, where objects are placed, and how energy flows through a doorway can either nourish or deplete you. The principle is simple — energy moves through space just as it moves through the body.

HOPE does not require you to master feng shui, but it does invite you to notice what feels aligned in your environment. Where light lands in your home, what objects rest on your desk, how clutter gathers at your door — all of these subtle details shape the flow of your energy. And once your space feels aligned, you can begin to notice the next layer of influence: the colors that surround you.

Color & Frequency Amplification

COLOR IS MORE THAN decoration — it is vibration made visible. Each shade interacts with your nervous system the way music does: some tones soothe, some energize, some overstimulate. This is why you might instinctively crave soft blues when anxious or lean toward golden tones when tired.

In HOPE, color is not magic or a quick fix. It is amplification. What you carry within is what color magnifies. A bold red might strengthen your confidence when you are grounded yet feel overwhelming if you are already scattered. Soft greens and blues can steady your system, though if your energy is already low, they may deepen your stillness rather than lift you.

The Color & Frequency Chart is a tool to help you choose with intention. Ask yourself: What do I need more of today — calm, energy, grounding, or clarity? Then allow color to support that choice. Whether worn on your body, placed in your workspace, or even woven into your meals, color becomes a gentle ally in shaping your vibration.

This is not about perfection or performance. It is about awareness. Simply asking, does this color bring me into alignment, or does it scatter me further? It is already an act of harnessing your energy.

Soul Scribbles Prompt

THINK ABOUT THE LAST outfit, room, or object you were drawn to because of its color. What did it do for your energy? Did it calm, uplift, or drain you?

Which color are you most drawn to right now? How does its frequency reflect the season of energy you are in?

WiSH-to-HEAL through HOPE Daily Rhythm Template

THINK OF THIS RHYTHM as gentle touchpoint to guide your day. Each one is simple, but together they help you harness your energy, stay aligned, and return to yourself.

Morning — Wisdom & Serenity

Begin with three deep breaths before reaching for your phone.

Speak one HOPE affirmation aloud.

Sip warm water with lemon or mineral salts.

Journal one intention for the day (Soul Scribbles).

Midday — Heart & Healing

Re-center with a walk, water, or gentle breath-work.

> Place your hand on your heart and ask: "What do I need right now?"

Notice: What needs clearing? What would feel restoring?

Evening — Expression, Acceptance & Love

Reflect: What gave me energy today? What drained it?

Cleanse your energy with an Epsom bath, energy brushing, or prayer. Close the day with gratitude, naming one small moment of light. This rhythm is not about perfection. It is about returning, again and again, to practices that anchor you in Wisdom, Serenity, Heart, Healing, Expression, Acceptance, and Love.

HOPE Blessing for Nourishment

"MAY THIS FOOD NOURISH not just my body, but my frequency. May it bring light to my cells and alignment to my spirit."

HOPE in Practice: The One-Minute Reset

PLACE ONE HAND ON YOUR heart, one hand on your belly. Inhale for four, exhale for six. Whisper gently, "I am safe in this moment. I am not who I was. I am who I am becoming." Do this before a difficult conversation, after a long day, or in the middle of a silent breakdown. It counts.

Which color are you most drawn to right now? How does its frequency reflect the season of energy you are in?

HOPEfully Human Moment

NOT EVERY HEALING MOMENT looks like a candlelit meditation or a perfect yoga pose. Sometimes it looks messy, awkward, or just plain human. These stories are here to remind you that healing is not about performance but more about presence.

I once tried to meditate after a particularly rough day, convinced I would emerge blissed out and balanced. Instead, I fell asleep sitting up, drooled on my shirt, and woke up to the sound of my dog barfing. It wasn't pretty. It wasn't holy. But it was real.

Harnessing your energy isn't about doing it flawlessly. It's about giving yourself permission to show up exactly as you are, even if that means falling asleep in the middle of meditation. Healing isn't always holy. But it's always human.

HOPE Frequency Activation

THIS PRACTICE IS OFFERED as a sacred close to the Revelation. It carries the energy of integration and the rule of three. So that the knowing isn't just read, but felt, spoken, and remembered deep within your cells.

Whenever you touch true alignment, even for a breath, you are already vibrating with God and the universe. Enlightenment is not a final destination; it is the felt moments when your body, your breath, and your spirit are in rhythm with something greater.

Here is how to begin:

Read it. Let the words land on your mind.

Speak it aloud. Let your voice vibrate with the truth.

Breathe it in. Place your hand on your heart and let the vibration settle into your body.

This is how knowledge becomes wisdom. When it is not only thought but embodied. This is HOPE in frequency: an activation that reminds you of your belonging to yourself, to God, and to the whole of creation.

HOPE in Practice: Harness with Sound

When you feel scattered, let sound become your anchor. Choose one tone, song, or frequency. Sit or lie still, close your eyes, and place a hand on your chest. Let the sound wash over you until you feel your body sync with its rhythm. In that moment, your energy is no longer scattered as it is gathered, harnessed, and whole.

Invocation: A Soul Whisper

THIS INVOCATION IS meant to be spoken aloud or in silence as a way of welcoming yourself into deeper knowing. Think of it as opening a door, reminding your body and spirit that you are safe to return to truth.

"I call upon the light within me, the voice that has never lied, the energy that remembers. May I release what is not mine. May I rise to what I came here to be. I am safe to shine. I am ready to reveal. I am returning to the frequency of truth."

Affirmation: To Anchor the Frequency

AFFIRMATIONS ARE NOT magic spells. They are reminders of the words you choose to plant in your mind and body until they become lived truth. When repeated with intention, they reshape your inner dialogue, soften old stories, and call your energy back into alignment.

Here is how to use this one:

Read it daily. Let the words settle into your awareness.

Speak it aloud. Feel the vibration move through your body.

Write it 3x in your journal. Writing engages a different part of the brain and helps integrate it more deeply.

I remember who I am. I am a soul of light, walking this earth with sacred purpose. My truth is not too much. My gifts are not too strange. I bring peace. I bring HOPE. I bring heaven to earth.

Soul Seed to Take With You

YOU DO NOT NEED TO be at your best to begin. You only need to bring yourself, just as you are.

Soul-Guided Journal Prompt: A Doorway Within

THIS PROMPT IS MEANT to help you listen inward and put words to what your soul has always known. Do not overthink it. Let yourself write freely, without judgment. You may be surprised at what flows out when you give yourself permission.

Ask yourself:

What truth have I always carried but rarely spoken aloud?

If fear wasn't steering me, what would I finally admit about who I am or what I'm here to do?

When have I seen light in places others only saw shadow and what did that teach me? How can I begin living more honestly and radiantly as a messenger of HOPE, starting today?

Harness is not about control — it is about return. Each breath, each pause, each whisper of presence calls you back into yourself. But once you have gathered what was scattered, a new question emerges: what will you do with what you now hold? Will you keep choosing what is familiar — even when it drains you? Or will you dare to choose what is Optimal — what expands your soul instead of shrinking it? That is where we turn next.

Chapter Eight

Optimal – Choosing What Truly Serves

There comes a point in healing when survival is no longer the goal. You have already survived. Now the question becomes: what serves me best?

The second pillar of HOPE — Optimal — is not about being perfect. It is about attunement. Alignment. It is the quiet bravery of choosing what nourishes your nervous system rather than what simply distracts it. And that's harder than it sounds. Because familiarity is seductive.

We return to the job that drains us because at least we know what to expect. We stay in friendships that shrink us because they have been around forever. We choose partners, patterns, or personas that feel like home, even if home was chaotic, conditional, or cold.

But healing asks us to get curious about the difference between what feels familiar and what is optimal.

Optimal is not always easy. It often requires unlearning. It might feel awkward. Foreign. Even "wrong" at first, not because it is wrong, but because your nervous system was trained to feel safe in discomfort.

Optimal doesn't always mean softer. Sometimes it means stronger boundaries. Sometimes it means resting instead of explaining. Sometimes it means walking away from what is good enough, so you can discover what's actually good for you.

Sometimes what feels familiar are the old thought patterns we've rehearsed for years: 'I'm not enough,' 'I'll never change,' 'This is just who I am.' Choosing Optimal also means learning to rewrite those inner scripts. Later in this book, I'll share more about a practice called cognitive self-change — a way of catching and reframing those thoughts so they align with truth and healing.

Optimal — The Choice that Changes Everything

OPTIMAL IS THE FOUNDATION of the HOPE Method because it is where theory becomes action. Harnessing your energy is essential, but it is the choice of what to do with that energy that directs your path. Optimal asks: What serves my healing, my wholeness, my true self — not just what feels familiar or easy? This is the moment when you stop repeating patterns that once kept you safe but now keep you small.

For many, smoking or vaping has become that kind of pattern. The inhale, the pause, the exhale mimic calm — but what you are soothing is not the craving, it is the scattered energy beneath it. In survival, the cigarette feels like a friend; in truth, it is only a substitute for the breath your body has been asking for all along.

Smoking is not only about soothing anxiety — it is also about patterned repetition. The hand-to-mouth motion, the break from routine, the familiar cycle of inhaling and exhaling all train the nervous system to expect relief. Optimal invites you to honor the need for ritual, but to choose one that truly restores your energy instead of depleting it.

Choosing Optimal does not mean choosing perfection. It means choosing alignment. It means noticing the crossroads — between fear and trust, depletion and renewal, suppression, and expression —

and stepping, even in the smallest way, toward what lifts you. Every time you choose what is Optimal for your soul, you strengthen your sovereignty, you reshape your nervous system, and you open space for HOPE to become embodied in real time.

HOPE in Practice: Breath Instead of Smoke

WHEN THE URGE TO SMOKE or vape rises, pause and notice: your body is asking for calm and ritual. Try this instead:

Inhale deeply through your nose, as though you are gathering scattered energy back into yourself.

Hold your breath for as many seconds as you comfortably can. This simulates the pause your nervous system craves and rewires neural pathways that once linked relief to smoke.

Exhale slowly through your mouth, imagining you are releasing tension like smoke leaving your body.

Repeat three times. If your hands feel restless, hold a pen, a stone, or a mug — giving your body the comfort of ritual while teaching it a new pattern of relief.

With practice, this breath ritual satisfies both the patterned repetition and the nervous system's need for calm. Each time you choose breath over smoke, you strengthen your freedom and reclaim your energy.

How Do You Know What's Optimal?

YOU LISTEN. YOU PAUSE. You feel. Your body knows. It always did. The shoulders that tense when a "friend" texts. The stomach drops when you open that email. The breath that shallows every time you try to "push through."

You listen. You pause. You feel. Deep down, your body already knows it always has. Think about the shoulders that tighten when a "friend" texts, the stomach that sinks when you open that email, or the way your breath goes shallow every time you try to force yourself to "push through." These aren't random reactions; they're signals. Your body is speaking, whispering what your soul has been trying to say all along: this isn't optimal.

Of course, optimal doesn't mean you'll avoid all discomfort. Growth has its aches and stretching pains. But there's a difference between the necessary discomfort of growth and the heaviness of suffering. To live optimally is to stop confusing struggle with sanctity, to stop believing that pain is proof of worth.

So, you begin to notice. You start asking yourself: Does this energize me or drain me? Am I choosing from love or from fear? Is this an old pattern I am repeating, or a new alignment I am stepping into? These questions may not always give you perfect answers, and you will not get it right every time. But that was never the point. The point is that you have begun to ask, and in the asking, you are already shifting. You are reclaiming awareness. You are learning to trust the wisdom that has been in you all along. Stirring quietly, steady, and waiting for you to return.

Rewiring the Familiar

NEUROPLASTICITY TELLS us the brain can change. HOPE reminds us: so, can your choices.

What feels familiar often feels safe. Even if it is the very pattern that has fragmented us. The body clings to what it knows: chaos disguised as love, exhaustion disguised as worthiness, silence disguised as peace. Familiarity becomes a kind of comfort, even when it keeps us divided within ourselves.

But safety can be rewired. You can begin teaching your body that joy is not dangerous. That stability is not boring. That calm is not the same as numbness. These new associations do not come overnight. They are formed slowly, through repetition, practice, and patience. The same way the old pathways of fragmentation were once carved. Every gentle choice in favor of your healing is a signal to your nervous system: it is okay to rest here.

To live in what is optimal is to begin making micro-decisions in favor of your future self. The one who is rested, aligned, whole. And when you choose differently, you are not betraying the self who survived through fragmentation. You are honoring them. You are giving your past self what they never had permission to choose: safety without fear, love without loss, peace without punishment.

This is the work of HOPE. To believe that no matter how deeply your brain or body has been trained to brace for fracture, you can choose again. You can rewire not just your mind, but your entire way of being in the world.

What Is Optimal Today?

OPTIMAL DOES NOT LOOK the same every day. Some days, it is a green smoothie and a morning walk. Other days, it is French fries and a long nap with your phone set to Do Not Disturb. Sometimes, optimal looks like a brave conversation where you finally speak your truth. Other times, it means protecting your peace by saying nothing at all.

This is not about optimization for productivity, perfection, or performance. It is not about squeezing more out of yourself. It is about optimization for presence. The more you choose what is optimal (even in the smallest ways) the more your nervous system begins to trust the now. Slowly, your body starts to learn that safety can exist in ordinary choices.

Optimal living is deeply tied to boundaries. Every time you choose what supports your well-being, you are drawing a line in the sand that says, this is where I honor myself. Boundaries are not walls; they are pathways back to alignment. They remind your nervous system that safety is not found in overextending, people-pleasing, or staying silent. Safety is found in truth. And each time you set one, you rewire your body to trust that it is safe to protect your peace.

You are not too much. You are not too sensitive. You are not dramatic, difficult, demanding, or broken. You are aware. And with each choice, you are remembering what it feels like to live inside a body that is aligned with truth.

Choosing what is optimal does not mean you have failed when you forget. It means you are practicing how to return. It is one thing to notice your energy. It is another thing entirely to choose what is optimal over what is familiar. And this is where the work of HOPE comes alive because what feels familiar is not always what is aligned.

Fragmentation has trained many of us to cling to the familiar, even when it is harmful. "Familiar," often masquerades as safe because the body recognizes it. We mistake chaos for passion. We confuse adrenaline for love. We settle for crumbs when our whole being is starving for sunlight. But once you begin to harness awareness, you gain the power to optimize your life in ways your past self could not imagine.

This chapter is about that sacred moment of choice. Not the loud decisions made in public, but the quiet pivots in the kitchen at midnight, or in the parking lot when your body says no but your mouth wants to say yes. It is in those small, almost invisible moments that you begin to reclaim yourself.

In the HOPE Method, "optimal" does not mean perfect. It does not mean easy. It does not mean pleasing everyone else. Optimal means aligned. It means life-giving. It means you have paused long enough to ask your nervous system a simple but powerful question: Will this expand me, or will it exhaust me? And when you choose what expands you (even once) you begin the slow, steady work of remembering yourself whole.

Stillness as a Soul Strategy

IN A WORLD THAT GLORIFIES noise and movement, stillness can feel almost rebellious. We are taught that to pause is to fall behind, that silence is emptiness, that being alone with ourselves is something to be avoided. But what if stillness is not weakness, but strategy? What if silence is not a void, but a sanctuary?

Stillness is where the nervous system recalibrates. It is where the body exhales, where the mind declutters, and where the soul remembers its own voice. Without stillness, we mistake adrenaline for aliveness and busyness for worth. With stillness, we begin to see clearly again. We realize that our deepest answers do not shout, they whisper in the stillness of our minds.

As a soul strategy, stillness is not about withdrawing from life but about returning to it with clarity. It teaches us to pause before reacting, to breathe before deciding, to listen before speaking. In the quiet, we remember that expansion is not forced—it unfolds.

This kind of silence is not empty; it is full. Full of breath. Full of presence. Full of the subtle wisdom that only emerges when we stop running from ourselves. When silence becomes sanctuary, stillness becomes strength.

To choose stillness is to choose alignment over urgency, presence over performance, truth over noise. It is to give yourself permission to "be" not as the world demands you to "be," but as your soul already is.

The Healing Frequency of Stillness

IN A WORLD OF HUSTLE, healing sometimes looks like not moving at all. We are taught to measure our worth in motion, to prove our value through doing, to equate stillness with laziness or falling behind. But stillness is not passive. Stillness is a frequency. A vibration that resonates with restoration. It is active listening. It is the sacred pause that says: I trust the unfolding, even when I don't control it.

For many of us, especially those shaped by fragmentation, stillness once felt unsafe. Silence was not a sanctuary; it was the space before impact. It was the waiting room for the next blow, the next rejection, the next loss. Rest felt like vulnerability, like lowering your guard in a world that had already taken too much. So, we learned to keep moving. We ran, we hustled, we over functioned because motion felt like survival.

But healing invites us into a different relationship with stillness. It teaches us that stillness is not absence. It is presence. It is where God whispers. It is where the body finally exhales after years of holding its breath. It is where the soul, long out of sync, has a chance to catch up and settle back into the body.

Stillness is not a void. It is fullness. It is the space where awareness ripens, where patterns loosen their grip, where your nervous system recalibrates toward safety. In the quiet, you may feel the ache of everything you once outran, but you will also feel the pulse of everything that is waiting to meet you.

This is why stillness is a healing frequency: it vibrates with restoration, with remembrance, with alignment. In stillness, the body begins to trust that rest is not weakness. The heart begins to believe that silence is not abandonment. And the soul begins to recognize that it is no longer fractured, no longer waiting, because it is home.

HOPE in Practice: The Optimal Question

YOUR PRACTICE BEGINS here: before saying yes to anything. It does not matter if it is a request, a relationship, a role, or even a calendar invite; take the time to pause and ask yourself:

"Is this optimal for my body, my energy, and my future self?"

This is not just a nice idea; it is a soul strategy. Every time you ask this question, you create space between the automatic yes you were conditioned to give and the aligned yes, your body is longing for. In that pause, you reclaim choice. You stop abandoning yourself in the name of being good, or kind, or easy to love. You begin to honor what is life-giving, not just familiar.

If your answer feels cloudy, uncertain, or conflicted step back. Don't rush clarity. Sometimes the most sacred act of devotion is not found in the yes, but in the courage to say no.

There was a time when I believed healing would come from fixing the outer world: a better job, a quieter house, someone else's apology. But real healing began when I stopped abandoning myself in the name of pleasing others. I realized that my definition of kindness had been twisted to mean, "Don't make anyone else uncomfortable."

But what about the discomfort of being half-alive in your own life?

To choose what is optimal is to be disloyal to the dysfunction that once kept you afloat. It is to admit: "I deserve more than survival." "I am allowed to live."

Wisdom Through the Ages: Stoicism & The Soul of Stillness

THE STOIC PHILOSOPHER Epictetus once taught: "First say to yourself what you would be; and then do what you have to do."

This is not hustle culture. This is HOPE culture. It is not about striving harder-it is about becoming clearer. Healing begins with naming who you long to be and then making choices that honor that becoming. Each decision is an act of alignment, not achievement.

Healing also means recognizing what depletes you. It means walking away, not only from people who drain you, but also from versions of yourself that once settled, shrank, or shut down just to stay loved. The Stoics would remind us: it is not about becoming a "better" person. It is about becoming a more honest one.

Epictetus also wrote: "Man is not disturbed by things, but by the views he takes of them." The Stoics were not emotionless; they were clear. They believed that inner peace is not found in controlling the chaos of the outer world, but in governing our response to it. It is a radical shift: from demanding life bend to our will, to learning how to bend our perspective toward truth.

Seneca added: "He who is brave is free." To the Stoics, freedom was not the absence of trial, but the presence of courage. Stillness was not weakness, but strength. It was restraint, grace, alignment with nature's rhythm. Seneca also wrote: "To bear trials with a calm mind robs misfortune of its strength and burden."

In this, we can see the bridge to HOPE. Stillness is not avoidance. It is power. It is the ability to pause long enough to ask: What is mine to carry, and what is not? It is the awareness that we may not control every storm, but we can choose the way we anchor ourselves through it.

Energy & the Nervous System

YOUR NERVOUS SYSTEM is always working to conserve energy. It does this by sticking to patterns, even destructive ones, because the familiar feels safer than the unknown. This is why so many of us find ourselves drawn back into old dynamics, repeating cycles that drain us, or mistaking chaos for passion. It is not weakness. It is wiring.

This is also why healing is less about raw willpower and more about neuroplasticity. The brain's ability to rewire and create new pathways. Each time you choose peace over panic, rest over running, alignment over approval, you are carving out a new trail in the brain. You are teaching your nervous system that safety can live in stillness, that calm does not mean danger, and that love does not have to hurt.

The process is slow, and that is by design. Your nervous system does not transform in a single moment of clarity. It does, however, shift through repetition, through gentle practice, through consistent signals that say: you are safe here. This is why in the HOPE Method; we emphasize micro-decisions. Each time you pause to ask the Optimal Question, you are feeding a new neural pathway. You are telling your body: this is what love feels like. I can choose this again.

Think of it this way: your old patterns were a map to survival, but they were drawn in scarcity, fear, and fragmentation. Now you are drawing a new map, one that leads not just to survival but to wholeness. With every small choice toward alignment, you invest in your future self. The one who is rested, grounded, and alive.

HOPEfully Human Moment

I ONCE SPENT AN ENTIRE afternoon convincing myself that frozen pizza was an "optimal choice" because it was quick, easy, and technically edible. But the truth? My soul wanted soup. Hot, nourishing, made-from-scratch soup.

We do this all the time. We justify the ten mini candy bars because they are "little." We excuse the handful of chips because it was not the entire bag. Once, I even talked myself into eating cookies in the middle of my "eat nothing purchased in a wrapper" plan, simply because they were homemade. I chose them over the healthy snack I had actually packed for myself. My logic? They were not in a wrapper, so they did not count the same as store-bought. In that moment, I was not following the rule. I was tweaking it just enough to satisfy my craving.

We laugh, but this is the work: noticing when you are settling, even with yourself. Noticing when you are making bargains that keep you from what you truly want. The HOPE Method does not ask you to be perfect; it asks you to be honest. Honest enough to admit that your frozen pizza is not soup, your cookies are not nourishment, and your body is asking for something better.

The power is not in never choosing the pizza, or the chips, or the candy. The power is in learning to pause long enough to ask yourself: What is truly optimal right now? And sometimes the bravest choice is to stop settling for "good enough" when your soul is hungry for more.

Grief, Sorrow, Solitude, and Divine Timing

THERE IS A STILLNESS that comes only after loss. Not the peace-filled kind of stillness, but the hollow kind — the kind that echoes in an empty room and makes hours stretch into years. It is the stillness of absence, of waiting, of not knowing how to go on.

And yet, even in that emptiness, something stirs. Stillness is where grief humbles us, where our defenses fall away and we are left bare with what is true. It feels like nothing is happening, yet beneath the surface, grace is gathering the pieces we thought were gone.

Grief, when unprocessed, can weave what I call sorrow bonds — invisible cords that tether us to what was lost. We replay the "what ifs" and the "if onlys." We cling to imagined futures that will never come, and we hold on so tightly that sorrow becomes a constant companion. These bonds are not a sign of weakness; they are proof of how deeply we loved. But when we mistake them for the only way to stay connected, we end up carrying grief as a chain instead of honoring it as a teacher.

Processing sorrow differently means loosening those bonds without severing the love. It means allowing memory to be a bridge, not a weight. It looks like creating new rituals of remembrance, telling the story with gratitude instead of only pain, and letting love express itself in presence rather than attachment.

Let your solitude be sacred. Let your grief be more than a wound — let it be a teacher. Grief teaches patience, perspective, and presence. It reminds us that love was real, and that loss is proof of connection. Solitude whispers that we are never as alone as we think; we are held by memory, by spirit, and by God's quiet hand.

Stillness teaches us this too: Not all seeds bloom on our timeline. Some require winters of waiting before they break the soil. Not every silence is punishment. Some silences are the womb of new creation. Sometimes the Divine holds us in stillness not to withhold, but to recalibrate our vibration — aligning us with what we could not yet carry.

Grief, sorrow, solitude, and divine timing are not detours from the path; they are the path. When you trust that stillness is not empty but pregnant with grace, you begin to see that loss does not end the story. It opens a new chapter. And in that opening, HOPE becomes the quiet ember that never goes out — waiting to rise again.

The Soul of Surrender

SURRENDER DOES NOT mean giving up. It means giving over to trust, to timing, to something wiser than your own agenda. When you stop demanding that life bend to your plan, you begin to experience the relief of being carried by a greater current. As Epictetus wrote: "Don't demand that things happen as you wish. Let events happen as they do, and your life will flow well."

So much of our stress and worry comes from trying to control what was never ours to manage. We grip tightly to outcomes, to people, to plans, as if the tighter we hold, the safer we will be. But the truth is, gripping only exhausts us. The mind spins, the body tenses, and our soul contracts under the weight of trying to solve what logic and effort cannot.

Surrender is the release. It is the moment you unclench your fists and take a breath. It is trusting that even if you do not understand the timing, there is timing. Even if you do not see the bigger picture, there is one. Destiny, path, divine order, whatever language you use; it is always moving in ways your mind could never map.

Stillness is the bridge between intention and manifestation. It is where you stop gripping and start receiving. It is the pause where your nervous system shifts from fight-and-force into flow-and-trust. And in that pause, you discover a freedom you did not know you were missing, the freedom of not having to figure it all out.

Surrender is not weakness. It is wisdom. It is the quiet confidence that your life does not depend on your endless striving, but on your willingness to align with what is already unfolding for your highest good.

And like all wisdom, surrender deepens when you take time to sit with it. Writing helps turn an idea into an embodied truth literally moving it from your head into your heart.

Soul Scribbles Prompt: Integrating Stillness

YOUR PRACTICE BEGINS here: take a quiet breath, set aside distractions, and let these questions guide your pen. Do not edit, do not overthink, just allow whatever rises to spill onto the page.

When was the last time I gave myself permission to be still without guilt, without explanation?

As I sit in silence, what emotions or sensations begin to rise? Do I resist them, or can I welcome them?

Where in my life am I confusing constant busyness with meaning or purpose?

What area of my life is asking me to release control and trust in divine timing?

When I soften into stillness, what truths about who I really am begins to surface?

Stillness Affirmations

"I AM SAFE IN STILLNESS." "I trust what comes to me in silence." "My power grows in rest." "Stillness restores my soul." Your practice begins here: Affirmations are not about forcing yourself to believe something you do not feel. They are gentle reminders, spoken often enough that your body begins to trust them. To work with affirmations, choose one that resonates and repeat it slowly out loud, if possible, while breathing deeply. You might place your hand on your heart, close your eyes, or write the words in your journal. Let the phrase settle into you like a seed. Return to it whenever your mind feels loud or restless.

Affirmations to guide you:

"I am safe in stillness."

"I trust what comes to me in silence."

"My power grows in rest."

"Stillness restores my soul."

HOPE in Practice: Optimal Choice: Entering Stillness

YOUR PRACTICE BEGINS here: Stillness doesn't have to be complicated. These practices are simple doorways—take time to choose one that calls to you or move through them in sequence. There is no wrong way to enter stillness; your only task is to pause, breathe, and allow yourself to be present.

Breath Ritual – Inhale for 4 counts, hold for 4, exhale for 8. Repeat slowly until your nervous system begins to soften.

Grounding Outside – Sit barefoot on the earth or rest your back against a tree. Let the earth hold you.

Soul Anchor Phrase – Whisper a mantra such as "I am here. I am safe. I am guided." Let the words sink deeper with each breath.

Stillness Journal – Open your journal and write what you hear in the quiet, even if it's just one word. Trust silence to speak in its own time.

Light & Listen – Light a candle, set a timer for 5 minutes, and simply listen — to your breath, to the quiet, to your soul.

Soul Seed to Take With You

FAMILIAR DOES NOT MEAN safe. Easy does not mean aligned. You are allowed to choose what heals you even if no one else understands.

Remember: stillness isn't absence. It's presence amplified. It is the space where you become reacquainted with your higher self, where you remember you are not here to chase the world but to align with it from the inside out. Carry this with you: The next time you feel pulled toward what is familiar but depleting, pause. Take a breath. Ask yourself: Will this heal me, or will this hollow me? Let stillness be the doorway back to alignment.

We learned: choosing what is Optimal means you stop settling for what is familiar and begin aligning with what actually serves your soul. But alignment is not only about the choices you make — it is also about what those choices create. When you choose what nourishes instead of what numbs, when you walk away from what drains and toward what sustains, something remarkable happens: your body begins to remember joy. And here is the paradox — joy is not the reward at the end of healing. Joy is part of the medicine itself. The question is: how do we reclaim joy without betraying our grief? How do we live in emotional integrity — where sorrow, laughter, rage, and love all have a place at the table? That is where we turn next.

Chapter Nine

Positive – Joy, Expression & Emotional Integrity

To be positive in a wounded world is not naive. It is radical. It means you have seen the darkness — and still choose to light a candle. It means you have been silenced — and still choose to sing. It means your joy is not a mask, but a reclamation.

This pillar is often misunderstood. Positive does not mean pretending. It does not mean bypassing your grief or forcing gratitude when your chest is on fire. In the HOPE Method, positivity is not performance. It's permission — to feel fully, to express yourself freely, and to choose your light without shame.

Positivity After Pain

WHEN YOU HAVE LIVED with trauma, joy can feel unsafe. You brace for its disappearance. You hold your breath when things get good. You may even sabotage peace because your nervous system mistakes it for danger. This is not dysfunction. It is defense.

The body remembers when joy was followed by loss. When laughter came before punishment. When being seen led to being hurt. So, it adapts. It learns to not feel too much. To stay "low" so it will not crash later. But that's not living. That's limbo.

And part of healing is letting yourself taste joy without apology. It is remembering that joy is a birthright, not a betrayal of your pain.

Emotional Integrity

BEING POSITIVE IS NOT about silencing your shadow, it is about being honest. Honest with your yes. Honest with your no. Honest with your rage, your radiance, and the ache in your bones that says, "I can't fake it today."

You do not owe anyone a curated version of your emotions. Positivity rooted in truth allows all parts of you to coexist. You can cry and still be hopeful. You can rage and still be rooted in love. You can feel messy and still carry light.

This is emotional integrity at that moment when your insides and outsides match. When you stop performing and start embodying.

Finding Your Joy Language

JOY LOOKS DIFFERENT to everyone. For some, it is dancing in the kitchen. For others, it is quiet mornings with tea. It might be painting, gardening, playing, poetry, running barefoot, or watching the wind flirt with the trees.

What matters is that you find what makes your energy hum. Start small. One moment of unforced delight. One hour of being deeply alive. One ritual that reminds you, you're more than your wounds.

You don't have to be cheerful. You just have to be true.

The Alchemy of Expression

EXPRESSION IS A SPIRITUAL act. When you speak, move, dance, scream, sob, laugh, these beautiful expressions from you move energy. And what does not get expressed becomes depressed.

The HOPE Method honors creative expression as a form of healing. Sing off-key. Journal like you are writing to God. Drum, stretch, paint, howl. Let your emotions be heard by yourself first, and maybe the world later.

You are not too emotional. You are awakening. Positive is not a mood. It's a movement that moves you toward truth, joy, wholeness, and liberation. It is what happens when you stop performing wellness and start living well. It does not mean plastering on a smile or chanting affirmations while your heart is breaking. It does not mean spiritual bypassing, ignoring pain, or denying the grit of your healing journey.

In the HOPE Method, positive means truthful. It means choosing light, not because you have never seen the dark, but because you have learned how to carry a lantern through it.

You do not heal by erasing what happened. You heal by finding a frequency that can hold what happened. And that frequency, more often than not, is love.

Being "positive" in the HOPE Method means choosing to work with your emotions, not against them. It means knowing that laughter is not a betrayal of your pain, but it is alchemy.

Here, positive is not the absence of shadow. It is the presence of light in the middle of it.

Positivity is resonance. Just as a single note can shift the tone of a whole song, a single choice toward joy, forgiveness, or creativity can shift the rhythm of your life. You are not pretending the sorrow isn't there — you are allowing vibration to move through it, carrying you somewhere new.

Ancient civilizations even built obelisks as pillars of resonance, symbols of energy linking earth and sky. In the same way, your body acts as a living transmitter: every word, breath, or song sends a signal through your whole being. And sometimes that signal comes in forms we least expect such as the words we resist.

Sometimes positivity looks like prayer, poetry, or song. Other times, it bursts out as raw language — a curse word shouted into the air, a sharp release that carries years of tension with it. Modern psychology has shown that swearing can actually reduce pain and release pent-up stress. From a HOPE perspective, this too is expression — vibration leaving the body instead of festering within it. It is not about hostility, but honesty. Sometimes the most healing thing you can do is give your feelings a voice, unfiltered, so that your nervous system can finally exhale. And that release, whether through words or through silence, you'll find it directly shapes how your brain encodes experience.

Positivity & the Brain

YOUR BRAIN REMEMBERS pain more easily than pleasure, a survival tactic known as the negativity bias. This is why joy must be practiced. HOPE teaches you to linger in beauty. To let a good moment soak in like sunlight. To wire in not just what you survived, but what you created from it. And as the brain rewires, the body responds, because positivity does not stop at thought, it ripples through biology.

Positivity & the Body's Healing Intelligence

POSITIVITY IN HOPE is not just emotional — it is biological. Research shows that hope and positive mindsets strengthen immunity, lower inflammation, and even speed recovery. The placebo effect itself is proof that belief has power: when the mind expects healing, the body often follows.

Gratitude, laughter, and joy are not luxuries; they are medicine. They shift brain chemistry, soften the stress response, and restore balance to systems thrown off by trauma. When you choose authentic positivity, you are not ignoring your wounds. You are signaling to your body: It is safe to heal.

One of the simplest, most researched ways this shows up is gratitude. Gratitude practice has been proven to reshape how the body and brain respond to stress.

The Practice of Gratitude

GRATITUDE IS NOT A bypass. It is not about ignoring pain or pretending you are fine. Gratitude is about presence — letting your body notice what is good, even in the middle of what is hard.

When you name a small gift — the way sunlight warms your skin, the softness of a blanket, the taste of tea, the laugh of a friend — you are inviting your nervous system to feel safe enough to soften. Gratitude helps shift your focus from what is missing to what is still here.

For trauma survivors, gratitude softens the brain's pull toward pain, teaching it to linger in beauty instead of threat — the survival instinct that clings more tightly to pain than to joy. Practicing gratitude teaches your mind to linger in beauty, to let goodness soak in like sunlight instead of slipping away unnoticed.

Gratitude does not erase sorrow, but it steadies you inside it. It is a form of emotional integrity, saying: yes, the ache is real... and so is this moment of grace.

Why We Laugh After We Cry

HAVE YOU EVER NOTICED how laughter sometimes slips in after a deep cry? This is not weakness or contradiction — it is healing intelligence at work.

When you cry, your body is releasing stress hormones and letting the nervous system discharge what it has carried. Once that release occurs, the body often swings back into balance through laughter. Endorphins rise, oxytocin softens your edges, and suddenly joy is possible again.

From a HOPE perspective, this rhythm is not random. It is proof that sorrow and joy are companions, not opposites. Crying makes room; laughter fills the space. Together, they remind you that healing is not about erasing pain but about allowing your body to move between states — contraction and expansion, release and renewal. Just as laughter restores balance after tears, sound restores balance after silence.

The Language of Frequency

THIS IS WHY SOUND AND music have always been companions to healing. When you sing, hum, or laugh, your nervous system responds: your breath deepens, your vagus nerve softens, and your body begins to regulate. A song can lift your spirit, a chant can steady your mind, a rhythm can remind you that you are not stuck. Vibration moves what words cannot.

Specific frequencies carry different invitations:

396 Hz eases fear and guilt, grounding you in safety.

417 Hz clears old patterns and helps you step into renewal.

639 Hz resonates with love and connection, softening isolation.

741 Hz supports clarity and self-expression.

852 Hz awakens intuition and restores inner light.

Positivity in HOPE is not about suppressing your humanity. It is about letting sound, movement, and joy bring you back into resonance with your wholeness. To choose positivity is to say: I will not bypass my shadow, but I will not let it silence my song.

At its heart, Positive is about joy, forgiveness, and creativity. It redefines positivity as a practice of truth-telling that makes space for both sorrow and light. And when you practice this kind of positivity, you discover that hope is not fragile — it is regenerative, multiplying each time you choose to meet life with honesty and wonder.

HOPE in Practice: Let Sound Move You

WHEN YOU FEEL HEAVY, let sound become your medicine.

Choose a sound. Play a frequency track, hum a tone, or pick a song that always stirs something in you.

Let your body respond. Close your eyes, sway, tap your foot, or simply breathe with the rhythm.

Notice the shift. As the vibration moves through you, ask yourself: What is softening? What is loosening? What feels alive again?

Anchor the moment. When the track ends, sit in silence for one breath, holding the resonance inside you.

This is positivity in practice: not a mask, but a vibration that carries you back to yourself.

HOPE in Practice: The Light Invocation

CLOSE YOUR EYES. IMAGINE a warm golden light surrounding your body. See it filling the room, the cracks, the wounds, the corners. Say aloud:

"I am safe to feel joy. I am allowed to feel peace. I will not dim to stay small."

Let that be your anchor. Even in stormy waters.

For many trauma survivors, positivity has been weaponized. We were told to "look on the bright side" instead of being held in our pain. We were asked to perform happiness instead of being allowed to feel grief.

But HOPE teaches that true positivity is not a mask. It's a muscle. And every time you reach for it whether, through joy, through forgiveness, through gentle laughter, you strengthen your ability to rise.

Wisdom Through the Ages

THE POET RUMI WROTE, "Don't grieve. Anything you lose comes round in another form."

This is the HOPE Method's definition of positive: not denial but transmutation.

Joy, in this work, becomes a radical act. It is sacred rebellion. Especially when you've lived a life that told you joy must be earned.

When you laugh while healing, you are not doing it wrong. You are reminding your body that it is safe to be fully alive. In fact, some people can realign their energy including all 7 of their chakras, through laughter alone. It is one of the body's most natural ways of restoring flow.

And yet, while laughter and joy are natural medicine, they don't always come naturally when you've lived through pain. The brain is wired to notice threats more than delights. Which is why joy doesn't just happen, it has to be practiced.

HOPEfully Human Moment

I ONCE CRIED THROUGH an entire episode of a cooking show. Not because it was sad, but because the woman made dumplings for her estranged daughter and said, "These are filled with my love."

Healing has made me so tender, even dumplings make me weep. That's the kind of positive I'm talking about — the kind that softens you into gratitude without asking you to deny the ache. Positivity doesn't just live inside us; it vibrates in the spaces we create. Just as sound can shift the body, color carries a frequency that can either soothe or amplify what is already present. I learned this the hard way...

Color Doesn't Lie: How Our Surroundings Amplify Energy

THERE WAS A SEASON when I painted my bedroom in deep purples. The walls, the pillows, even the curtains shimmered in shades of lavender and plum. I believed I was creating a sanctuary for my weary soul. But I wasn't alone in that room. I was still living inside a painful marriage, commuting to a toxic job, pouring my longing for peace into a space that wasn't energetically safe.

I thought I was raising the vibration. In truth, I was amplifying the frequency of what was already there. Purple, tied to the crown chakra, is a high-frequency color — but instead of ushering in serenity, it magnified dissonance: neglect, resentment, confusion, spiritual numbness.

That experience revealed a truth I now carry into the HOPE Method: color is not a cure; it is a conductor. It doesn't erase what exists; it amplifies it. Surround yourself with color, and you are tuning into its frequency. If your space — or your inner state — is steeped in fragmentation or sorrow, even the most beautiful hue will echo distortion.

Soul Seed to Take With You

"POSITIVITY IS NOT THE absence of pain. It is the presence of light in spite of it. And you, beloved, are becoming luminous. This is the promise of the HOPE Method."

This is why the P in HOPE — Positive — matters so deeply. Once we clear what is toxic and choose what is optimal, color becomes an ally. It magnifies what is authentic, sustaining alignment instead of masking hurt. We must clear before we amplify. We must align before we adorn.

Color is one conductor in a greater symphony of energy. Every sound, every breath, every choice vibrates at a frequency that shapes your reality. When truth and peace are present, color brightens not just the room but you. And when positivity is real, even your surroundings begin to heal alongside you.

Chapter Ten

Energy – Vibration, Frequency & Healing in Motion

Energy is the "First Language" of every human being, because everything is energy. From the beat of your heart to the heat in your palms. From the buzz of anxiety to the ache of unspoken grief. From sunlight dancing across your skin to the pull in your belly when someone walks into the room. Energy is not woo. It's what we're made of: movement, vibration, charge, resonance.

The ancient mystics knew this. The quantum physicists now prove it. Energy is the language of the body, the soul, the cosmos.

Science may not yet have an instrument that measures qi or prana the way it measures blood pressure, but it has been proven that the practices built around these concepts create measurable changes in the body. EEGs show shifts in brainwaves during meditation. ECGs reveal the heart's electromagnetic field moving into harmony during prayer or breath-work. Stress hormones drop. Immune cells strengthen. The nervous system steadies.

In other words, science is beginning to confirm what the ancients have always known: when you work with your energy (through breath, intention, or presence) you change your state. You shift from chaos into coherence, from depletion into restoration. Call it biology or call it spirit; the truth is the same. Energy moves us, and we can learn to move with it.

And because energy is always moving, it is always being influenced. Every thought you think, every action you take, every environment you step into contributes to your energetic field. In The HOPE Method, we don't just explore how to protect and restore that field, but we learn how to elevate it.

Your vibration that frequency you emit, is the signal you send into the world. And what surrounds you either supports that signal or distorts it. This includes people, media, emotions... and surprisingly, even the materials in your daily life.

Let's explore one of the most underestimated yet energetically dense materials we encounter daily: plastic.

Plastic surrounds us everywhere, from our kitchens to our closets. And while it's practical, it carries a kind of density, similar to an energetic heaviness that doesn't harmonize with our bodies. It lingers, it clutters, it dulls. And this is the deeper truth: everything we live with, consume, or wear is shaping our energetic field. Materials hold memory. Environments hold vibrations. Which means the things we overlook, like a water bottle, a synthetic shirt, a cluttered corner, are also part of the frequency we carry through the world.

Plastic and the Vibration of Cluttered Energy

WHAT SURROUNDS YOU shapes you. Take a look around. How many things within arm's reach are made of plastic — your cup, your chair, the wrapper from your lunch? We live in a world wrapped in it. Plastic doesn't breathe, change, or return to the earth with ease. It carries no life force. Energetically, it acts like a block — stagnant, dulling, and lifeless. Surrounding ourselves with it, especially in what touches our skin or food, can numb our sensitivity. It's like filling a garden with artificial flowers: colorful, but not alive.

Our bodies know the difference. The comfort of linen sheets, the grounding weight of wool, the softness of worn cotton — natural fibers carry traces of the earth. Plastic does not. The nervous system responds to this, even if our minds don't notice.

This isn't about eliminating plastic overnight. It begins with awareness. Notice how it feels to drink water from glass instead of plastic, or to wear cotton instead of polyester. These small shifts attune you to the vibrations you're living with.

To raise your frequency is to choose more consciously. Every material that touches your skin, enters your home, or fills your sacred space shapes your energy. The more we welcome life-giving substances, the more life we invite back into ourselves.

When Energy Stalls: Depression as Blocked Flow

DEPRESSION is often misunderstood as a flaw of character or a permanent state. From an energy perspective, it is what happens when flow collapses into stillness. Too much rest without release becomes stagnation. The spirit longs to create — to take thought and turn it into form — and when that expression is blocked, heaviness sets in.

This is not weakness. It is energy waiting for direction. Healing begins by moving that energy, even in small ways. Writing a page in a journal, walking barefoot in the grass, humming a single note — each act of creation reminds your nervous system that life is still moving forward.

Journaling is especially powerful because it takes the invisible weight of thought and gives it form on paper. Each word becomes proof that your energy is flowing again, transforming what was once stuck into momentum.

When Energy Gets Stuck: Energy Leaves Clues

FRAGMENTATION OFTEN leaves imprints not only in memory, but in frequency.

You've felt it before: the room that carries an "off" feeling, even if no one speaks of what happened there. The person who gives you chills without saying a word. The heaviness that settles in your body after a conversation primarily not because of what was said, but because of what was exchanged.

This is the language of energy. Our bodies are brilliant translators. They don't just store memory; they broadcast and receive. They tune in to what is unseen. And when your energy feels stuck, fractured, or overstimulated, it doesn't mean you're broken. It means your system is signaling that it's due for attunement.

This is where HOPE becomes practical. It teaches you to notice the clues: the tension in your shoulders, the sudden drop in your stomach, the sense of lightness or expansion when you're aligned. These are not random sensations; they are your soul's navigation system, reminding you that energy is always speaking.

To reclaim your frequency is to stop dismissing these signals as "just feelings" and start honoring them as truth. Because every environment, every interaction, every thought leaves a trace, and you have the power to choose which ones you keep.

Your Energy Field Is Sacred

IMAGINE YOUR ENERGY as a garden. Who are you letting walk through it? What are you allowing to take root there? What deserves to bloom, and what is ready to be composted back into the soil? The way you tend this inner garden shapes the way you move through the world.

Energy hygiene matters. Just as you brush your teeth or wash your face, your energetic field needs regular care. It doesn't always require elaborate rituals. It is just not necessary because you don't need sage smoke or a sound bath every day (though they can certainly support you). More often, it's the small, ordinary choices that clear and strengthen your field.

Sometimes clearing your energy looks like turning off notifications and giving your nervous system a break. Sometimes it looks like setting a boundary and saying no without apology. It might mean sinking into a salt bath, lying on the ground, and breathing deeply into your belly, or crying until the heaviness releases. Clearing can also come through laughter, singing, movement, or whispering to yourself: "That's not mine to carry."

Even the simplest acts like drinking water as if it were holy or calling back the parts of yourself that have wandered too far. Are perfectly acceptable ways of tending your sacred field. Each of these choices sends a signal to your soul: I am worthy of care. I am whole enough to protect my energy. I am allowed to return to myself.

Your energy field is not just background noise; it is the atmosphere of your being. When you treat it as sacred, you begin to live aligned with the truth that your presence matters.

Vibration & Frequency Are Felt First

THE WAY YOU TEND YOUR energy field doesn't stay hidden; it becomes the vibration you carry into every space. Think of it as the atmosphere of your presence. You don't have to announce your mood or your stress because others feel it before you ever speak.

Ever walk into a room and feel the tension hanging thick in the air? Or meet someone who immediately soothes you, even without words? That's vibration. It's the first language we all speak, the undercurrent that connects us before logic or language ever has a chance to explain.

Your vibration is the tone of your being. Your frequency is the song your energy sings. When fragmentation has shaped your life, your body often learns to play the background music of defense, depletion, or hyper-vigilance. You don't have to judge this as it was survival. But it isn't the only soundtrack available.

HOPE doesn't ask you to turn those signals off. It asks you to tune them as gently, consciously, slowly. Through presence. Through breath. Through rhythm. Through choice. Each time you choose stillness, laughter, gratitude, or a boundary that protects your peace, you are tuning your frequency closer to truth.

And here's the beauty: vibration shifts are felt first, too. Others may not know why they feel lighter in your presence, but they do. You may not recognize why a space feels more supportive, but your body does. Energy doesn't lie. And as you learn to honor this, you begin to live in harmony with the song your soul has been waiting to sing all along.

Raising Your Vibration Isn't Pretending

RAISING YOUR VIBRATION is not skipping sadness. It's not "good vibes only." It is refining your signal to be mindful, so that even when sorrow visits, it doesn't own the whole station.

Sound healing, color therapy, essential oils, touch, dance, chanting, stillness — all of these are ancient tools of vibrational recalibration. You are not just flesh and thought. You are frequency. You are resonance.

Even the design of this book reflects that truth. The faded gray behind the bright orange poppy is not decoration — it is vibration made visible. Gray holds the neutrality of pause, the quiet between notes, while orange carries the frequency of creativity, vitality, and renewal. Together, they remind us that raising your vibration is not about erasing shadow, but allowing color, energy, and life to rise through it.

And when you choose what raises your vibration — from food, people, practices, language — you will find that you don't just feel better. You become better at feeling. Fully. Honestly. Softly. With strength.

Blood, Water, and Vibration

BLOOD CARRIES WATER, and water carries vibration. More than half of our blood is plasma, and plasma is mostly water. This water flows with every beat of the heart, carrying not only oxygen and nutrients but also the subtle signatures of our inner life.

Science tells us that water is a conductor — of electricity, of sound, of resonance. Some researchers, like Masaru Emoto, suggested that water responds to intention and emotion, holding memory and reflecting vibration. While his findings have been contested, symbolism remains powerful: water is impressionable. It reflects what surrounds it. And if the body is mostly water, then our inner waters inevitably mirror the frequencies we live in.

Trauma, loss, and grief can mark these waters. The body remembers what the mind tries to forget, and the vibration of sorrow can lodge itself into the bloodstream, echoing as fatigue, tension, or dis-ease. Yet water is never fixed. It can shift, change form, and carry new imprints.

This is where self-love becomes medicine. Not the shallow affirmation that tries to gloss over pain, but the steady practice of kindness toward the self — gentleness in thought, compassion in breath, patience in healing. When you begin to practice self-love, the vibration of your inner water's changes. Blood becomes more than circulation; it becomes a messenger of healing. With each pulse, it carries compassion into the places that once only remembered pain.

Even if the science of water's memory is debated, the lived truth is undeniable: your body feels different when bathed in love. The bloodstream hums with a new rhythm, tissues soften, the nervous system steadies. Slowly, the places fractured by trauma, loss, and grief begin to restore themselves.

Every heartbeat, then, is more than survival. It is a chance to carry love through your body, to remind your cells of what wholeness feels like, and to let vibration become the quiet language of healing.

Researchers like Dr. Masaru Emoto became widely known for experiments suggesting that water responds to vibration. In one classroom demonstration, students were asked to speak harsh, negative words to one jar of water and gentle, loving words to another. When frozen, the negatively spoken-to water appeared jagged and distorted, while the water spoken to with love formed crystals as symmetrical and beautiful as snowflakes.

While many scientists debate these findings, the metaphor is undeniable. If water can hold the vibration of words, and our bodies are made mostly of water, then what we speak — especially to ourselves — matters more than we realize.

Every thought, every word, every breath of self-love is not wasted. It imprints into the bloodstream, carrying harmony where there was once distortion. Trauma, grief, and loss may leave jagged edges in our inner waters, but love has the power to re-pattern the flow. With practice, each heartbeat becomes a snowflake — carrying symmetry, grace, and wholeness into the places that once only held fracture.

HOPE in Practice: Journaling to Move Energy

SET A TIMER FOR 5 MINUTES. Write without editing or stopping, even if all you can say is, "I feel heavy." Let the words spill. When the timer ends, pause. Notice your breath. Notice your chest. Do you feel even slightly lighter?

Healing is not static. It moves. And so can you.

Healing Is Not Static — It Moves

ENERGY IS MEANT TO move — through body, voice, or creative expression. When it gets stuck, so does emotion. That's why grief presses on the chest, why anxiety buzzes in the belly, why unspoken words lodge in the throat.

Healing isn't about "getting over it." It is about giving what's inside of you a way out. Journaling is one way. But so is song. So is dance. So is silence. So is the bath water drawing sorrow from your bones.

This is not spiritual fluff. This is energetic truth: the moment you allow energy to move; you invite your whole being back into flow.

Healing happens at the speed of presence, not performance. It cannot be forced, faked, or rushed. Yet the instant you open to movement — a breath, a word, a tear — you begin to shift your field.

Vibrations in the Material World

AS STATED IN THE BEGINNING: everything is energy. This is not just philosophy but quantum truth. From the chair you're sitting on to the thoughts you think, everything vibrates. That vibration influences everything it touches, including you.

This is why the HOPE Method invites you to notice not only your inner patterns, but also your outer environment. Because sometimes it isn't only the grief in your chest or the fear in your throat that weighs you down — it is also the vibration of what surrounds you.

One of the most overlooked culprits is plastic. It fills our kitchens, coats our food, hides in our closets, even wraps our so-called wellness tools in a film of lifelessness. Plastic may be practical, but it is not neutral. It is stagnant. It does not breathe, shift, or return to the soil. It carries no rhythm, no memory, no soul.

And while it promises convenience, it leaves us cluttered — not just physically, but vibrationally. You may not hear its drag, but you feel it: in the fog that lingers in your mind, in the dull fatigue of your body, in the loss of sacredness around your simplest daily rituals.

Natural materials hum differently. Glass carries clarity. Wood breathes. Stone remembers. Clay grounds. These substances belong to the Earth; they resonate with ancestral rhythm.

A HOPEful Return to Living Light

SO, WHAT DO WE DO? We return, gently. We reclaim reverence, not rigidity. This is not about perfection. It is about attunement.

We begin by noticing: a wooden comb instead of a plastic brush. A glass jar instead of disposable packaging. A candle in a ceramic vessel instead of another plastic diffuser. Clothe bags. Bamboo utensils. Simple, soul-honoring choices that remind us: life belongs to life.

And as you choose, ask yourself: Does this support my soul's vibration? Does this align with the Earth I belong to? Does this help me live lighter in body, home, and spirit?

Because you are not only a consumer. You are a conductor of light. And even the smallest swap matters. Healing doesn't happen in a single purchase; it happens in the steady remembering that what surrounds you shapes you.

Soul-Aligned Fabric Field Guide

EVERY THREAD CARRIES energy. Some fabrics breathe life into your body's vibration; others dampen it. This guide is not about fashion: it's about frequency.

You may notice that fabric frequency shows up more than once in these pages. That's not by accident. Repetition is a reminder: the materials we live in and live on matter. We return to this teaching because it's one of the most overlooked ways that energy is shaped in daily life and one of the simplest places to begin shifting it.

Natural fibers such as cotton, linen, wool, hemp, and silk carry the resonance of the Earth. They move with your body, allow your skin to breathe, and create a sense of grounding and ease. When you wrap yourself in natural fibers, you are literally clothing yourself in something alive, something that still hums with the memory of the soil, the sun, the seasons. These fabrics harmonize with your energy field instead of fighting against it.

Synthetic fabrics such as polyester, nylon, acrylic, spandex are different. They are born of petroleum and plastic, not soil and sunlight. They do not breathe, and energetically, they often create subtle dissonance in the body. Over time, this dissonance can feel like low-level fatigue, agitation, or simply a dullness that makes it harder to sustain a higher vibration. That $3 clearance shirt may feel like a bargain, but it carries a hidden cost for your energy field.

This is not about perfection. It is about awareness. I'll be the first to admit: I still struggle with letting go of my spandex leggings and tank tops. They're comfortable, they're easy, and that's okay. What matters is that I've begun to choose more consciously when I invest in new pieces. I started by making sure my bedding (the place where I spend a third of my life) was all natural fabrics. Each mindful choice raises the baseline vibration of my environment. And over time, these small shifts add up.

When you choose what to wear or wrap yourself in, ask: Does this bring me home to myself? Does it breathe with me, or block me? Does it harmonize with the frequency I want to carry into the world?

Frequency lives in the weave. And every choice you make is a thread in the fabric of your healing. But it's not just texture that carries energy, it's color too. What we wear, what surrounds us, and even what we paint on our walls can either harmonize with our vibration or amplify what is already present.

Color & Frequency Amplification

RED: Frequency Range: ~400–480 THz. Energy it Amplifies: Passion, vitality, survival, grounding. When to Use: When you need courage, to take action, or to feel rooted in your body.

Orange: Frequency Range: ~480–510 THz. Energy it Amplifies: Creativity, joy, sexuality, renewal. When to Use: To spark inspiration, restore playfulness, or reignite vitality after heaviness.

Yellow: Frequency Range: ~510–540 THz. Energy it Amplifies: Confidence, clarity, optimism, personal power. When to Use: When you need focus, empowerment, or a reminder of your inner light.

Green: Frequency Range: ~540–580 THz. Energy it Amplifies: Balance, compassion, healing, growth. When to Use: To restore calm, open your heart, or align with nature's rhythms.

Blue: Frequency Range: ~580–620 THz. Energy it Amplifies: Communication, peace, truth, integrity. When to Use: For clear expression, deep listening, or to soothe anxious energy.

Indigo: Frequency Range: ~620–670 THz. Energy it Amplifies: Intuition, insight, wisdom, inner vision. When to Use: To strengthen discernment, deepen meditation, or trust your inner knowing.

Violet / Purple: Frequency Range: ~670–750 THz. Energy it Amplifies: Spiritual connection, transmutation, higher consciousness. When to Use: When seeking divine alignment, clarity of purpose, or to release old patterns.

White (All Colors): Frequency Range: Full spectrum. Energy it Amplifies: Purity, wholeness, unity, illumination. When to Use: To cleanse, reset, or call in protection and divine light.

Black: Frequency Range: Absorbs all. Energy it Amplifies: Mystery, depth, protection, transformation. When to Use: For grounding, shadow work, or creating a sacred container.

Gray: Frequency Range: Neutral field. Energy it Amplifies: Balance, pause, reflection, neutrality. When to Use: In times of transition, discernment, or when integrating shadow and light.

Note: The higher the frequency, the more it interacts with our spiritual and emotional layers. The lower the frequency, the more it roots into the physical and primal body.

HOPE in Practice: The Vibration Check-In

YOUR PRACTICE BEGINS here: Pause for a moment and ask yourself:

"How do I feel in my body right now is it heavy, buzzy, tight, or free?"

Then ask: "What raised or lowered my vibration today?"

This is your tuning fork. These questions teach you more about your life than any to-do list ever could.

A vibration check-in is simple, but it's also profound. Here's how it works:

What you notice: heaviness, tension, or exhaustion may point to energy drains. Lightness, warmth, or expansiveness often signal alignment. Neither is "good" or "bad," but both are information.

Why it matters: your body feels energy before your mind makes meaning. These sensations are your nervous system's way of saying, "This is safe" or "This is draining."

How to use it: once you identify what raises or lowers your vibration, you can choose more wisely. You begin to set boundaries, protect your peace, and lean toward what fuels you instead of what fragments you.

We've been taught to dismiss energy as 'woo,' but scientific evidence affirms that everything modern medicine does is based on energy: the electric rhythm of your heartbeat, the measurable waves of your brain, the oxygen carried through your blood. Ancient systems like Chinese medicine, Ayurveda, and Reiki never forgot this. They always treated the body as more than a machine. They understood it as a field of life force: Qi, Prana, the Divine One. Modern research now echoes this truth. Breath-work, meditation, and energy-based practices show measurable changes in brainwaves, hormones, and immune function. The language may differ, but the principle is the same: when energy flows, the body thrives. When it becomes disrupted by fragmentation, grief, repression, or disconnection, symptoms appear, not because you are broken, but because your body is signaling: 'The frequency is scrambled — please return to alignment.'

The vibration check-in is your first step toward that realignment. It's not about fixing everything at once. It's about listening, gently and consistently, until your body begins to trust that you are paying attention.

Ancient Wisdom, Modern Science: Science + Spirit: What Research Affirms About Energy

HEART COHERENCE → Studies from the HeartMath Institute show that the heart generates the body's largest electromagnetic field. When people experience emotions like love or gratitude, this field shifts into a measurable state of harmony called coherence, positively influencing the brain and nervous system.

Brainwaves & Meditation → EEG studies confirm that meditation changes brainwave patterns — moving from high-stress beta waves into slower alpha and theta waves linked with calm, creativity, and healing.

Breath & Prana → Research on pranayama (yogic breath-work) demonstrates lowered cortisol (stress hormone) levels, improved lung function, and enhanced nervous system balance.

Touch & Qi → Clinical trials on acupuncture and Reiki suggest reductions in pain, anxiety, and fatigue with outcomes consistent with the idea that balancing "life force" restores wellbeing.

Ancient words like Qi and Prana may not show up in scientific journals, but their effects do. Science affirms what sages taught long ago: when energy flows, the body thrives.

HOPE Anchors

THESE ARE NOT RULES to cage you. They are gentle laws of alignment similar to touchstones to help you return when life feels scattered. Post them somewhere visible. Whisper them to yourself when you forget. Let them become the rhythm of how you walk with HOPE.

I honor my energy before I offer it to anyone else. Your energy is sacred. When you tend to yourself first, you give from overflow instead of depletion.

I choose what is optimal, not merely familiar. Familiar patterns feel safe, but they often keep us stuck. Optimal choices move you toward alignment.

I clear what does not align with my light. Release what drains you such as clutter, relationships, old stories. Clearing makes room for your energy to rise.

I forgive myself and others to lighten my load. Forgiveness frees your energy. It is not forgetting but rather it is choosing not to carry the weight anymore.

I move my body with reverence, not punishment. Movement is a celebration of life, not a debt to be paid. Let it be joy, not judgment.

I trust my inner compass. Your intuition is a map. The more you listen, the more clearly it guides you back to yourself.

I harness HOPE — even in the dark. Light is not the absence of darkness, but the presence of truth. HOPE is the steady flame that carries you through.

Soul Scribbles Reflection: Which of these Anchors feels easiest to live by right now? Which feels hardest? Notice what that reveals about where your energy is asking for attention.

Wisdom Through the Ages

THE HOPE ANCHORS OFFER a modern framework for living in alignment, but they are not new. Across time, humanity has wrestled with the same question: how do we live at peace within ourselves in a turbulent world?

The Bhagavad Gita teaches stability — a mind steady like a lamp in a windless place. The Hermetic Principles remind us that energy never rests, life moves in rhythm, and our choices set the frequency of reality.

Ayurveda echoes this truth: balance is vibrational, shaped by food, rhythm, and environment. Each tradition affirms that we are not machines to be fixed, but energy beings to be aligned.

The HOPE Anchors distill these timeless teachings into simple, livable reminders. They steady you when life feels stormy, return you when you drift, and call you home when you forget.

And while these traditions speak in the language of spirit, today science is catching up with what sages have always known. What the mystics called vibration, physics calls frequency. What Ayurveda described as balance, biology names homeostasis. What the ancients whispered as rhythm, neuroscience records as regulation. Different words, same essence: we are fields of energy, and the way we tend that energy shapes every part of our health.

Science + Spirit: How Energy Heals

MODERN SCIENCE AND ancient wisdom may use different languages, but they point to the same truth: healing is energetic.

Neurons fire. Hormones pulse. Cells regenerate. These are all energetic processes, driven by tiny electrical signals that keep us alive. What most people don't realize is that thoughts carry their own measurable electromagnetic frequency. A thought of fear vibrates differently than a thought of gratitude. One contracts the body; the other expands it.

Your heart's electromagnetic field is said to be 5,000 times more powerful than the brain's. This means that when you feel love, genuine, embodied love, your entire system shifts into coherence. In this state, the rhythms of your body harmonize. Your breath deepens, your blood pressure steadies, your nervous system recalibrates. Love doesn't just feel good; it literally heals.

This is why practices like music, touch, breath-work, movement, and even scent is so transformative. They don't just relax you; they change your frequency. They remind your body that it is not fixed matter, but frequency made flesh.

The HOPE Method bridges science and spirit by showing you how to work with this truth instead of against it. You don't have to control every thought or heal every wound all at once. You simply begin to notice: What am I broadcasting? What am I receiving? And then you choose, gently and consistently, to shift your signal toward love, coherence, and life.

HOPEfully Human Moment

ONE TIME I TRIED MEGAHERTZ sound healing for stress. I put on a 528Hz track, lit a candle, and promptly fell asleep in my jeans with mascara all over my pillow. I woke up oddly peaceful, deeply wrinkled, and with eyebrows going in entirely new directions.

It's not the only time this has happened. I once signed up for a three-hour meditation and made it through the first hour... before falling asleep sitting upright. Honestly, I am always drifting off during meditation because I rarely rest properly. My body isn't sabotaging me but it's seizing the first chance it gets to repair.

And that's the hidden lesson: healing doesn't always look holy. Sometimes it just looks like your body saying, "Thank you for finally being still enough to let me rest." Sometimes it's not a vision, or a download, or a perfect lotus pose but it's mascara on your pillow, askew eyebrows, and a nervous system that finally got to exhale.

HOPE in Practice: Energy Hygiene Ritual

THINK OF THIS AS BRUSHING your energetic teeth. Just as you wash your face or brush your hair, your energetic body benefits from a quick daily cleanse. You don't need sage, crystals, or special tools, you just need your own hands, your breath, and your imagination.

How to practice (2 minutes):

Sweep with your hands – Using your own hands, gently brush down the front, sides, and back of your body, from head to toe. Imagine you are sweeping away static or dust. Move slowly and intentionally, as if you are clearing your field of anything that doesn't belong.

Ground into the Earth – Place both feet on the floor (barefoot if you can). Picture cords of light or roots growing from your soles deep into the earth. Feel yourself steady and supported.

Claim your field – Place one hand on your heart. Breathe deeply and say aloud (or silently): "I cleanse and reclaim my field. I carry only what is mine." Repeat this until you feel lighter or calmer.

Why it matters: This is energetic sovereignty. It helps you release other people's energy, quiet your nervous system, and anchor into your own truth before the day begins. When you keep your field clear, you move through the world as both soft and strong — compassionate without being drained, open without being overwhelmed.

You don't have to chase healing. You become healing. One breath, one choice, one vibration at a time.

Soul Seed to Take With You: Your energy doesn't lie. It may be subtle, but it is sacred. You don't have to fix the world — you just must keep your own signal clear.

Energy is not just something you hold in rare, radiant moments. It is shaped by the quiet choices of every day — the food you eat, the space you keep, the thoughts you allow, the movements you repeat. Frequency isn't only raised in ceremony or meditation; it is woven into the rhythm of dishes washed, walks taken, breaths remembered. The real question becomes: how do you sustain this vibrational state, not for a moment, but for a lifetime? That is where integration begins — not as theory, but as rhythm. Rituals, daily practices, and sacred self-regulation are the vessels that keep your energy steady when life tries to scatter it again. And that is where we turn next.

Chapter Eleven

Integration – Rituals/Daily Practices, Rhythm & Sacred Self-Regulation

Healing doesn't happen in the breakthrough. It happens in the days after — when you choose to stay awake to the truth you touched. Integration asks us to take what we've learned and embody it, one choice at a time. And the most reliable way to do that is through consistency. Not rigid rules or complicated routines but simple daily practices that help us stay aligned.

I sometimes use the word rituals because these small practices can be deeply sacred. But for many, the word "ritual" feels heavy, sometimes even forbidden. So, let's call them what they are: daily practices. Gentle anchors that steady your nervous system, quiet your mind, and remind your soul that healing is safe.

Why do daily practices matter? Because they create rhythm. Rhythm builds trust. And trust is what allows your body to believe the transformation you're seeking is real. Without daily practices, even the most beautiful breakthrough can fade. With them, healing becomes not just something you experienced once, but something you live every day.

Healing doesn't happen in the breakthrough moment. It happens in the days after. When you choose to stay awake to the truth you touched. Breakthroughs are bright and inspiring, but they are only beginnings. Integration is what makes transformation stick.

Think about it: you can read every book on self-care, listen to every podcast, and follow every teacher online. But until you live what you've learned until the wisdom moves from your head into your body it remains theory. Wisdom that doesn't reach the body stays as noise in the mind.

Integration is about weaving truth into the fabric of your everyday life. It's not about grand gestures; it's about the rituals that ground you, the rhythms that steady you, and the small choices that bring your nervous system back into balance again and again.

HOPE teaches that healing is not performance. It's practice. Integration is the daily devotion to showing up for that practice and not because you are broken, but because you are remembering how to stay whole. It is learning to anchor yourself in rituals of breath, stillness, movement, and nourishment so that healing doesn't remain a fleeting high but becomes a steady way of living.

Integration is where the work gets real. It's where you meet yourself on Monday morning after a weekend retreat. It's in how you handle the hard conversation, how you wind down before bed, how you return to yourself after being pulled in a thousand directions. This is where healing becomes durable, not dramatic, but dependable.

Why Daily Practices Matter

A DAILY PRACTICE IS repetition with reverence.

It's brushing your hair slowly while whispering, "I'm not in a hurry anymore." It's lighting a candle before journaling. Taking three deep breaths before you respond. Laying your hand on your chest before sleep. These are the moments when you speak to your soul in the language of presence.

Daily practices don't need to be long or elaborate. They only need to be intentional. Think of them like hygiene for your nervous system. Just as you brush your teeth or wash your face each day, these practices cleanse, regulate, and strengthen your inner world.

Your nervous system heals through patterns. It craves rhythm. Safety isn't built through grand gestures, it's built in small, repeated acts of remembrance. Each time you choose to pause, to breathe, to return to yourself, you lay another brick in the foundation of your wholeness.

Self-Regulation Is Sacred

SELF-REGULATION IS not about control. It's not about forcing yourself to "calm down" or pretending to "get over it." It is the art of learning how to stay with yourself when the world feels like it is too much.

This means holding space for your own overwhelm instead of shaming it. It means choosing presence over panic, even when your body is trembling, aching, or shutting down. Self-regulation is not about silencing what you feel; it is about befriending it. It's whispering to your nervous system: "I won't abandon you again."

This work is sacred because it is tender. And it is hard. It asks you to feel — fully — without fleeing. But it also gives you something precious in return: your power. When you know how to regulate your energy, you no longer have to wait for life to be calm before you can feel safe. You carry safety within you.

Through breath, touch, sound, movement, time in nature, daily practices, and silence, you begin to shape a life that knows how to soothe itself. These are not tricks to fix you; they are anchors that remind you who you are beneath the storm.

This is integration. Not the dramatic moment of healing that happens once, but the steady devotion of coming back to yourself again and again. And the more you practice, the more your body begins to believe safety is possible, even here.

Building Rhythm, Not Rigidity

A HEALING LIFE is not built on strict routines. It's built on relationships with yourself, with your energy, with your becoming.

Rhythm is different from routine. Routine can feel like a cage, something forced and rigid, where you measure your worth by how well you "stick to it." Rhythm, on the other hand, is alive. It moves with you. It's felt more than scheduled.

Think of the ocean: waves come in, and waves go out. Some days your rhythm will be fast and full on with productivity, connection, movement. Other days it will be slow and quiet full of stillness, silence, softness. Both are sacred. Both belong. Integration honors these cycles instead of trying to force one pace for every day of your life.

This is important because so many of us have been taught to see healing as another performance or as another checklist to master. And when we miss a day of journaling, meditation, or exercise, we think we've failed. But healing isn't about perfection. It's about presence.

The HOPE Method doesn't give you one rigid path. It gives you a lens. A way of seeing yourself clearly enough to know what you need today, not just what you needed yesterday. It invites you to pause, to listen, and to choose repeatedly what aligns, what serves, what soothes.

Healing through rhythm means learning to trust that your body knows the beat. Some days that beat is strong and quick, other days it slows to a whisper. Your task is not to control it; however, your task is to notice, to honor, and to move with it.

You don't need another plan. You need presence. You need permission to begin where you are. To mess it up. To get tired. To come back. Again, and again.

This pillar is where the real magic happens not because it's glamorous, but because it's sustainable. Healing becomes who you are, not just what you do.

The soul doesn't shout. It hums. It pulses beneath the noise, waiting for you to get quiet enough to hear it.

Your soul is not a concept or a theory. It is not a metaphorical "you." It is you. It is your essence the part of you that was never wounded, never abandoned, never lost. The part that remembers who you were before the world told you what you had to be.

In the HOPE Method, soul is your compass. When the map is missing, soul shows the way and not through logic, but through resonance. You don't think your way into alignment; you feel your way there.

And this is where presence becomes practical. Because if the soul is always humming, the question becomes: how do you hear it? How do you tell the difference between the noise of fear and the whisper of truth?

That is where the next practice comes in. The Soul Whisper Test will help you pause long enough to feel the difference and to notice when your energy expands in alignment or contracts in resistance. It is your body's built-in language of yes and no, waiting for you to listen.

HOPE in Practice: The Soul Whisper Test

SO OFTEN WE CONFUSE the loudest voice in our head with the truest one. The voice of fear shouts. The voice of shame nags. The voice of "should" never seems to stop. But the soul doesn't work that way. The soul doesn't shout because it whispers. And learning to hear that whisper is one of the most life-giving practices you can ever cultivate.

How to practice:

Find a quiet space. Sit comfortably and close your eyes.

Place one hand on your heart and the other on your belly. Take a slow breath in, and an even slower breath out.

Ask gently: "What does my soul know that my mind keeps forgetting?"

Wait. Don't analyze. Just notice what arises and scribble a word, an image, a sensation, or even a memory. Write it down without editing. Your soul speaks in first drafts.

What this does: This practice creates a pause between your survival mind and your deeper knowing. It gives you access to a truth that often gets buried under roles, expectations, and noise. Even a single word or phrase can become an anchor for your day.

Why it matters: So many of us have been taught to value personality over presence. To survive, we perform, we please, we hide behind roles and achievements. But underneath those layers is the remembering: a flicker of truth, a sacred ache, a whisper that says: "This is not all I am."

The soul is not wounded by fragmentation, but it can become obscured. Shame, repression, and disconnection act like clouds covering the sun. And yet, the soul never leaves. The moment we return to our breath, our body, or the beauty of a single sunset, we feel it again. We don't awaken the soul; we awaken to it.

Wisdom Through the Ages

LONG BEFORE MODERN psychology talked about "thought patterns" or "mindset," ancient sages were already exploring the link between thought, desire, and destiny. Their writings, known as the Upanishads, are among the oldest spiritual texts in the world. Composed in India thousands of years ago as part of the Vedic tradition. The word Upanishad means "to sit close," describing the way students would gather around their teachers to receive wisdom about the nature of life, self, and spirit.

One teaching from the Upanishads says:

"As a man acts, so does he become. As he thinks, so does he act. As he desires, so does he think."

This spiral of being is not meant to trap us, but to reveal the truth: our lives are shaped from the inside out. Desire influences thought, thought shapes action, and action creates the person we become.

The question then becomes: Where does our desire arise from? If it comes from fear, shame, or fragmentation, our actions will reflect that distortion. But when desire arises from the soul —from the quiet, steady hum of our truest self — our actions naturally align with wholeness.

The HOPE Method carries this same thread of wisdom forward. When we pause long enough to listen to our soul and align our energy, we interrupt old cycles and create new ones. What the sages taught thousands of years ago is what you are practicing now: remembering that healing begins with the energy you choose to embody.

Soul and Neurobiology

WHILE THE SOUL IS NOT bound to the brain, your connection to it is influenced by the state of your nervous system. When your body is locked in fight, flight, or freeze, survival takes over. The nervous system prioritizes safety, not soul. In that state, it can feel impossible to access intuition, clarity, or inner wisdom, it's not because your soul has disappeared, but because your body is protecting you.

This is why so many of us struggle to "hear ourselves" when we're anxious, exhausted, or overwhelmed. It's not a moral failing or a spiritual weakness. It's biology doing its job. But what biology can block, it can also be soothed into reopening.

The HOPE Method teaches that through grounding, safety, and stillness, you can gently shift from survival mode into connection. Breath slows the heart. Grounding reminds the body of stability. Stillness creates space for the subtle hum of the soul to rise again. In this way, neurobiology and spirituality are not at odds as they are dance partners. One creates the conditions for the other to be felt.

The soul doesn't need fixing. It doesn't vanish when you're dysregulated. It waits, steady and unchanged, beneath the noise. What it needs is listening. And listening becomes possible when your body feels safe enough to soften.

HOPEfully Human Moment

ONCE, WHILE LISTENING to a song that reminded me of childhood, I burst into tears in the grocery store aisle between crackers and olives. The memory came out of nowhere like the rush of a scent, sound, and longing wrapped in a melody.

The truth is, I don't usually cry. As a child, I was often told to stop or made fun of when I did, so I learned to hold it in — to be strong, to stay busy, to keep moving. And maybe that's why my tears sneak out at the most inconvenient times now.

But here's the part that really made it a scene: after a few tears fell, I suddenly burst out laughing. Laughing at myself — for being too strong, too busy, too practiced at keeping it all together — until it all unraveled between crackers and olives. I must have looked completely unhinged, half-crying and half-laughing, while strangers walked past probably questioning my mental stability.

One woman just smiled kindly and asked, "Good song?" I nodded, mascara smudged, cheeks wet, still chuckling at myself.

Sometimes the soul says "remember" at exactly the wrong time, which might actually be the right time. And sometimes the most healing thing isn't to hold it in, but to let the tears and laughter mingle, proof that your body is finally catching up to what your soul already knows: you're allowed to feel.

HOPE in Practice: Soul Tending Daily Practice

LIGHT A CANDLE.

Write a letter from your soul to your current self. Let the words flow unfiltered.

Read it aloud. Let the vibration anchor into your field.

Close with this: "I remember who I am. I trust what I carry."

How to practice:

Light a candle – this will signal to your body and mind that you are entering a sacred space, even if it's just for a few minutes at your kitchen table.

Write a letter – begin with the words: "Dear [your name], this is your soul speaking..." and then let the words pour out unfiltered. Don't edit. Don't judge. Let your pen move faster than your doubt.

Read it aloud – your voice carries vibration. Speaking the words helps anchor them from thought, to paper, to sound, and finally into your energetic field.

Close with an affirmation – place your hand on your heart and say: "I remember who I am. I trust what I carry."

What this does: This practice bypasses the analytical mind and opens a direct line to your deeper wisdom. The act of writing lets the unconscious surface, the act of reading aloud amplifies it, and the closing affirmation seals it into your energy field.

Why it matters: Most of us live in constant conversation with our fears, doubts, and fragmented selves. Rarely do we pause to listen to the soul — the part of us that is steady, clear, and whole. Soul tending is how you build that relationship. Over time, this daily practice teaches you to recognize the difference between the noise of survival and the whisper of truth. It reminds you that you are not broken — you are remembering.

Soul Seed to Take With You

THE SOUL DOESN'T NEED to be found. It needs to be followed. It knows the way. It always has.

Why this matters: So often we go searching — in books, in teachers, in achievements — for what was never missing. The soul has always been present, steady beneath the noise. The real work isn't finding it but remembering to listen and letting it lead.

What this means: Your soul's guidance rarely arrives as a thunderclap. It comes as a whisper, a nudge, a pull in the direction of peace. It shows up in synchronicities, in the body's signals, in the quiet knowing that doesn't demand proof. Following your soul means honoring these subtle cues, even when they don't make logical sense.

How to live it: Pause daily and ask: "What is my soul whispering to me right now?"

Notice when your energy expands (that's alignment) or contracts (that's resistance).

Take one small step that honors the whisper — even if it feels inconvenient, even if no one else understands.

Each time you follow instead of force, you deepen the trust between you and your soul. And that trust becomes a rhythm — one that carries you back, repeatedly, to your truest self.

Nourishing your vessel is where intention begins to settle into the body. It's the point where healing asks to be lived, not just understood. To support you in carrying this forward, you'll find a HOPE Method Quick Start Guide and a 14-Day HOPE Rhythm in the back of this book — simple frameworks to help you integrate what you've learned into daily practice. And now, we turn to what happens when nourishment, rhythm, and presence begin to root more deeply: embodiment.

Chapter Twelve

Embodiment – Living the Light You Cultivated

There comes a moment when healing moves out of the mind and into the marrow.

You no longer have to explain yourself — you simply are. You don't need to repeat the mantras or consult the journals before making decisions. You move differently. Breathe differently. You pause before reacting, not out of discipline but because your nervous system remembers peace. This is embodiment.

It is not a finish line. It's a frequency. A lived resonance. And it's what happens when HOPE is no longer a method — but a way of being.

You Are No Longer Just Surviving

WHEN YOU BEGIN TO EMBODY your healing, you stop negotiating your worth. You don't chase closure. You don't beg for validation. You don't shrink to fit into rooms that can't hold your truth. You walk with a quieter power — one that doesn't need to be seen to be real. You find yourself saying "no" with softness, and "yes" with sovereignty. You protect your peace like a sacred inheritance, because now you know you are the sanctuary.

The Body Doesn't Lie

EMBODIMENT IS PHYSICAL. Tangible. It's in your posture, your breath, your voice. It's in the way you touch your own arm. The food you choose. The way you walk away from what hurts, without needing to justify the exit.

Trauma taught your body to shrink, to freeze, to override. Embodiment invites it to expand, to feel, to trust again. When you live from this place, your intuition grows louder. Your choices align faster. Your relationships soften or recalibrate. The external may stay chaotic — but internally, something has changed.

Living the Light

LIVING THE LIGHT doesn't mean being endlessly radiant. It means being real. It means honoring your shadow. It means laughing from your belly and crying in the car. It means staying present when others check out and choosing peace even when anger feels easier.

You become the light when you no longer abandon yourself in darkness. The light isn't a performance — it's a practice. A daily returning. A sacred remembering. HOPE, in its embodied form, looks like joy that doesn't need to be photographed. Boundaries that don't require permission. A heart that still opens, even after it's been broken.

The Return Is the Revolution

YOU'RE not meant to become someone else. You're meant to return to yourself as the you that existed before fear got loud, before shame distorted your reflection, before the world told you who to be.

The return to your own body, your own rhythm, your own voice — that is the revolution. This is embodiment. And it's not perfect. It's honest.

You don't need to know all the answers. You just need to know where to listen. And the more you practice being with yourself, the less you'll fear losing anything else.

You are no longer the seeker. You are the source.

The Nervous System — Sacred Wiring

BEFORE THERE WAS LANGUAGE, before there was memory — there was sensation. Your nervous system is the oldest storyteller you have. And it doesn't lie. It tells the truth about what you've lived through, what you've held inside, what you're still bracing for. Not in words, but in symptoms. In clenching. In shutting down. In over-apologizing, overachieving, over-functioning.

In the HOPE Method, we honor the nervous system as sacred wiring. Not something to conquer, but something to befriend. Because the body doesn't misbehave — it protects. It has always tried to keep you safe. Even when it makes you freeze. Even when it made you hide.

HOPE in Practice: Befriend the Body

PUT ONE HAND ON YOUR chest. One hand on your belly. Whisper: "Thank you for protecting me. I am safe to feel. I am safe to heal." Repeat until your breath slows. Repeat again tomorrow. Your nervous system is built to respond to threats. But when you've lived through trauma, it can confuse familiar discomfort with actual danger. It's not your fault. It's wiring. And wiring can be rewritten. This is where regulation comes in.

Regulation is not about never feeling anxious — it's about knowing how to return to center. The more you practice, the faster your body learns: We don't have to live on high alert anymore. We are no longer at war.

Polyvagal Theory Made Simple

THE POLYVAGAL THEORY teaches that your nervous system is like a ladder:

Top rung – Safe, social, connected (ventral vagal)

Middle rung – Fight or flight (sympathetic)

Bottom rung – Shutdown or freeze (dorsal vagal)

The goal isn't to always stay at the top — it's to know where you are and climb back up gently.

The HOPE Method helps you do just that — not with force, but with frequency. Through touch, breath, ritual, play, and attunement.

Wisdom Through the Ages

THE TAO TEACHES, "KNOWING others is intelligence; knowing yourself is true wisdom. Mastering others is strength; mastering yourself is true power."

Across history, wisdom traditions have leaned on the power of seven steps to describe the journey of the soul. The number seven has long carried spiritual weight — a symbol of completion, initiation, and wholeness. From the creation story told in seven days, to the seven heavens of mystic texts, to the seven metals of alchemy, humanity has always recognized that transformation unfolds in sevenfold rhythm.

Stoicism: Marcus Aurelius called the self "the inner citadel" — a fortress of presence that remains unshaken even when storms rage outside.

Buddhism: Embodiment is mindfulness — returning to breath, body, and presence as the path to liberation.

Christian Mysticism: Teresa of Ávila described the "interior castle" of the soul, where one walks through inner chambers until resting in union with God.

Alchemy: The Ladder of Transmutation spoke of seven stages of transformation. Fire to burn illusion, water to soften rigidity, air to lift vibration, spirit to embody wholeness. The final "gold" was not metal, but wisdom itself.

Mystical Philosophies: Sacred geometry, the seven heavens, the seven rays of divine light — all mapped the soul's climb.

Modern Psychology: Stages of development, integration, and healing now echo these truths in clinical language.

The **WiSH-to-HEAL** practice was not copied from these teachings — it was born from lived experience, forged in the fire of grief and healing. Yet when placed beside these ancient maps, it reveals itself as part of the same timeless pattern of sevenfold transformation:

Wisdom mirrors Separation — the courage to see what is true.

Serenity echoes Dissolution — softening what is rigid.

Heart is the great Conjunction — emotion and soul reuniting.

Heal (Accountability) recalls Calcination — burning away what no longer serves.

Express parallels Fermentation — awakening voice and spirit.

Accept aligns with Distillation — refining what remains in clarity.

Love becomes the final Coagulation — not a concept, but an embodied truth.

What the alchemists hid in symbols and sacred texts, WiSH-to-HEAL makes accessible through simple, embodied practice. Both point to the same truth: healing is not about bypassing pain but transforming it into light.

HOPEfully Human Moment

I ONCE HAD A FULL-ON anxiety spiral because I forgot to return a library book. Not because of the book, but because my body read "you messed up" as "you're in danger." I found myself breathing into a paper bag, laughing and crying all at once.

Sometimes, the nervous system is just doing its old job in a new world. You're not crazy. You're catching up to safety.

HOPE in Practice: Anchoring Techniques

RUB YOUR PALMS TOGETHER and place them over your eyes

Tap your chest gently (thymus thump)

Press your feet firmly into the ground and name five things you can see

Sip warm tea and hum softly for 30 seconds

These are not silly. These are sacred — they help you climb the ladder.

Soul Seed to Take With You

YOU ARE NOT YOUR PANIC.

You are not your shutdown.

You are the brave, breathing being

learning to come home to your own body.

Integration is where the pieces finally touch, where practice becomes pattern, and where safety becomes a rhythm, you can return to again and again. But there is a difference between weaving healing into your days and becoming the healing itself. The question is not only: Can I integrate this? The question is: Can I live it so fully that it shines through me without effort? That is where embodiment begins.

Chapter Thirteen

Nourishing the Vessel - Reclaiming the Body as Sacred Ground

Your body is not a problem to fix. It is a sacred vessel — a living, breathing temple that carries your soul through this life. When we speak of nourishment, we are speaking of more than nutrition or diet plans. We are speaking of vibration. Of frequency. Of the way energy itself is exchanged every time you eat, drink, breathe, or even think.

Every bite, every sip, every breath carries a frequency. Food is not only fuel — it is information. It speaks to your cells, your nervous system, and your emotional body. A ripe mango ripened in sunlight vibrates differently than a processed snack engineered for shelf life. One expands the body's field, the other contracts it. Neither is inherently "good" or "bad," but each carries a message — and your body feels the difference.

Think of food the way you think of fabric. A natural cotton shirt allows your skin to breathe, carrying the imprint of the earth. A polyester one, made from petroleum, may look fine but often feels suffocating against the body. Food is no different. When it comes wrapped in plastic, loaded with chemicals, or processed into something unrecognizable, it tends to carry a lower vibration and less nutrient density. When it comes whole, fresh, and close to its natural state, it holds life force. If buying fresh feels overwhelming, frozen fruits and vegetables are still infused with vibrational life — they are harvested at peak and preserved, making them an accessible bridge back to vitality.

But nourishment is never only about what you eat. It is also about how. A rushed, guilt-ridden meal communicates one thing to your nervous system. A warm, intentional meal eaten with presence communicates another. Your body digests not only the food, but also the mood you're in, the thoughts you entertain, the emotions you swallow, and even the environment you sit in. This is why food often feels so comforting — not because of the calories, but because of the vibration it carries. The key is not to shame that comfort, but to become conscious of what kind of comfort it brings: temporary numbing, or genuine nourishment.

Your body is always seeking balance — what science calls homeostasis. Left to its own design, your system returns to what feels familiar, even if that "normal" isn't supportive of healing. This is why drastic diets fail: the body resists when it feels unsafe. The invitation here is not to force your body into submission, but to gently help it create a new rhythm — one rooted in ease, clarity, and vitality.

Simplicity is the key. Instead of overhauling everything at once, start with one choice. Replace a food or drink that no longer serves you with something that does. Keep that promise long enough for it to become a rhythm, then make another. Over time, these small shifts gather momentum, creating a lifestyle that feels less like restriction and more like reverence.

Nourishing the vessel, then, is not about perfection. It is about alignment. It is about seeing food as frequency, meals as medicine, and your body as the sacred ground where spirit and matter meet.

Food as Frequency

WITH THAT IN MIND, let's explore how each food group carries its own vibration. None are inherently "good" or "bad." Each carries qualities — light or heavy, expansive or contracting, enlivening or dulling — and your body responds to them in real time.

Fruits: Light & Renewal: Fruits are some of the highest-vibration foods on the planet. They carry sunlight, water, and natural sweetness in a form that the body recognizes immediately. Their vibration is one of lightness, joy, and cellular renewal. When eaten in the morning or early afternoon, they support the body's natural rhythm of detoxification and clearing.

A handful of berries deliver antioxidants and vibrational brightness. An apple cleanses the system and symbolizes fresh beginnings. A ripe mango feels like solar energy turned into sweetness. Fruit doesn't just feed the body — it uplifts the spirit.

Vegetables: Grounding & Balance: If fruit is the sun, vegetables are the soil. They anchor, cleanse, and mineralize the body. Leafy greens like kale and spinach carry iron and chlorophyll — plant "blood" that strengthens and restores. Cruciferous vegetables like broccoli and cauliflower support the liver, our detox powerhouse. Root vegetables like beets, carrots, and sweet potatoes embody the grounding energy of the earth itself.

Vegetables balance the nervous system and bring steadiness to the body. Their vibration says: Be rooted. Be strong. Be here.

Nuts & Seeds: Sacred Carriers: Compact, potent, and protective, nuts and seeds hold sacred fats and energy reserves. They stabilize hormones, fuel the brain, and provide sustainable energy in small amounts. A handful of walnuts nourishes cognition. Pumpkin seeds offer zinc and grounding. Chia and flax hydrate and regulate with omega-3s and fiber.

Their vibration is one of stability, protection, and slow, sustained strength. They remind us that nourishment doesn't always come in volume — sometimes it comes in concentration.

Proteins: Repair & Resilience: Protein is the builder. It repairs tissues, regulates blood sugar, and provides the body with resilience. But its vibration depends on source and intention. Eggs symbolize life itself — concentrated beginnings in a shell. Lentils hold earthy heart energy. Clean poultry or fish carry the focus and vitality of movement.

Animal proteins, when sourced with care, can feel grounding and strengthening. Plant proteins often carry gentler vibrations, encouraging balance and renewal. Each serves differently, and your body will tell you what it prefers in each season of your life.

Grains & Roots: Warmth & Memory: Grains and starchy roots are optional in vibrational eating, but when tolerated, they bring warmth, satiety, and a sense of ancestral memory. Quinoa offers a complete amino acid profile, a gift of balance. Sweet potatoes root us in steady nourishment, while rice — humble and accessible — offers easeful digestion.

Their vibration is one of comfort, tradition, and grounding. Too much, and they may weigh the body down. The right amount, and they help anchor your energy when life feels untethered.

Hydration & Ritual Drinks: Flow & Focus: Water is life-force in its purest form. It is the element of flow, of cleansing, of emotional movement. Every sip you take carries vibration — and the way you drink is just as important as what you drink. A gulped bottle of cold water in the car holds a different resonance than a warm cup of lemon water savored in the morning sunlight.

Warm lemon water signals clarity and detox. Herbal infusions like tulsi, nettle, and rooibos nourish and fortify at a cellular level, reminding the body of its natural rhythm of renewal. Chamomile whispers rest. Rosemary brings clarity and focus.

Coffee: Fire in a Cup. Coffee carries the vibration of fire — sharp, quick, and awakening. In moderation and with presence, it can be medicine: igniting focus, sparking creativity, and helping us rise into the day. But when used as a crutch to override exhaustion, its fire becomes depletion. Best received as ritual, not fuel.

Chocolate: Heart Medicine. In its purest form, cacao is one of nature's deepest gifts. It carries magnesium, mood-elevating compounds, and a vibration that opens the heart. But heavily processed chocolate loses its medicine and becomes shadow. Choose dark, minimally processed cacao and savor it with intention.

Carob: Gentle Ally. Naturally sweet, caffeine-free, and grounding, carob offers warmth and ritual without stimulation. A reminder that indulgence can be soft, gentle, and restorative.

Alcohol: A Word of Caution. Alcohol carries a fragmented vibration. A glass of wine may hold antioxidants and tradition, but frequent or unconscious drinking scatters energy and numbs emotion. If included, let it be with awareness, not escape.

Hydration and drink rituals are powerful not just because of their chemistry, but because of their frequency. A mindful sip can recalibrate your system. A careless pour can deplete it. The choice is always yours.

Fats, Oils, Herbs & Seasonings: Carriers of Light: Fats, oils, and seasonings are often treated as extras — the things we add after we've chosen the "real" food. But they are anything but secondary. They are carriers of light, memory, and medicine. Each drizzle, pinch, and sprinkle reshapes not only the flavor of your food but the way your body receives and integrates nourishment.

Butter holds the vibration of comfort and tradition — grounding, warming, and tied to hearth and home. Olive oil flows with the radiance of the Mediterranean sun, protective and heart-centered, supporting circulation and vitality. Avocado oil is steady and harmonizing, strong enough to withstand high heat without losing integrity. Coconut oil carries tropical warmth and antimicrobial qualities, stabilizing both body and aura with its sweet steadiness.

Mineral-rich salts like Celtic or Himalayan return us to the earth, grounding the body and restoring electrolyte balance. Vinegars cut through heaviness, enliven digestion, and brighten both palate and spirit.

And then come the herbs and spices — the true frequency shifters. Ceylon cinnamon steadies blood sugar while warming the spirit. Ginger sparks circulation. Turmeric soothes inflammation and infuses food with the golden glow of the sun. Cayenne activates and energizes. Rosemary clears mental fog, while chamomile whispers rest to a weary nervous system.

These are not random add-ons. They are micro-medicines — sparks of vibrational alignment woven into daily meals. A drizzle of oil, a pinch of salt, a sprinkle of spice: each is an offering, reminding you that nourishment is not only about fuel but about frequency. When chosen with reverence, fats, oils, and spices transform your kitchen into a space of everyday alchemy.

Fermented Foods: Living Frequencies: Fermented foods are alive — quite literally. They carry beneficial bacteria that support microbiomes, aid digestion, and stabilize the nervous system. Beyond science, they hold the vibrational imprint of transformation. Something simple — cabbage, milk, soybeans — becomes something greater through time, care, and microbial alchemy.

Sauerkraut, kimchi, kefir, kombucha, and miso all teach us that nourishment is a living, evolving process. Their sourness sparks the palate, while their enzymes and probiotics awaken the gut. Fermented dairy, like kefir or yogurt, transforms milk into something easier to digest and more supportive of gut health.

In vibrational terms, fermented foods remind the body that transformation is possible — that life is not static, and even what seems "spoiled" can, with guidance, become medicine.

Not all bodies welcome fermentation. For some, especially with histamine sensitivities or gut imbalances, these foods may agitate rather than soothe. The key is attunement: if they make you feel vibrant, embrace them. If not, pause. Fermented foods are a metaphor: when tended with care, what is fermented does not rot — it evolves.

Dairy & Alternatives: Dairy is one of the most nuanced food groups when it comes to vibrational nourishment. For many, it creates congestion — not just in the sinuses, but in the gut, the lymphatic system, and even the emotional field. It can bring heaviness, fatigue, or inflammation, especially when sourced from stressed animals in industrial systems.

And yet, not all dairy is the same — and not all bodies respond the same way. Some find small amounts tolerable, even supportive. Swiss, goat, or feta cheeses often feel lighter and more digestible. Cultured and aged forms like kefir, sheep's yogurt, or artisan cheeses may even support gut health.

Plant-based alternatives provide nourishment without the weight. Homemade nut and seed milks — almond, cashew, oat, hemp — are simple to make, cost-effective, and vibrationally clean compared to many processed versions. Coconut milk is one of my staples, carrying a smooth, grounding energy. Goat and sheep milk, when sourced ethically, can also serve as gentler bridges.

The point is not to demonize or sanctify dairy. It isn't "bad." It's simply dense. In some seasons of healing, density supports you; in others, it overwhelms you. The invitation is to listen. Choose what aligns with your body's current needs.

Sweeteners & Treats: The Frequency of Sweetness: Sweetness is not the enemy. It is a vibration. At its best, it carries the frequency of joy, playfulness, and celebration. At its worst, it can numb and scatter energy. The difference is intention.

Refined sugar delivers a fiery rush but leaves the body depleted. Its vibration is erratic, often leading to cravings, crashes, and mood swings. Artificial sweeteners carry a hollow, discordant frequency — a sweetness without life force.

But nature offers gentler allies, forms of sweetness that still carry the imprint of the earth. Raw honey with its healing enzymes. Maple syrup infused with the wisdom of trees. Dates packed with fiber and minerals. Coconut sugar, with its low glycemic impact and mineral content. Allulose — a modern sweetener that provides sweetness without the crash. And even unprocessed cane sugar, in its raw or minimally refined form, retains some of its natural minerals and life force, making it a more balanced choice than its heavily processed counterpart. It's also a smarter option for baking, since it maintains consistency and texture better than liquid sweeteners, while still offering a gentler vibration.

When used sparingly and with intention, these sweeteners remind us that life is meant to be savored. A drizzle of honey in tea, a spoonful of maple syrup on roasted squash, a date blended into a smoothie, or a sprinkle of raw cane sugar or coconut sugar in baking can feel like offerings of joy. The key is presence: if sweetness is your way of avoiding feeling, its vibration contracts. If it is your way of honoring celebration, its vibration expands.

Weight, Compassion & the Healing Journey

FOR MANY OF US, WEIGHT is not just physical — it is emotional, spiritual, and energetic. Extra pounds can feel like heaviness, but often that heaviness is protection. It is grief the body hasn't released, the weight of burnout or trauma stored in tissues. It is the nervous system saying: I must hold on until it's safe to let go.

If you've carried extra weight, know this: you are not broken, and you are not a failure. The body is not stubborn — it is loyal. It guards you until it believes you can live without the armor. That's why shame and punishment rarely work. Healing begins when the body feels safe, nourished, and seen.

Compassion does not mean resignation. It means aligning with wise support. Working with a physician or dietitian can provide clarity that self-blame cannot. Blood panels, hormone screenings, and micronutrient tests reveal hidden imbalances that no diet book will uncover. Testing for inflammation markers, thyroid function, gut health, or adrenal fatigue provides tools, not guesses.

If you are beginning again, start gently. Replace one non-serving food or drink at a time and keep that promise. The body thrives on safety and small consistencies more than grand declarations. Over weeks and months, those choices accumulate into a new rhythm — a new baseline.

Our modern world adds burden our ancestors never knew heavy metals in soil, pesticides in food, endocrine disruptors in plastics, chemicals in processed meals. Parasites and chronic low-level infections can drain energy and distort appetite. This is why detoxification — done safely, with practitioner guidance — can be part of healing. Hydration, fiber, mineral balance, liver-loving foods, and practices like sauna or sweating help clear stagnation. Deeper cleanses should always be overseen by professionals.

The goal is not thinness. It is alignment. It is vitality. It is feeling at home in your body again.

Sacred Skincare & Daily Practices

NOURISHMENT doesn't end at the plate. How we touch and tend the body also carries frequency. Touch is a language of healing. Whether through applying tallow-based or plant-based cream, soaking in an Epsom salt bath, or oiling your skin with intention using plant-based oils, you send signals of safety to your nervous system. These daily practices are not vain — they are vital.

I began simply, with castor oil and ginger oil, using them faithfully for nearly two years before expanding into other plant-based oils. That exploration became the foundation of my skincare and aura care line: natural oils that are organic, hexane-free, and cold-pressed. These are not only nourishing for the skin but vibrationally pure — carrying the energetic imprint of plants that heal.

We aren't taught these skills the way we're taught cooking or cleaning. But tending the vessel with oils, herbs, and touch is wisdom we can reclaim. One oil at a time, one plant at a time, you begin to notice what soothes, what uplifts, what aligns.

Sacred skincare is not about perfection. It's about presence, consistency, and choosing ingredients that honor your body instead of burdening it. Each time you oil your skin, you're not just moisturizing yourself, you're whispering: You are safe. You are worthy. You are home.

HOPE in Practice: The Reclaim Ritual Soak

DRAW A WARM BATH AND add 1-2 cups Epsom salt, 1 tablespoon bentonite clay, 2 tablespoons of baking soda, and a few drops of a grounding essential oil (lavender or frankincense, if tolerated). Dim the lights. Give yourself at least 20 quiet minutes.

As you soak, imagine the water pulling out what you no longer need—stagnation, shame, heaviness. With each exhale: "I return to my vessel with love."

Why it helps: Magnesium helps muscles release and calms the nervous system; clay absorbs heaviness; warmth signals safety. Paired with visualization, this is both nervous-system care and spiritual reset.

HOPE in Practice: The Soul Whisper Test

WHAT IF YOUR BODY ALREADY knows?

Your body already knows. Before you eat, fast, start a workout, or sign up for a plan—pause.

Hand to belly, hand to heart. Breathe. Or in the alternative; hold the food you are about to consume with both hands, close your eyes. Breathe.

Ask: "Is this for my healing or for my hiding?"

Notice: Does my body lean in (soften/expand) or tense (contract/brace)?

Choose: the action that feels like safety, not self-punishment.

Wisdom Through the Ages: Ayurveda & the Sacred Body

AFTER YEARS OF TRYING every diet in the book — portion control, calorie counting, vegetarianism, veganism, even becoming a weight loss coach for a popular brand — nothing ever felt sustainable. It wasn't until I worked closely with my primary care provider and dietitian that I began to make meaningful changes. By focusing on higher protein foods, fruit, and mindful fasting, I released 85 pounds and returned to a healthier state. But even then, I sensed there was more to nourishment than weight management.

That's when I began to explore Ayurveda — one of the world's oldest healing systems — and eventually enrolled in practitioner training. Ayurveda taught me what modern culture often dismisses: that the body is not just a machine to be fueled or fixed, but a sacred system designed for balance. Long before calorie charts or diet trends, Ayurveda understood that food carries prana — life force. It understood that digestion isn't only chemical, but energetic, tied to the rhythms of nature and the constitution of the individual.

In Sanskrit, the word for health is svastha, meaning "to be established in the self." That teaching alone shifted everything for me. Health was not about forcing my body into compliance; it was about listening to my unique constitution and aligning with the rhythms of the earth. Ayurveda doesn't ask, "How little can you eat to lose weight?" It asks, "What do you need right now to feel balanced, grounded, and alive?"

This perspective reframes nourishment from punishment into partnership. It reminds us that food is not an enemy to battle, but a teacher to walk with. By tuning into qualities like heavy vs. light, warming vs. cooling, grounding vs. uplifting, we learn to choose foods not just for their nutrients but for their vibration — the way they shape how we feel in body, mind, and spirit.

The Soul of Neurobiology

THE BODY WILL NOT RELEASE what it believes it needs to survive. This is why so many of us feel "stuck" despite our best efforts. When we live in survival states — whether from trauma, chronic stress, or lack of sleep — the nervous system sends a message: hold on, conserve, protect. That's not failure. It's intelligence.

When the body senses starvation, the amygdala — the brain's alarm center — is triggered, shifting us into fight-or-flight. In this state, metabolism slows, fat is preserved, and cravings intensify. The body isn't betraying you; it's trying to save you. Chronic stress adds another layer, as high cortisol levels drive both fat storage and emotional eating. Shame only compounds the problem, lighting up the same neural pathways as physical pain. No wonder dieting feels like a battle — your biology is literally fighting to keep you safe.

But here's the good news: the body is also wired for healing. Self-compassion, nervous system regulation, and consistent nourishment create signals of safety. Practices like deep breathing, gentle movement, restorative sleep, and eating whole foods in rhythm with your body's needs all strengthen vagal tone — the body's ability to shift out of survival and into calm. And when the body feels safe, it finally let's go.

The truth is simple: you can't hate yourself into healing. Force only deepens the body's defenses. Safety, compassion, and presence are what rewire patterns that willpower never could. Your body isn't stubborn. She's loyal — holding on until she knows you're truly safe to let go.

Human Moment: My Body Isn't Stubborn—It's Loyal

WE OFTEN CALL IT "STUBBORN fat" or say our bodies "won't cooperate." But the truth is softer, and far more sacred: your body is loyal. When it holds on, it's not defying you — it's protecting you. Crash diets, starvation, and shame only convince your biology to cling tighter. Homeostasis doesn't care about your "glow-up"; it cares that you survive.

For me, this truth came into focus when I found myself 100 pounds overweight and my doctor prescribed medication as an alternative to bariatric surgery. At first, I wrestled with shame — was I "cheating"? Was I taking the easy way out? But the truth was, I had already begun laying the foundation: working with my doctor, my dietician, and my mental health providers to repair the rhythms I'd broken. The medication wasn't a shortcut — it was a tool that gave my body the safety to reset while I rebuilt healthier patterns. And because of that foundation, when the prescription ended, the weight stayed off.

Still, I learned something even deeper: weight is not always physical. It is often energetic. Extra pounds can be the body's way of holding grief, shielding against stress, or storing unprocessed trauma. Until we deal with the root cause of that stuck energy — the heartbreak, the exhaustion, the constant survival mode — weight will not release safely, no matter how "perfect" the diet or how many hours are spent in the gym. The body waits for trust, not tricks.

This is why hype diets and shame-based health plans don't work. They bypass the deeper truth: healing requires safety, not punishment. If you're considering weight loss or major health changes, don't let culture, commercials, or comparison dictate your choices. Sit with trained practitioners — a physician who can order full labs and do a comprehensive check-up, and consider a referral to a sleep specialist for a study if sleep issues are suspected, a dietician who can help you rebuild, a therapist who can help untangle emotional patterns, a physical therapist or movement specialist who can gently retrain the body, restore function, and reconnect you to safe, aligned movement, and alternative medicine practitioners — such as acupuncturists, herbalists, or energy healers — who honor the mind-body connection.

Ask the hard questions. Look beyond quick fixes. You are not just reprogramming your weight — you are reprogramming your life force. "You are going to have to decide that you love yourself too much to stop settling for less than what you really deserve." — Brianna Wiest, *The Mountain Is You: Transforming Self-Sabotage Into Self-Mastery*

Your body isn't stubborn. It's loyal. It will carry the weight literally and energetically until you show it that it's safe to let it go. And when you finally treat it as a sacred ally instead of an enemy, it releases, not out of defeat, but out of trust.

HOPE in Practice: Soul Tending Ritual

FIND A QUIET SPOT. Light a candle or sit by a window. Hand on heart, hand on lower belly. Whisper:

"I forgive myself for trying to earn worth through restriction."

"I honor the vessel that carried me through pain."

"I nourish you now."

Breathe. Let what comes, come—tears, warmth, gratitude. Let nourishment be homecoming.

Soul Seed to Take With You

HEALING HAPPENS IN rhythm, not in rush. One swap. One breath. One kept promise. Consistency is love made visible.

Optional: One Gentle Day

LET THIS RHYTHM GUIDE your day – gentle, grounded, consistent.

Morning: Warm lemon water; fruit + protein (e.g., berries, chia pudding, or mango with soft-boiled eggs).

Midday: Big greens + clean protein + healthy fat (olive oil, avocado); add a grounding starch if desired (quinoa, sweet potato, rice).

Afternoon: Simple snack that steadies (cucumber + pinch of salt; handful of nuts/seeds).

Evening: Protein + two vegetables; optional small starch to anchor; herbal tea.

Practice: Gratitude line at night; 3 calming breaths before meals; light self-massage with oil after a shower. To nourish the vessel is to honor the sacred ground of your own body — feeding it with rhythms, rituals, and choices that keep your light steady. But vessels were never meant to hold light only for themselves. A lamp shines brightest when it illuminates a room. A river flows strongest when it joins the ocean. The question is: what happens when the nourishment you cultivate spills over into others — when your healed energy becomes a collective current of HOPE?

Chapter Fourteen

Expansion – HOPE in the Collective, Community & Service

Healing is not just about feeling better inside your own skin. It's about what your energy, your choices, and your presence release into the world. When you heal, you change the story your family inherits. You interrupt cycles of harm that would otherwise echo into the next generation. You become a safer partner, a truer friend, a steadier neighbor.

Your healing matters because it ripples. And those ripples are what make collective transformation possible.

Healing is never just personal. Though it begins within, the impact does not stop there. Each choice to tend your own wounds ripples outward — shaping families, touching relationships, and influencing the wider currents of community and culture.

Expansion is not about doing more. It is about becoming more fully yourself, shedding what is false, and allowing your authentic presence to move naturally through the world.

While you heal, you may encounter resistance. Not everyone will understand, welcome, or even believe in your transformation. Some will shower you with genuine praise, surprising you with encouragement you didn't expect. Others may respond with sarcasm, passive-aggressive remarks, or even outright criticism. This mix can be confusing—because it's not all negative, but it's not all supportive either.

That's why it helps to prepare in advance. Decide now how you'll respond—to the enthusiastic praise, the cutting sarcasm, the unexpected kindness, and the dismissive comments. This preparation gives you a steady center. You'll know what belongs to you and what doesn't.

In doing so, you protect your energy. You remind yourself that your healing is not up for debate, approval, or rejection—it's your sacred work. When you stand rooted in your truth, the external noise—whether sweet or sharp—loses its power to sway you.

You are not separate from the collective. You are one of its vital threads. Every time you choose healing over harm, presence over performance, honesty over hiding, you are helping to shift the collective field toward wholeness.

This is the sacred expansion of HOPE: the inner light that becomes an outer force for renewal.

From Individual Healing to Collective Resonance

EARLIER, WE EXPLORED the sovereignty of self — the work of reclaiming your energy, raising your vibration, and tending to your nervous system. That inner healing was essential. But healing never ends with the self. Once your roots grow stronger, you are ready to branch outward into the wider world.

Your nervous system is not an island. It speaks to other nervous systems, often more powerfully than words. When you regulate, you help others regulate. When you live with joy, you give others quiet permission to remember their own. And when you set a boundary, you declare what you will no longer carry, tolerate, or transmit.

Boundaries are not walls of separation — they are bridges of clarity. They model what is possible for others and protect the integrity of the field you are co-creating.

We heal together, or not at all. Trauma isolates, disconnects, and divides. But HOPE restores the web. It brings us back into resonance — with ourselves, with Spirit, with each other.

Living the HOPE Method is not only about improving your personal life. It is about reweaving the communal fabric. Every act of truth-telling, every boundary honored, every choice for healing becomes a stitch — sewing torn places back together until what was once fragmented begins to feel whole again.

Boundaries as Collective Healing

BOUNDARIES ARE OFTEN misunderstood as barriers that keep people out. But in truth, boundaries are declarations of clarity. They communicate what you will allow, what you will not, and what you are actively choosing to cultivate. Boundaries are not walls of rejection — they are invitations into healthier, more honest relationships.

When you set a boundary, you are not only protecting your own nervous system; you are also reshaping the energetic field around you. Every "no" to dysfunction creates space for a "yes" to integrity. Every moment of clarity interrupts the cycle of confusion that trauma perpetuates. Boundaries stabilize the collective, not just the self.

In families, boundaries prevent generational patterns from being passed down. A parent who says, "I will not use shame as discipline," stops an old wound from echoing into the next generation.

In workplaces, boundaries shift culture. The person who refuses to glorify burnout gives permission for others to honor their limits, too.

In communities, boundaries draw lines of dignity. Saying, "We will not tolerate exclusion or cruelty here," restores belonging and creates a safe space for collective healing.

This is why boundaries are not selfish. They are sacred acts of service. By standing firm in what you will and will not carry, you are modeling freedom, stability, and resonance for others. You become a living reminder that healing is possible — not just for one life, but for the web of lives connected to yours.

The Community Mirror

COMMUNITY IS NOT JUST where you are seen — it is where you are reflected. Others help you remember who you are, especially when you forget. They become mirrors of your growth, your blind spots, and your light.

Healing in isolation is possible. But healing in community is exponential. Neuroscience affirms this: our nervous systems are relational and co-regulate with one another (as described in Stephen Porges' Polyvagal Theory). What one heart steadies can ripple into others.

Fragmentation isolates and divides, but community restores the web. When you find your people — or when you choose to become that mirror for someone else — you weave resonance back into the fabric of belonging. The HOPE Method encourages collective practice: shared breath, shared witness, shared presence. Because healing is more powerful when echoed.

Let Your Light Spill

YOU DON'T NEED TO BE a coach, a healer, or a leader to live in service. You simply need to be willing to radiate what you've remembered. Social learning theory tells us that people learn more by watching behavior than by instruction. A single moment of courage — saying no, saying yes, standing in your wholeness — can plant a seed in someone else's soul.

You never know who your truth might touch. The way you hold yourself at a family dinner, the way you model rest in a workplace addicted to hustle, the way you choose honesty over hiding — all of these are forms of service.

You don't have to save the world. Just meet it with your presence. And as you do, HOPE expands — not through force, but because it naturally wants to be shared

Daily Practice as Collective Renewal: There is something primal in practice. Across cultures, humans have always created rhythms to anchor meaning, mark time, and survive the in-between. Anthropologists like Victor Turner describe these shared practices as essential for transition, while neuroscience shows that rhythm and repetition help regulate the nervous system. What ancient traditions have always known, science now affirms: we are wired for patterns that sustain us.

Daily practice is the soft architecture of the soul. They do not demand performance; they offer permission. In the HOPE Method, daily practice is the bridge between intention and embodiment. It is how we translate healing into rhythm, turning ideas into lived experience.

Healing is not a linear checklist — it is cyclical. Daily practice reminds us that regulation and renewal are not luxuries; they are lifelines. And when practiced together — whether through shared breath, reflection, or stillness — daily practice becomes a collective drumbeat, guiding us back into harmony again and again.

Belonging After the Break: Rebuilding Community from the Inside Out

THERE COMES A POINT in healing when you begin to glow again. Not perform. Not pretend. But glow — from truth, from restoration, from remembering who you are. And in that glow, a new ache often arises:

Where do I belong now? Who sees me now that I've stopped dimming?

For many of us, fragmentation created a version of belonging rooted in survival. We performed to be accepted, tolerated relationships that drained us, and tiptoed around those who felt unsafe. We stayed not because we were seen, but because we feared being alone.

Healing invites a new question: What if I only allowed relationships that honor the light I worked so hard to reclaim?

This is where HOPE begins — Harnessing your energy back from old survival patterns and redirecting it toward truth. And as you do, you move through the rhythm of W-S-H-to-Heal — choosing wisdom, serenity, and heart-led belonging that restores love to your connections.

Belonging, in its truest form, is not about fitting in. It is about being seen and celebrated as you are — and that is where HOPE expands into community.

And yet, to truly belong — to yourself and to others — your energy must be available. When unseen forces are siphoning your vitality, it becomes harder to stay present, to trust connection, and to share your light. This is why tending to the integrity of your energy field matters just as much as nurturing your soul.

Hitchhiking on Your Energy: Parasites, Pathogens, and the Energy They Steal

YOUR BODY IS NOT JUST a biological machine; it is a sacred vessel of life force energy. When it is clear, you feel grounded, intuitive, and vibrant. But just as fragmented emotions or cluttered environments can drain you, so too can hidden invaders — parasites, stealth pathogens, and microbial overgrowths that hijack your vitality.

In medicine, these intruders often reveal themselves quietly: persistent fatigue, foggy thinking, cravings, looping emotions, or unshakable anxiety. Spiritually, they mirror energetic invasion — toxic patterns, codependent ties, or grief that clings. Whether biological or symbolic, they steal clarity, intuition, and strength.

"You are the gatekeeper of your energy. And sometimes, the invaders are internal, hidden, and hungry for your light."

Clearing these drains is part of living the O in HOPE — choosing what is optimal for your body and soul. Through W-S-H-to-Heal, you learn to honor your body with wisdom, meet your healing with serenity, and reclaim the love that fragmentation tried to steal.

Reclaiming Sovereignty

NOURISHMENT IS ONLY half the equation. To live in energetic integrity, we must also clear what does not belong. This chapter is a reclamation of sovereignty — exploring how parasites, pathogens, toxins, and energetic intrusions can cloud your field and dull your light.

Through the lens of both science and spirit, we will look at how these disruptions affect your vibration and emotional clarity. You'll also be introduced to HOPE in Practice: The Sovereign Cleanse — a soul-centered approach to clearing and reclaiming. We'll explore the healing power of sleep, the vibrational importance of sacred rest, and accessible daily practices like Epsom and clay baths, environmental awareness, and dreamwork. Each of these tools helps recalibrate the body's field back to coherence.

A Gentle Sovereignty Cleanse: If you feel called to clear what no longer serves you, approach it gently. Align with the waning moon, prepare your body with rest, and choose practices that nourish as much as they release.

Light broths, grounding foods, and mineral-rich teas support the body as it lets go. Castor oil packs, salt baths, and journaling can help move stagnant emotional energy. Herbal protocols, if used, should be guided by a trusted practitioner.

This is not a punishment — it is a return to sovereignty. A reclamation of your body's brilliance and boundaries. Let it be sacred. Let it be kind.

And remember, in a world full of invisible pollutants — chemical, emotional, energetic — even simple practices like regular Epsom or clay baths can be acts of spiritual protection. Each rinse is a reminder: Release what is not mine. Recalibrate to what is true.

Fragmentation — whether from pathogens, toxins, or unresolved emotions — clouds our energy field and makes it harder to live in alignment. Science shows that parasites and stealth pathogens can disrupt digestion, immunity, and mood, while psychology affirms that emotional clutter weakens resilience. Spiritually, these intrusions can be seen as energetic "hitchhikers" that dim our light. The Sovereign Cleanse exists to restore clarity, resilience, and vibrational strength.

The Sovereign Cleanse is not a harsh detox or extreme regimen. It is a soul-centered approach to clearing what doesn't belong while nourishing what does. It combines gentle physical support (hydration, minerals, gut balance) with energetic daily practices (Epsom salt baths, grounding, breathwork, journaling, and sacred rest). Together, these clear stagnation from both body and soul.

HOPE in Practice: Your Sacred Pause

BEFORE YOUR NEXT TRANSITION — from work to home, from scrolling to sleep — pause. Breathe deeply. Brush your hands gently down your arms. Whisper: "I honor the ending. I open to what's next." That alone is a daily practice.

Daily practice doesn't need to be elaborate. It doesn't require altars or chants. It can be a morning stretch done with intention, stirring tea while repeating a mantra, or slipping into a bath and letting sorrow dissolve into the water.

What makes it powerful is not the form — but the presence you bring to it.

This is the E in HOPE — Energy. Each pause is an act of tending your life-force, protecting it from fragmentation, and replenishing what the day has asked of you. And through W-S-H-to-Heal, a sacred pause becomes more than a break: it is wisdom choosing reflection, serenity entering the body, heart opening to the moment, healing unfolding in breath, expression finding voice, acceptance softening the edges, and love infusing the next step forward. A sacred pause is how you carry HOPE into the ordinary — one transition, one breath, one moment at a time.

HOPE in Practice: Belonging by Vibration, Not Obligation

YOU DON'T NEED TO FIT in where your soul is shrinking. You need connection that expands you — that honors your full presence.

Belonging is not about performance; it's about resonance. True belonging happens when you can speak your truth without fear of exile, when you're celebrated instead of merely tolerated. When you are healing, you stop dimming yourself just to stay connected. This can feel lonely at first — not because you are broken, but because you are becoming whole. And wholeness changes your radius. It naturally filters who can meet you where you are now.

This is why so many on the healing path feel disconnected from old groups or roles. The truth is you are not losing belonging — you are rediscovering it. Real belonging by vibration means choosing connections that honor your authenticity instead of demanding your performance. It looks like spaces where you can be both soft and strong without being asked to choose. These spaces expand you instead of shrinking you, allowing your full self to be welcomed.

To live this out, begin by noticing how your body responds in relationships. Where do you contract? Where does your energy grow heavy or your voice go silent? These are signals that obligation has replaced resonance. Belonging by vibration invites you to release ties that cost you your authenticity and to seek or create spaces that allow you to expand. Sometimes this looks like a supportive community, sometimes it begins with one trusted friend, and sometimes it starts with choosing to be that safe space for yourself.

Through the flow of WiSH-to-HEAL, wisdom rises as you begin to discern who is truly safe for your spirit. Serenity follows as you release the ties that no longer honor your path. Your heart learns to stay open, even in the tender places, so connection remains possible. Healing unfolds as new patterns replace the old, offering you steady ground. Expression becomes natural, as your voice no longer hides in silence. Acceptance deepens, teaching you to trust the gentle filtering of relationships. And in the end, love remains — the kind of love that celebrates you exactly as you are, without condition, without performance, simply in truth.

Daily Practices & the Nervous System

DAILY PRACTICES HAVE a profound effect on the nervous system because they offer both rhythm and predictability. The human brain is wired to seek patterns; when life feels chaotic, practices that repeat with consistency signal to the body, "This is safe. This is familiar. You can settle here."

Neuroscience shows that rituals and daily practices engage the prefrontal cortex — the part of the brain that helps regulate stress — while also calming the amygdala, the brain's built-in alarm system. Over time, this predictability allows the nervous system to anticipate calm even before the practice begins. It's why a warm cup of tea, a morning walk, or even brushing your hands down your arms with intention can bring such immediate relief. The body remembers the signal: you are safe.

In the HOPE Method, this is the E — Energy. Daily practice isn't about performance or perfection; it is about creating rhythms that regulate and restore. And through the flow of W-S-H-to-Heal, these small moments weave wisdom into your day, serenity into your body, heart into your presence, healing into your rhythms, expression into your choices, acceptance into your transitions, and love into the spaces you inhabit.

Wisdom Through the Ages

ACROSS CULTURES AND centuries, human beings have instinctively turned to daily practices to regulate the mind, body, and spirit. From the Japanese tea ceremony to Native American smudging, from Catholic communion to the Ayurvedic dinacharya (daily rhythm), we see a common thread: repetition combined with reverence brings regulation. These practices ground us, reminding both body and soul: I exist. I matter. This moment belongs to me.

Modern culture often pushes us in the opposite direction. We are sold the myth that faster is better, that stillness is wasted time, that productivity proves our worth. But daily practices return us to the speed of soul. They slow us down until we can hear our own breath again, until we can remember that life is not only about doing it, it is about being. And in that slowing, we are reintroduced to our essence.

These practices also hold space for the paradox of being human: grief and joy existing side by side. Lighting a candle in remembrance, playing your grandmother's favorite song, journaling after a long cry — these are not merely coping strategies. They are medicine, soothing the emotional body, nourishing the spiritual heart, and even influencing cellular health by calming the nervous system. Science now confirms what ancient wisdom always carried: when we give reverence to rhythm, we create resilience.

HOPEfully Human Moment

ONCE, IN THE MIDDLE of heartbreak, I decided to take an Epsom salt and bentonite clay bath. Only, the bag of clay slipped while I was pouring it in — and half of it dumped into the tub at once. The water turned thick and murky, and by the time I sank into it, I wasn't sure if I was bathing or sitting in a puddle of wet cement.

It wasn't glamorous. It definitely was not worthy of social media. And later, I had to scoop clay out of the drain so the pipes wouldn't clog. But it was sacred. Because for that one evening, I let the heaviness leave my body and trusted the mess to hold it.

Afterward, gritty-skinned and heart still aching, I whispered, "I still choose me." That was enough. That was practice.

HOPE in Practice: Build Your Daily Practice

ASK YOURSELF: WHAT soothes me? What grounds me? What helps me remember that I am alive and healing? The answers don't have to be elaborate. It might be taking three slow breaths, stepping barefoot on the grass, writing one honest sentence in your journal, or lighting a candle at the same hour each day.

The key is not complexity — it's consistency. Choose one simple action and repeat it at the same time, in the same way, with the same intention. Over days and weeks, your nervous system will begin to anticipate calmness before the practice even begins. This is how the body learns: through repetition and rhythm. Predictability says to your brain, "This is home. This is safe. You can rest here."

In the HOPE Method, this practice connects to the E for Energy. By tending to your energy daily, you create resilience. And through W-S-H-to-Heal, this repetition becomes wisdom for the mind, serenity for the body, heart for the soul, healing in rhythm, expression in action, acceptance in presence, and love woven into ordinary time.

Soul Seed to Take With You

DAILY PRACTICE IS NOT about control — it is about teaching your nervous system that change does not always equal danger. Some change is devotion. Some changes are divine. Each time you repeat a practice with reverence, you plant a soul seed. Over time, these seeds grow into trust: trust in your body, trust in your rhythms, trust in your capacity to hold both joy and grief without breaking.

This is the essence of HOPE — Harnessing Optimal Positive Energy — and it begins not in the extraordinary, but in the ordinary moments you choose to treat as sacred.

Belonging Reflection Journal Page

BELONGING BEGINS WHEN you stop performing for connection and start honoring your true vibration. Journaling can help you discern where that shift is needed. Reflect:

Who taught me that I had to earn my place?

What relationships still require me to shrink or shape-shift?

What does belonging feel like in my body when it is true and safe?

What kind of community would reflect the person I am becoming?

Where am I being invited to create new, soul-aligned spaces of connection?

These questions are not just about relationships with others — they are about your relationship with yourself. Each answer brings you closer to the H in HOPE — Harnessing your energy back from old survival belonging. And through the flow of W-S-H-to-Heal, you gather wisdom from the past, serenity for the present, heart for the ache of change, healing in your honesty, expression in naming truth, acceptance of what no longer fits, and love for what is waiting to be born.

Spiritual Boundaries vs. Isolation

BOUNDARIES ARE NOT barriers; they are thresholds. Isolation is rooted in fear — it pushes everyone out and leaves you carrying heaviness alone. Boundaries, on the other hand, are rooted in love. They create clear thresholds where you decide what energy may enter and what must remain outside.

When you say no, when you take space, when you protect your peace — you are not being cold, you are being sacred. You are honoring the light within you. Boundaries feel clean, empowering, and soul honoring because they align you with truth.

This is the O and P of HOPE — choosing what is optimal and positive for your soul. And through W-S-H-to-Heal, boundaries allow wisdom to guide your choices, serenity to protect your nervous system, heart to remain open, healing to continue without intrusion, expression to find its voice, acceptance to hold reality, and love to define the terms of connection.

Affirmation

"I DON'T CHASE CONNECTION. I cultivate alignment — and trust the rest will rise to meet me."

Say it aloud. Write it on a card. Place it on your mirror. Let it become part of your nervous system's new language — one that affirms that you belong not because you shrink to fit, but because you stand in the full truth of who you are.

Expansion is remembering that your healing does not end with you. Every choice to live in alignment ripples outward — softening a family pattern, inspiring a friend, steadying a community. But even as your light touches the collective, the question remains: How do you keep from pouring so much outward that you forget the most essential relationship of all — the one you hold with yourself? That is where we turn next: the practice of self-love, not as a concept, but as the foundation of everything HOPE expands into.

Chapter Fifteen

Self-Love – Returning to the Center of Your Own Heart

In Chapter 11, we explored what it means to nourish the vessel — the foods, practices, and rhythms that sustain the body. But the body is only one layer of nourishment. The vessel is also filled with thoughts, beliefs, and choices. What we feed ourselves with wisdom, honesty, and compassion matters just as much as what we place on our plates.

Self-love is the next expansion of nourishment. It isn't a bubble bath or a catchy phrase. It's not always soft or pretty. Sometimes it's fierce. Sometimes it's quiet. Sometimes it's messy. But always, always — it is necessary.

Self-love is the act of returning — again and again — to the sacred center of your own heart. Not for ego. Not for image. But for truth. For life. For peace.

Love Isn't a Feeling — It's a Frequency

WE'VE BEEN TAUGHT TO chase love. To earn it. To prove our worthiness for it. Sometimes this training came from those who claimed to care for us — a parent who withheld affection to "teach us respect," a teacher who shamed us to "build our character," a partner who withdrew to "make us try harder." They may have believed they were shaping us, but what they really shaped was our fear.

Those small unintentional cuts — the disapproving look, the sarcastic remark, the silent treatment — taught us to question our own worth and to perform for belonging. Over time, those lessons dimmed our light. We learned to hide pieces of ourselves, to mask our desires, to abandon our needs in the name of being "good." We became experts at self-betrayal because we thought it was the price of love.

But the deeper truth is this: Love is not something you have to prove, win, or maintain by performance. Love is not fragile, nor is it conditional. Love is essence. Love is unconditional. It does not vanish when you falter or wait until you are perfect to arrive.

This is the kind of love described in ancient wisdom that describe love as patient, kind, enduring. Not transactional. Not earned. A love that never fails but always calls you home.

And that essence is who you are. Before the betrayals. Before the masks. Before the abandonment. Before anyone told you that you were too much or not enough — you were love. You still are.

The invitation now is to extend that same form of love to yourself. To be patient with your own becoming. To be kind with your flaws. To offer grace when you stumble and gentleness when you are weary. Self-love is not a performance of confidence; it is the daily practice of treating yourself the way unconditional love always has — with compassion, with endurance, with the quiet promise: I will not leave you, no matter what.

Even now, beneath the scars, beneath the stories, beneath the armor, that love remains. It waits not to be earned, but to be remembered — and practiced first toward yourself.

And when you return to self-love, you are returning to the innocence of love — the way your inner child once knew it. The child who reached out with open arms, unafraid of rejection. The child who lived in curiosity, who explored with wonder, who trusted joy as the most natural thing in the world. That part of you has not disappeared; it has only been covered. Self-love is the uncovering. It is remembering what it feels like to belong to yourself first, before the world taught you to earn it.

HOPE teaches that self-love isn't something you find in someone else's eyes — it is something you remember within your own heart. And the remembering itself is healing.

The Many Faces of Self-Betrayal

TO LOVE YOURSELF, YOU must first acknowledge the ways you've been taught not to.

Self-betrayal rarely begins with grand gestures. It slips in quietly, often in childhood, in the moments when innocence met someone else's conditions. The curious child who asked too many questions was told to be quiet. The adventurous child who dreamed too wildly was told to be realistic. The tender child who laughed too loud or cried too long was told they were too much.

Those lessons may have come with good intentions, but they taught us to dim our light in exchange for love. Over time, that dimming became second nature.

Self-betrayal sneaks in through subtle disguises: saying yes when your body screams no. Silencing your truth just to be accepted. Abandoning your needs to avoid conflict. Staying where you are unseen just to avoid being alone. Believing love has to hurt to be real.

People-pleasing when you long for freedom. Staying when you want to go. Compromising on or settling for second best because you've been told you can't do better.

Each of these disguises began the moment the child within learned it was safer to shrink than to shine. What was once protection has become a pattern. These are not failures. They are survival strategies. But survival isn't the same as self-love.

And some forms of self-betrayal cut even deeper. Beyond the daily disguises are the larger wounds — the broken promises, the shaming doctrines, the inherited scripts that taught us our worth was conditional. These leave imprints not just on our choices, but on the very way we see ourselves.

It's here that we must slow down and name these wounds for what they are — because only by naming them can we begin to reclaim the truth beneath them.

Vow Betrayal, Religious Shame & Reclaiming Your Truth: The child within us is born trusting, wide-eyed and open-hearted. But when that trust is betrayed, the wound runs deep. For some, it came in the breaking of vows — words once spoken with devotion that later unraveled through silence, infidelity, neglect, or choices that slowly pulled two lives apart. For others, it came through religion, where what began as devotion was twisted into fear, where honest questions were branded as rebellion, where shame was used to quiet the innocent child who only longed to belong.

These betrayals teach us to believe that love and safety must be earned by sacrifice. That belonging requires us to shrink. That to be "good" is to surrender our own power in order to keep the peace. Such lessons carve themselves deep, not only into our choices, but into the way we see ourselves.

But HOPE offers another way. Breaking these inherited scripts may feel like rebellion, but it is not destruction — it is reclamation. It is the moment we take the hand of our inner child and whisper: you never had to earn love by betraying yourself. You never had to carry shame that was never yours.

Self-love means choosing differently now. It sounds like a quiet vow to yourself: My worth is not for sale. My silence is not required. The shame I carried is set down. I return, gently, to my truth.

And yet, returning is never just a single moment. It is a practice — a rhythm of remembering and forgetting, of wandering and coming home again. The work of healing is not to love yourself perfectly, but to keep finding your way back.

The Practice of Returning: Self-love isn't a destination. It's a relationship — a homecoming.

There will be days you forget. Days when the old patterns call you back. Days you speak to yourself in tones you would never use on a friend or even a stranger. And still, you are invited to return.

To return is to reach again for the hand of your inner child — the one who still waits for you beneath the noise. The child who once laughed freely asked boldly, and trusted joy as the most natural thing in the world. Every time you soften, every time you pause instead of punishing, every time you choose kindness over criticism, you are reminding that child: we are safe now, and we belong to ourselves first.

Return through words that affirm your truth. Through movements that honor your body. Through food that nourishes instead of punishes. Through boundaries that protect your peace. Through touch that reminds you you are real. Through stillness that lets your soul breathe.

Self-love doesn't erase the past — it redeems it. Each return is another stitch in the fabric of wholeness, weaving back together the pieces that were once scattered.

Wholeness Doesn't Require Perfection: You don't have to love yourself perfectly to live with HOPE. You don't have to get it right every time. What matters is that you are willing — willing to show up, willing to soften, willing to begin again.

Think of your inner child: they never needed a perfect parent, only a present one. In the same way, you don't need flawless self-love. You just need to be there for yourself, even imperfectly.

Every time you pause instead of punishing. Every time you choose to rest instead of proving. Every time you speak to yourself with even a whisper of kindness — you are practicing self-love. You are proving to your inner child that love is safe here, that care will not be withdrawn when mistakes are made.

It's not always a grand gesture. Sometimes it's as simple as whispering, I forgive you, I love you, or even I am beautiful to the mirror. Sometimes it's letting yourself rest without guilt. Sometimes it's daring to eat in a way that feels kind instead of punishing.

This is how we return. This is how we remember. This is how we begin to belong to ourselves again.

Nourishing the Vessel: What We Feed Ourselves Reflects What We Believe We Deserve

SELF-LOVE IS NOT ONLY emotional and spiritual — it is also physical. The way we nourish our bodies is a mirror of how deeply we believe in our own worth.

We've been taught that nourishment means discipline — counting, restricting, subtracting. But in truth, nourishing the vessel is about connection. It is about recognizing what makes you feel alive, aligned, and able to carry your light forward with both strength and softness.

And nourishment comes in many forms. Yes, it is in the foods you choose — not as punishment or performance, but as an act of listening to what your body truly needs. But nourishment is also found in self-care — in rest that restores, in movement that strengthens, in boundaries that protect your peace. And it is spiritual as well — in devotion, in journaling, in grounding practices that root you back into yourself.

Healing is not about the perfect diet or flawless routine. It is about reclaiming your relationship with energy, emotion, and embodiment. And sometimes... the biggest shift begins not with what you add, but with what you stop forcing — the foods, practices, or expectations you thought were helping but were actually weighing you down.

Nourishing the vessel means honoring the whole of you: body, mind, and spirit. It is a daily reminder that you are worth feeding with kindness, worth caring for with gentleness, worth rooting in practices that remind you — you belong here, in your own skin.

And yet, knowing this in theory and living it in practice are not always the same. Sometimes, the very ways we try to care for ourselves can become another form of pressure or punishment. That's why I don't share theory alone — I share from lived experience. What I teach, I have had to walk through myself.

When Nourishment Becomes Noise

FOR YEARS, I TRIED to do everything right. And sometimes, it isn't a straight line — it's a puzzle. One you can't always solve alone. This is where the right practitioners matter: those who look deeper than surface numbers, who honor what your body is telling you instead of dismissing it. Because I've been told, more than once, that according to my bloodwork I was a "perfectly healthy fat person." As if numbers on a chart could erase the swelling in my joints, the exhaustion in my bones, the heaviness I carried that had nothing to do with calories.

To move forward, I had to become a detective of my own body. That meant examining everything I put into and onto myself — every supplement, every food, every lotion, every capsule — to find the hidden triggers my body was quietly reacting to. It wasn't about obsession. It was about listening with new eyes and ears, honoring that my system was sensitive and asking for a different kind of care.

I followed the detoxes, the green powders, the vegan trends, the mushroom elixirs. I took the popular supplements, filled my plate with leafy greens, and swapped out my morning coffee for adaptogenic blends that promised clarity, calm, and a faster metabolism. And yet — my body held on to inflammation like armor. The scale wouldn't move. My joints felt swollen, my energy unpredictable, my mood flatlined. And worst of all, I felt like I was failing.

But I wasn't failing. I was just following protocols that weren't designed for my body. And that's when I began to understand real nourishment is not about proving your discipline or chasing the next wellness trend. It is about listening inward — honoring the signals of your own body with the same patience, kindness, and curiosity that define self-love.

For me, that listening began with simple but radical choices. I stopped eating processed foods altogether. That meant bread and grains, canned or bottled drinks, and pretty much anything that came in a wrapper. If I wanted a sweet treat, I had to make it myself — with ingredients I trusted, in a way that felt kind to my body.

At first, it felt restrictive, but soon I realized it was actually liberating. I was no longer outsourcing my nourishment to packages and promises. I was choosing presence. I was choosing to know what was going on in my body — and more importantly, how it made me feel.

The truth is that a lot of "healthy" advice is built for the average body — not the sensitive, empathic, allergy-prone, fragmentation-touched body that absorbs everything more deeply. I didn't know that salicylates (natural compounds in plants) were triggering inflammation. I didn't realize that cellulose capsules — the same ones in so many "clean" vitamins — were wreaking havoc on my digestion and nervous system. I didn't know that "detox" meant different things for different people.

I thought I was helping myself. But I was overwhelming a system already trying to survive.

What I've learned is that weight is not just about calories or willpower — it's about inflammation, nervous system overload, and what your body is protecting you from. And often, the very supplements or meal plans that work wonders for someone else can create chaos in the body of a person like me.

Now, I choose what's optimal, not just what's trendy. I listen to how my body feels, not just what a protocol promises. And I trust that my path is slower, softer, and far more sacred.

Healing, for me, means less is more. It means warm carob drinks, gentle minerals, peeled fruit instead of greens I can't tolerate. It means forgiving my body for not responding the way I wanted it to — and thanking it for holding out until I finally learned how to listen.

And perhaps the most important shift? I began to trust my intuition again — that soft, knowing whisper that rises beneath the noise. I stopped outsourcing my wellness to trends and experts and started asking my body directly: Does this feel safe? Does this feel nourishing? Do I feel lighter, brighter, more like myself after this choice?

Sometimes the healing isn't what you add. It's in what you stop forcing.

A Gentle Reminder

IT'S IMPORTANT TO LISTEN to your body when it comes to nourishment. We covered this thought at length in Chapter 10. Sure — something might taste good in the moment... but how long does it linger in your system? Does it drag you down, or lift you up?

One of the most powerful ways to uncover this is to keep a daily journal. Write down every food you eat, every drink you sip, every supplement you take. Track the rhythms of your day as well — your shower schedule, your lotion routine, your bedtime. And add in your daily weight. Not as judgment, but as data. Over time, you'll notice whether certain foods add water weight, leave you inflamed, or help you wake up feeling lighter and more energized.

You don't need a fancy system. The notes app on your phone works beautifully — especially on busy days. You can even use simple symbols to keep it easy: a moon for sleep quality, a water drop for hydration, a plate for meals, a sleeping face for fatigue, and a lightning bolt for energy. A few quick marks can tell the story at-a-glance.

In just a few short months, you'll begin to see patterns you might have missed for years. For me, I discovered that if I eat after 8 p.m., I wake up sluggish, with low energy, almost as if I didn't sleep at all. Without journaling, I might have blamed stress or age. But by tracking daily — food, weight, rhythms, and morning energy — I could see the direct link between timing, choices, and how my body responded.

This practice isn't about obsession or perfection. It's about resonance — testing each choice, listening deeply, and noticing: What energy did it bring, and what energy did it quietly take away?

We've just covered a lot of ground — nourishment, patterns, betrayals, and the ways our bodies carry stories that diets and routines can't always touch. Now it's time to step back and soften. Healing isn't only about information; it's about integration. And one of the most powerful ways to integrate is through reflection — letting your thoughts spill onto the page without judgment, like soul scribbles.

Quiet Journal Prompt

BEFORE YOU BEGIN, PREPARE yourself. Gather what you need — a notebook or your phone's notes app, maybe a blanket or a cup of tea. Choose a time when you can be present: late at night when the house is quiet, early at 5 a.m. before the day begins, or during a still weekend moment. However, you create it, let this be mindful and intentional. Think of it as a sacred appointment with your own heart — a chance to hear what your body and spirit have been whispering beneath the noise of daily life. You may answer the first two questions, or you may also explore the other questions as they resonate in this moment:

What has my body been trying to tell me — beneath the noise of shoulds and trends?

What does it need to feel safe enough to release, shift, or soften?

Where in my life do, I still confuse discipline with care?

What small act of nourishment (physical, emotional, or spiritual) feels most loving to me right now?

When have I felt most at home in my own body? What supported that feeling?

If my inner child could choose one way to be cared for today, what would they ask for?

What am I ready to release — not just from my diet, but from my patterns of self-betrayal?

HOPE Insight:

SOMETIMES THE WEIGHT we carry isn't just on our bodies — it's in the rules we followed that were never made for us.

Emotions are not obstacles to healing — they are the healing. They are the messengers, the medicine, and sometimes the storm. But if we allow them, they become the gold.

In the HOPE Method, we practice emotional alchemy — the sacred art of transforming inner chaos into clarity. We don't bypass pain. We meet it. We don't deny grief. We honor it. And in doing so, we extract meaning from the very things that once tried to break us.

This is the "H" in HOPE — Harnessing. Each time we allow ourselves to feel, we reclaim energy that was once spent suppressing, avoiding, or pretending. That energy becomes fuel for healing, creativity, and deeper truth.

The truth is you cannot heal what you will not feel.

HOPE in Practice: The Emotional Check-In

PAUSE. ASK YOURSELF:

"What am I feeling right now — not what I should feel, but what's truly there?"

Then ask: "What does this emotion need from me — space, movement, expression, or release?"

This is how we begin the alchemy — with honesty. Most of us were taught to fear our feelings. We were told to stop crying, to calm down, to "be strong." But in truth, strength is found in sensitivity. Sensitivity is presence. Presence is power.

Emotional suppression may have kept you safe in childhood — but in adulthood, it keeps you disconnected. It separates you from your needs, your voice, your vitality. The HOPE Method invites you to feel — not to drown, but to integrate.

The Neuroscience of Feeling

RESEARCH BY DR. JILL Bolte Taylor, a Harvard-trained neuroscientist, found that when an emotion is allowed to move through the body without resistance, it lasts an average of 90 seconds in its purest form. It's not the feeling itself that overwhelms us — it's the story we attach to it, the way we replay it, resist it, or identify with it, that keeps it alive.

Emotional alchemy begins when we stop making feelings wrong and start seeing them as data and direction — signals that guide us toward what needs healing, honoring, or releasing.

Wisdom Through the Ages

THIS IS NOT POETIC fluff — it's emotional truth. Your capacity to feel pain expands you, making room for a fuller experience in life. The mystic poet Khalil Gibran once wrote: "The deeper that sorrow carves into your being, the more joy you can contain."

These are not just poetic lines; they are a reflection of emotional truth. Gibran, written in the early 20th century, was known for weaving spirituality and psychology long before modern science caught up. His insight reminds us that sorrow is not a defect to be erased — it is an opening. The very places where grief, loss, and disappointment carve us hollow are the same places where love, joy, and tenderness later find room to dwell.

This is the essence of alchemy: transforming what feels unbearable into something that expands us. Neuroscience now echoes what mystics have long taught — that emotions are energy, and energy cannot be destroyed, only moved and reshaped.

Some emotions require movement: the shaking off of anger through a run, the trembling release of tears, the guttural scream into a pillow. Others require stillness: the quiet presence of grief held in silence, the breath that steadies panic, the gentle rocking that soothes much like a child being cradled. There is no single formula, no perfect prescription.

And this is where it ties to self-love. Practicing self-love is to allow yourself to feel without judgment. It is to meet sorrow with compassion, to hold anger without shame, to cradle grief without trying to rush it away. Emotional alchemy is the practice of honoring your feelings as messengers rather than enemies.

Self-love is not about bypassing your inner weather but learning to walk with it, trusting that even sorrow makes you more spacious. In honoring your emotions, you return to your own heart — and in that return, you rediscover that you are worthy of gentleness, patience, and care.

HOPEfully Human Moment

I ONCE TRIED TO DO a guided anger release practice but was too polite to yell into the towel. Instead, I ended up whisper-screaming, "I'm upset!" in a British accent. Within seconds, I burst out laughing — and then cried anyway.

What I learned at that moment is that emotional expression is not about performance — it's about release. Self-love isn't making your healing look impressive, dramatic, or worthy of social media. It's about giving yourself permission to feel in whatever way your body allows you to, even if it comes out sideways, silly, or soft. The point isn't how it looks. The point is that you honored the truth of your emotion enough to let it move.

HOPE in Practice: Create an Alchemy Space

NOT EVERYONE HAS AN extra room in their home, and you don't need one. What matters is creating a small, intentional corner that signals safety to your nervous system. An "alchemy space" is less about where it is and more about what it represents: a place where every emotion is welcome, where nothing must be fixed or hidden, where self-love is practiced in real time.

It can be as simple as a chair in the corner of your bedroom, a basket tucked under your desk, or a spot on the floor by a window. Gather a few items that help you feel supported — a journal to release your thoughts, a soft blanket for comfort, tissues for tears, music that grounds you, or a stone that feels steady in your hand.

Think of it as your "alchemy cave" — not a shrine to sadness, but a sanctuary of truth. Here, no feeling is too much. Here, you can let sorrow carve you, let laughter bubble up, let anger move through, and let stillness settle in. This is the space where transmutation happens — where feelings shift from chaos into clarity simply because you gave them a place to exist.

Soul Seed to Take With You

THIS IS THE HARD PART of self-love — the part most of us were never taught. Write these words down. Carry them in your pocket. Tape them to your mirror. Let them remind you that even the heaviest feelings are holy ground, and walking through them is how you come home to yourself.

Your emotions are not a burden.

They are your birthright.

They are the language of your soul —

Let them speak, and they will set you free.

Self-love is not only an act of the heart — it is an agreement with your whole being. But love, no matter how deeply felt, must eventually make its way into muscle and memory, into posture and breath. Because while the mind can forget, the body never does. It carries every vow you've broken to yourself, every moment you've abandoned your own needs, every truth you've silenced. The question is: how do we teach the body to remember love instead of loss, safety instead of survival? That is where we go next.

.

Chapter Sixteen

The Body Remembers – Somatic Healing, Touch Points & Frequency Repair

In this section, we'll explore how the body carries the fragments of our experiences — not only pain, but also the memory of repair — and how listening to its signals becomes the first step in healing.

The body holds the fragments of our experiences until they are ready to be healed. They are often stored in the fascia — the connective tissue that weaves through every muscle, organ, and bone. This is why we sometimes develop aches, tension, or pain without any obvious explanation or injury. The body remembers. It holds and holds… until those fragments surface as fatigue, tightness, or discomfort that refuses to be ignored.

But here's the miracle: the body doesn't just store what has hurt us. It also carries memory of joy, resilience, and repair. Just as it holds fragments of fear, it also remembers how to release, how to breathe again, how to find rhythm. When we learn to listen, the body becomes not just a record of the past, but a doorway into healing in the present.

Up to this point, we've explored what it means for the body to hold memory and how fragmentation lives beneath the skin. Now we can turn to what helps the body repair. Support can take many forms — from energy-based practices like Reiki, to body maps like reflexology, to touch points like tapping or self-holding. Each of these approaches invites the body to release what it has carried and to restore the natural frequency of safety, flow, and vitality.

Now that we've named what the body holds, we can begin exploring how to support its repair. That begins with somatic healing — the practice of returning to the body's wisdom.

Somatic Healing: Returning to the Body's Wisdom

HERE, WE'LL DISCOVER what somatic healing really means, why it's essential for repairing fragmentation, and how both ancient traditions and modern science affirm the body as a pathway to wholeness.

Somatic healing simply means healing through the body. The word soma comes from the Greek for "living body," reminding us that our bodies are not shells we inhabit — they are living, breathing storytellers. Every ache, every tremor, every sigh is part of the body's language.

For generations, healing was attempted mostly "from the neck up." We analyzed experiences, searched for meaning, and tried to talk our way into peace. But fragmentation — those breaks in safety, belonging, and flow — does not live only in the mind. It lodges in the nervous system and shows up as clenched jaws, shallow breathing, digestive distress, or sudden fatigue when nothing "seems wrong."

This is why somatic healing matters. Fragmentation is a felt experience, so repair must also be felt. The body cannot be ignored in the process of wholeness — it must be invited back into the conversation.

Modern somatic approaches were pioneered by Dr. Peter Levine, whose work in Somatic Experiencing showed how animals in the wild shake off fear rather than store it, and by Dr. Bessel van der

Kolk, whose research confirmed that the body holds memory long after the mind moves on. These insights affirm what ancient traditions like yoga, qigong, and indigenous medicine have always known: the body is both the witness and the pathway to repair.

In the HOPE Method, somatic healing is woven into Harnessing Optimal Positive Energy. It is the practice of returning home to your own body, reading its signals, and responding with compassion rather than judgment. Through breath, movement, sound, stillness, and sensation, you renegotiate your relationship with yourself. You learn how to listen. You learn how to respond. You learn how to stay — even when it is uncomfortable.

Somatic healing is not about forcing the body to "get over it." It is about creating safety so the body can remember what it already knows: how to release, regulate, and heal.

Touch Points: Tapping, Brushing, Holding, Reclaiming

THIS SECTION INTRODUCES the body's natural access points for soothing and repair, showing how simple, intentional contact can restore safety and flow to the nervous system.

There are places on the body where healing can enter through intentional contact — we call these touch points. These are not quick fixes or trendy hacks. They are ancient reminders that healing lives in relationship — even if that relationship is with your own skin.

Touch points can take many forms. Sometimes it looks like tapping gently on the body's acupressure points, a rhythm that interrupts the stress response and helps energy move again. Other times it's the simple act of brushing the arms or chest with soft strokes, coaxing the nervous system back into rest. You may find it in the quiet intimacy of placing a hand over your heart or belly, giving yourself a moment of attunement, a pause that says, "I am here." Or perhaps in the steady sway of cradling or rocking, a motion that comforts the vagus nerve and restores the body's rhythm of safety.

Touch points can also come from others: massage or reflexology that presses into knots of tension or maps energy through the feet and hands, releasing what has been carried too long. Reiki and other energy-based practices remind us that presence itself can be medicine, a way of re-tuning the body's field without words. And sometimes the earth is the healer — walking barefoot in the grass, pressing your palms to the bark of a tree, or simply standing still under the open sky. These moments of connection recalibrate the nervous system and return you to your natural frequency.

This is only a glimpse, a handful of possibilities. Every culture carries its own wisdom of touch and energy. The invitation is not to master them all, but to gently experiment, notice what resonates, and create a personal toolkit that feels safe and true to you. In the HOPE Method, these small practices are part of Harnessing Optimal Positive Energy — reclaiming your body as an ally, one gentle touch at a time.

Frequency Repair: Healing the Body's Vibration

YOUR BODY IS A SYMPHONY of vibration — electrical, emotional, energetic. Every heartbeat sends an electromagnetic wave beyond your skin. Every breath shifts the rhythm of your nervous system. Every thought alters the chemistry that shapes your frequency. You are music in motion, a living field of resonance.

But fragmentation can distort that harmony. Stress, fear, and prolonged survival states create static or even silence, leaving you feeling heavy, restless, or out of sync. Just as an instrument slips out of tune, so too can the body. And just as an instrument can be tuned, so too can you.

Frequency repair is the practice of returning your body to resonance — realigning with rhythms of safety, vitality, and flow. Modern science affirms what ancient traditions have always known: sound, breath, movement, and connection to the elements can shift measurable frequency in the body, restoring balance to the nervous system and coherence to the heart.

Sometimes this repair begins with the breath — deep inhales that clear stagnant energy and bring oxygen back to the cells. Other times it is sound: solfeggio tones, the ring of singing bowls, the layered hum of binaural beats, or even the simple act of humming, chanting, or singing aloud to soothe the vagus nerve. Movement too becomes a form of repair: shaking, stretching, or dancing with abandon to loosen what has long been held. Minerals and salts — whether in a warm bath, in mineral-rich foods, or through the grounding of bare feet on the earth — restore cellular balance. So does water, in all its forms: clean hydration, soothing herbal teas, or the weightless release of floating in a pool, lake, or ocean. And then there is light — the rise of the sun, the fresh air of the outdoors, the reset of circadian rhythms when you let nature set the tempo again.

Each of these practices is a tuning fork for the body, reminding you of the frequency you were born to carry.

In the HOPE Method, frequency repair lives in E – Energy. It reminds you that you are not broken. You are not lost. You are not beyond repair. You are simply out of tune — and tuning is always possible.

The Sacred Art of Staying

IN THIS SECTION, WE'LL talk about how to remain present in your body, even when it feels uncomfortable. For many of us, being in the body has not always felt safe. It is where the fragments of our experiences rise first — in the clench of the jaw, the knot in the stomach, the racing of the heart. The body remembers what the mind has tried to forget, and so we learned to leave it: to dissociate, to distract, to numb.

But leaving may have protected us once; it also kept us from repair. Healing begins with the art of staying — learning to breathe through discomfort, to anchor in the present moment, and to trust that the body is not the enemy but the portal. This capacity to remain is not about forcing yourself into pain, but about gently returning to yourself so that repair and resilience can unfold.

Many of us learned to leave our bodies — to dissociate, disconnect, or distract. Because to stay meant to feel... and feeling wasn't safe. The ache in the chest, the tightness in the gut, the racing of the heart were signals we wanted to escape. So, we left.

But healing requires our return. Through the HOPE Method, you begin to build the capacity to stay. To anchor. To breathe. To rest inside your own being without needing to run from it. Somatic healing doesn't ask you to push through the pain; it invites you to come closer — not to the wound itself, but to the part of you that knows how to tend it.

Your body is not the problem. Your body is the portal. When you choose to stay, even for a few breaths longer than before, you create the conditions for repair. Regulation begins not in perfection, but in presence.

And staying isn't only about you. We do not heal in isolation. We heal in connection — but only when that connection is safe, steady, and sovereign. Every relationship is an energetic exchange. Every conversation, every glance, every memory leaves an imprint in the field between us. That field can nurture or deplete, expand or constrict.

The difference often lies in one sacred skill: boundaries. Boundaries make staying possible — with yourself, and with others. They create the safety needed for connection to become healing rather than draining.

HOPE in Practice: Energetic Boundary Reset

SIT OR STAND WITH YOUR feet grounded. Take a slow breath, then sweep your arms in a gentle circle around your body — as if drawing an invisible bubble of light. Say aloud: "This is my space. This is my signal. I am allowed to protect it."

You don't need permission to have boundaries. You need practice. For many of us, boundaries were never modeled. We grew up equating love with self-abandonment — learning to read others' moods like weather patterns, adjusting our own energy to keep the peace. We became hyper-attuned to danger, disconnection, and disapproval. That's not dysfunction. That was survival.

But survival is not the same as belonging. Through HOPE, we begin to reclaim the right to exist fully in relationships — without disappearing. Boundaries are not walls that shut people out. They are the sacred architecture of your energy. They say: "I want connection — and I want it to be real, respectful, and reciprocal."

Attachment & the Nervous System

THE FIRST LESSONS OF love are not learned in books or classrooms — they are etched into our nervous system before we even have words. As children, we learn how safe it feels to reach for comfort, how secure it is to cry out for help, and how much of ourselves we must hide or perform in order to be held. These patterns, often invisible, become the blueprints for how we seek closeness, navigate conflict, and carry love into adulthood.

Attachment styles are not character flaws. They are survival strategies — ways the body learned to either keep connection or protect against pain.

For some, this looks like an anxious attachment, where the nervous system hums on high alert. Love feels fragile, so you work hard to preserve it — over-giving, over-apologizing, or holding the quiet fear that abandonment is always around the corner.

Others learn an avoidant attachment, where distance feels safer than closeness. To need too much is to risk rejection, so independence becomes a shield. Emotions rise, and the body retreats, building walls that feel like safety but often breed loneliness.

Still others live with a disorganized attachment, where the heart longs for closeness but fears it at the same time. Relationships feel like both sanctuary and threat. The nervous system swings between approach and retreat, leaving confusion, intensity, and pain in its wake.

And then there is the experience of secure attachment — a steady rhythm of connection. In this state, love does not demand perfection or disappearance. Trust is possible. Disagreements don't feel like danger, but as opportunities for understanding.

Most of us do not live permanently in one style. We may shift depending on the relationship, the season of life, or the stress we're carrying. These are not permanent labels but living patterns that can be softened and reshaped.

The HOPE Method doesn't demand that you suddenly become "secure." Instead, it helps you gently regulate your system so that trust becomes possible again. Through mindfulness, daily practices that root the body, inner child repair, and truth-telling in safe spaces, you begin to build what psychologists call earned security. This is the slow, steady practice of teaching your body that love doesn't have to cost your peace. It is how we return, little by little, to the kind of love that feels like home.

Wisdom Through the Ages

OVER 2,500 YEARS AGO, Siddhartha Gautama — the man we now call the Buddha, meaning "the awakened one" — taught a simple but radical truth: "You, yourself, as much as anybody in the entire universe, deserve your love and affection."

In a time when worth was often tied to social role, gender, or status, this teaching broke the mold. Buddha was saying that no title, no ritual, no approval from others is required for you to be worthy of love. Worth is inherent. It lives inside you.

This is the core of what we now call energetic sovereignty — the practice of no longer outsourcing your value to the reactions or recognition of others. When you live in this truth, you stop waiting for someone else to confirm your place in the world. You stop measuring yourself against shifting standards of beauty, productivity, or perfection. You root your worth in your own being.

The HOPE Method invites us to remember this wisdom not as philosophy, but as practice. Each time you pause to honor your needs, speak your truth, or extend compassion inward instead of criticism, you are embodying Buddha's reminder: self-love is not selfish. It is the ground of all love.

HOPEfully Human Moment

ONCE, IN A CONVERSATION that had already grown tense, someone told me I was too sensitive. A few breaths later, they snapped that I wasn't sensitive enough. I couldn't help but laugh at the contradiction — how could I be both, in the same moment?

That experience reminded me of something important: we can never be everything to everyone. If people are given room to complain, they often will — even if there's nothing real to complain about. You cannot shape-shift enough to keep everyone satisfied.

The only way through is to hold yourself steadfast and root in your boundaries. You cannot be everyone's friend. And when you can read people's energy, remember — they may be able to read yours as well, which can place you in interesting situations. In those moments, communication becomes the key. Clear, honest words can deflect conflict before it spirals into confusion.

And yet, boundaries are not about shutting people out with hardness. They're about staying rooted in who you are while still leaning into kindness. Everyone you meet is walking their own fragmented journey, carrying burdens you may not see. Sometimes the grace you extend — even while holding your ground — becomes a healing frequency in itself.

Practiced with both clarity and compassion, boundaries stop being defenses and become a spiritual practice of self-remembrance.

HOPE in Practice: Loving Detachment Ritual

LOVING DETACHMENT IS not about cutting people off with bitterness or building walls of indifference. It is about releasing the energy of responsibility you were never meant to carry. Sometimes we absorb the emotions, expectations, or pain of others — believing we must fix, soothe, or save them. Over time, this drains us, leaving little space for our own healing.

Detachment becomes loving when it honors both sides: I care for you, but I will not abandon myself in the process.

Try this simple practice the next time you feel weighed down by someone else's energy:

Find a quiet place and light a candle, letting the flame remind you of your own steady light.

Place your hand over your heart and breathe in through the nose and out through the mouth calmly and slowly, anchoring into your body.

Whisper aloud: "I release the need to fix or absorb what is not mine. I send love, and I return to myself."

Imagine their energy gently flowing back to them and yours flowing back to you, like two rivers returning to their rightful courses.

The HOPE Method teaches that detachment doesn't mean absence of love — it means creating the conditions where love can remain pure, without distortion or depletion.

Soul Seed to Take With You

AS WE CLOSE THIS CHAPTER, remember: Relationships are not meant to strip you down or demand your disappearance. They are meant to mirror back your wholeness. Boundaries, presence, and loving detachment all lead to the same truth — that real love does not cost your essence, it protects it. Carry these words with you as a gentle reminder:

Love does not require your erosion.

Real love reveres your edges.

The energy between you and others should reflect the energy within you — sacred, steady, and whole.

Affirmation to Carry: "Real love reveres my edges. I am sacred, steady, and whole."

Your body remembers what your mind has long tried to forget — but memory is not destiny. Each breath, each touchpoint of somatic healing, begins to restore your frequency. Yet for healing to last, the mind must join the body in telling a new story. Because while the body holds the imprint, the mind holds the narrative. And when you rewrite the words you speak to yourself, you are no longer just repairing energy — you are reshaping reality. That is where we turn next: the power of neuroplasticity, belief work, and self-speak to anchor your body's healing into a life you can fully live.

Chapter Seventeen

The Mind Rewrites – Neuroplasticity, Belief Work & Self-Speak

The mind is not a passive observer of life; it is a storyteller, constantly weaving meaning from experience. What you think shapes how you feel, and how you feel shapes what you believe. Over time, those beliefs harden into invisible scaffolding — an internal architecture around which your entire reality is built.

When the mind has been trained in fragmentation, its stories often sound harsh, anxious, or self-critical. The inner voice may whisper, "You're not enough," or shout, "You'll never be safe." These thoughts feel permanent because they've been rehearsed for years. But the miracle of the human brain is this: it can change. Neuroplasticity — the brain's ability to rewire itself — means the story you've been carrying is not the story you're bound to live.

This chapter explores the art and science of rewriting. Not erasing the past but reframing the mind's narrative so it begins to speak in the language of HOPE. Through belief work, self-speak, and compassionate awareness, we'll learn how to harness the mind's plasticity to create patterns that serve rather than sabotage.

In the HOPE Method, this is where O – Optimal meets P – Positive: choosing the thoughts that align with truth, cultivating self-talk that uplifts rather than diminishes, and building beliefs that anchor you in possibility. The mind may have rehearsed fear, but it can just as faithfully learn to rehearse love, safety, and freedom.

This is the invitation of Chapter Fourteen: to discover that your mind is not a prison, but a canvas — and you hold the brush.

Neuroplasticity: The Mind's Power to Heal

THE HUMAN BRAIN IS one of life's quiet miracles. It does not stay frozen in the patterns of the past. Instead, it is alive, fluid, and endlessly adaptive. This gift is called neuroplasticity — the brain's ability to rewire itself, to form new connections, and to reshape old ones.

Not long ago, science told a different story. For decades, researchers believed the brain was fixed after childhood — that once its wiring was set, change was impossible. But the evidence began to whisper otherwise. In the 1940s, psychologist Donald Hebb observed: "neurons that fire together, wire together." Later, scientists like Michael Merzenich revealed how stroke patients could relearn lost functions, how blind individuals' brains adapted to process touch and sound, how imaging technology captured the brain reorganizing itself in real time. What once seemed impossible became undeniable: the brain is not rigid. It is resilient.

Think of every thought, every belief, as a trail through the forest of your mind. The more often you walk it, the clearer it becomes. If that trail was carved by fear, shame, or survival, it may only lead to anxiety or self-doubt. But here is the hope: you are not confined to that trail forever. With intention and repetition, you can begin to step off the old path and create a new one. At first, the ground may feel uncertain — grass unbent, leaves crunching underfoot — but the more often you return, the stronger that new pathway becomes.

This rewiring is not only shaped by thought and repetition — it is also supported by how we care for the body. Just as soil nourishes a garden, your body's chemistry and environment nourish the neural pathways that are trying to grow. Nutrient-dense foods, minerals, and natural compounds provide the raw material for repair. Even supplements such as chlorella and spirulina, long celebrated for their nutrient density, are believed to support cellular renewal and brain health. Hydration and minerals help conduct the brain's electrical signals. And your gut — often called the "second brain" — produces neurotransmitters and communicates directly with your nervous system, meaning gut health is brain health.

Science now confirms what ancient traditions have always known: the body itself is a partner in reshaping the mind. Cold exposure — whether through ice baths or a brisk cold shower — floods the body with norepinephrine, sharpening focus and helping the brain reset. Breath practices, including breath-holds or slow rhythmic cycles, increase vagal tone and oxygen efficiency, regulating the nervous system and teaching it safety. High-intensity interval training (HIIT) — raising the heart rate for thirty seconds, then resting, then rising again — stimulates powerful growth factors like BDNF (brain-derived neurotrophic factor) that encourage new neural pathways to grow. Even movement in softer forms — stretching, shaking, dancing — clears stagnation and restores vibrational flow. Together, these practices act like tuning forks, calling the brain back into coherence.

This is the miracle of neuroplasticity. Old beliefs can fade. New ones can take root. But like any living thing, these new pathways require nourishment: repetition, safety, embodiment — and sometimes, the courage to step into cold water, to move until your heart pounds, to breathe until you feel the body's quiet reset. Each choice becomes a signal, a new spark, a fresh alignment of the inner architecture of your brain.

The HOPE Method leans on this truth. Through Harnessing your awareness, choosing what is Optimal instead of familiar, practicing the Positive even in the midst of grief, and aligning with Energy that uplifts rather than depletes, you begin to rebuild the scaffolding of your mind. Slowly, steadily, you create a structure that supports self-trust, emotional safety, and possibility.

Your brain is ever changing. And so are you.

Self-Speak: Rewriting the Inner Dialogue

EVERY DAY, THERE IS a voice that follows you into every room. It greets you in the mirror, it lingers in your thoughts, it whispers when the world grows quiet. This voice — your self-speak — is the most influential relationship you will ever have.

For many of us, that voice was trained in fear. It repeats the echoes of teachers, parents, or partners who once told us we were too much, not enough, or impossible to love as we are. If your inner dialogue is sharp, cruel, or dismissive, it is not a flaw in you. It is a reflection of what you were taught to believe. But here is the truth: you are not the voice. You are the one listening to it. And as the listener, you hold the power to shift the story.

Rewriting self-speak begins with gentle substitutions — phrases that honor your humanity instead of punishing it. Where the old voice might insist, "I always mess this up," the new voice can breathe, "I'm learning, and mistakes are allowed here." When the echo says, "No one understands me," your self-speak can remind you, "I am beginning to understand myself." Instead of "I can't trust anyone," you might whisper, "I am learning to trust my own discernment." And where the harshness claims, "I'm too much," your new voice can declare, "I am allowed to be full."

The words you choose become pathways for your nervous system. Each gentle rewrite is a new trail laid down in the forest of your mind, one that leads not to shame but to self-compassion. The HOPE Method reminds us that self-speak is not performance — it is practice. Every phrase you shift toward kindness is a moment of reclamation. Every softer word is a step back into belonging.

Your inner world begins to soften when your words do.

Belief Work: Excavating & Replanting

EVERY BELIEF YOU HOLD began as a seed — often planted by someone else. A parent's warning, a teacher's scolding, a partner's silence — repeated often enough, it took root. Over time, it grew into a structure inside you, shaping how you see yourself and what you expect from the world. Some of those beliefs have sheltered you. Others have kept you small.

Belief work is the gentle art of excavation. It invites you to kneel down beside the roots of your own mind and ask: Where did this belief come from? Was it born of truth — or simply repetition? What has it cost me to keep it? And what might I grow in its place?

This is not about plastering false positivity over real pain. The HOPE Method never asks you to deny what you feel. Instead, it invites conscious choice — the courage to plant a new belief, even if it feels foreign at first. To say, "Maybe I am worthy of joy." To whisper, "Perhaps love doesn't have to hurt." To imagine, "Safety can live in me."

This is the slow, sacred reparenting of your inner narrative. One belief at a time, you learn to unearth what no longer serves and to replant what allows you to grow. Over time, the garden of your mind begins to look less like survival and more like sanctuary.

The Mind & the Body Must Talk

HEALING CANNOT HAPPEN in fragments. You cannot think your way out of pain while your body still trembles, nor can you feel your way into safety without words to guide you there. The mind and the body must learn to speak to each other again.

When the body feels safe, the mind begins to open. When the mind softens, the body responds in kind. This dialogue is delicate, but it is powerful. And self-speak is the bridge — language that soothes, steadies, and signals to your body: you belong here, you are safe here, you are worthy of care.

Why does this matter? Because before the world speaks to you each morning, you have already spoken to yourself — countless times. In the mirror. In the quiet. In the words you do not even realize you are rehearsing. If those words are harsh, your nervous system contracts. If they are kind, your body breathes easier. Words are not empty; they are signals, carried through the nervous system, shaping your chemistry, your posture, your sense of possibility.

So, ask yourself: is the voice within you a sanctuary, or a battlefield?

In the HOPE Method, self-speak becomes sacred speech. It is the language of re-parenting the wounded child within, of befriending the self you once abandoned, of calling yourself home again and again. Not just once. But daily. Not just kindly. But consistently.

Words shape worlds. And the first world you ever inhabit is the one you build inside yourself.

HOPE in Practice: Self-Speak Reset

FIND A QUIET MOMENT. Place your hand gently over your heart. Let your breath settle, and whisper: "What would I say to my younger self in this moment?"

Say it once for the child you once were — and then say it again for the one breathing in your chest right now.

Most of us inherited an inner narrator. Sometimes it wore the voice of a teacher, a parent, a religion, or a culture that scolded, shamed, or measured us against impossible standards. Over time, we repeated it until it sounded like our own. But it was never truly ours.

Here is the miracle: the voice inside can be rewritten. The tone can be softened. The script can be made new.

Because the words you speak to yourself matter more than any external tool. They shape your chemistry. They color your choices. They become the air you breathe inside your own skin — your inner ecosystem.

In the HOPE Method, this is where self-speak becomes sacred speech: the daily practice of choosing language that does not betray you but restores you.

Neuroplasticity and Inner Dialogue

YOUR BRAIN IS NEVER still. With every thought, every repetition, every word, it is wiring and rewiring itself — a living tapestry of connection, a forest of pathways being cleared and grown anew. This process, called neuroplasticity, is not abstract science; it is the quiet miracle happening within you each day.

When you speak to yourself with compassion, patience, and affirmation, you do more than lift your mood. You signal safety to your nervous system. You invite the parasympathetic response — the body's natural rhythm of rest and repair — to take its rightful place. Your heart rate slows. Your breath deepens. Your mind softens.

Even one kind word can act as a neural seed, planted in the soil of your brain. With repetition, it takes root. With gentleness, it grows into a pathway. Over time, these pathways become the trails you walk most easily — not of criticism and fear, but of trust, calm, and belonging.

Through the HOPE Method, this is how inner dialogue becomes inner architecture. What you whisper to yourself today becomes the scaffolding of tomorrow's peace.

Wisdom Through the Ages

CENTURIES AGO, THE Persian mystic and poet Hafiz wrote: "The words you speak become the house you live in."

Hafiz lived in the 14th century, writing verses that blended humor, devotion, and piercing insight into the human soul. His words still reach across time because they remind us that language is not decoration — it is foundation. Every sentence we whisper to ourselves lays another stone in the house we inhabit within.

Self-speak is spiritual architecture. What kind of home are you building inside your own heart? Is it a place of shelter or a place of scorn? Do your words make walls of shame, or do they open windows of compassion?

This is where self-speak becomes more than habit — it becomes the way we heal self-betrayal. Each time you ignore your needs, minimize your truth, or abandon your knowing to make someone else more comfortable, you chip away at your own foundation. But when you speak gently to yourself afterward — when you pause and whisper, "I see you. We'll do it differently next time" — you begin the work of repair.

Through HOPE, this becomes a practice of re-building. Brick by brick, phrase by phrase, you turn the ruins of self-betrayal into the sanctuary of self-love. And you don't do it all at once — you do it through the rhythm of WiSH-to-HEAL: finding Wisdom in where your old beliefs began, choosing Serenity as you let them go, opening your Heart to new truth, allowing Healing to unfold in new patterns, giving Expression to words that honor you, practicing Acceptance for the slowness of change, and rooting in Love as the foundation that carries you forward.

HOPEfully Human Moment

ONE WINTER, I WAS OUTSIDE shoveling the walk, being so careful not to slip. And then — you guessed it — I hit a patch of ice. My feet went flying, the shovel scooped me up like a cartoon, and the handle smacked me right in the head.

For a moment I just lay there, head throbbing, backside aching, muttering how careless and silly I was. The old voice was quick to scold: "You should have been more careful. You always mess things up."

But then the ridiculousness of it hit me. I pictured myself on America's Funniest Home Videos, arms flailing, landing flat on the shovel like some slapstick routine. And I laughed. Hard.

That laughter broke the spell. I realized I wasn't careless — I was human. And sometimes being human looks ridiculous. Instead of berating myself, I whispered, "Sweetheart, let's try again. And maybe this time we salt the ice first."

Self-speak isn't about avoiding mistakes. It's about how you talk to yourself when you're flat on your back in the snow — learning to trade self-blame for a little compassion, and maybe a laugh.

When was a time you hurt yourself even though you thought you were being careful — and struggled to give yourself grace?

HOPE in Practice: Mirror Work Ritual

FIND A QUIET MOMENT and stand before a mirror. Do not rush. Let your gaze meet your own until you recognize the soul behind your eyes. Then, with a steady breath, speak aloud:

"I forgive you for the ways you've hurt yourself. I thank you for the ways you've survived. And I love you enough to speak kindly to you, from now on."

Do this daily. Even when your voice trembles. Even when your mind resists. Especially then. For every awkward beginning is the seed of a new intimacy — a remembering that you are worthy of your own tenderness.

Soul Seed to Take With You

THE VOICE YOU SPEAK to yourself with becomes the landscape you live in. This chapter has shown you how words can wound — and how they can also rebuild. So, carry this truth with you: Healing is not only in the body's repair or the mind's resilience - it is in the daily choice to speak with kindness to the soul inside your skin. Tuck it in your pocket, whisper it to your reflection, and let it remind you: you are listening.

When the mind rewrites, the body listens. New neural pathways form, old patterns loosen, and your inner voice begins to echo with truth instead of trauma. But even this is not the end. Because beyond the mind's rewiring lies something deeper — the soul's remembering. The nervous system may restore safety, and belief work may reframe your story, but the spark that animates you has always been more than body and brain. The question is: once your mind learns to speak in healing tones, will you dare to listen for the voice beneath thought — the one that rises from spirit, from energy, from the greater whole you already belong to? That is where we turn next.

Chapter Eighteen

Spirituality & Soul – Guidance, Kundalini, and Returning to the Greater Whole

There is a place within you that fragmentation cannot touch. A place deeper than wounds, freer than fear, older than any story you've carried. It is your soul. And she remembers. And when you finally touch that remembering, you begin to see what was hidden all along: the lie about HOPE — that it was fragile, external, or out of reach. The truth is, HOPE was never outside of you. It has always been the vibration of your soul calling you home.

Up to this point, the HOPE Method has guided you step by step. You have learned to Harness your energy, to call back what was scattered. You have chosen what is Optimal, discerning between the patterns that kept you bound and the truths that set you free. You have embraced the Positive, not as shallow cheer, but as authentic joy, forgiveness, and creativity. You have honored your Energy as vibration, learning how to clear, protect, and raise it. Through the WiSH-to-HEAL framework, you have practiced wisdom, serenity, heart, healing, expression, acceptance, and love — weaving them like threads through your daily life.

Each chapter has been a layer of remembering: returning to the body, rewriting the mind, softening the inner voice, nourishing the vessel, restoring boundaries, rediscovering belonging. And now we step into the deepest layer — the soul.

This is where spirituality becomes the bridge. Not religion. Not doctrine. But resonance. The pulse beneath the noise. The whisper that steadies you in the dark. The current of guidance that has been with you since the beginning — the HOPE that never left.

But before we cross that bridge, let us pause to reclaim what HOPE really means. Too often, just as a teacher or parent once shamed us into silence, modern manifestation gurus have unintentionally shamed us out of hope — dismissing it as weakness, calling it "low vibration," as though to hope were to settle for less. That is another fragment, another distortion.

Because HOPE is not weakness. HOPE is survival. It is why prisoners dream of freedom, why refugees carry their children across oceans, why grieving mothers plant flowers in spring. HOPE is not passive. It is pulse. It is grit. It is the lifeline that whispers: keep going — there is something worth reaching for on the other side.

HOPE is also not the opposite of manifestation — it is its foundation. To manifest, you must first believe that something better is possible. HOPE is the spark that begins the vision, the backbone of grit that steadies you when everything else wavers. It is not idle wishing. It is a compass, a goal-setting word that points you toward what is possible. To hope is to declare that your story is not finished. To hope is to plant the first seed of self-awareness, the root that grows into self-love, the path that flowers into self-actualization.

And this brings us to abundance. So often, we've been taught to measure abundance in numbers and bank statements. But true abundance lives first in the body, flowing through your energy centers as stability, love, and belonging.

At the Root, abundance is not millions. It is enough — enough food on the table, enough warmth to feel safe, enough ground beneath your feet to stand on your own. For many of us, abundance simply means living a little better than our parents and grandparents, easing the struggles they carried. It is peace where once there was survival.

At the Heart, abundance shifts into a higher frequency. It is joy that cannot be purchased, laughter shared without condition, and love that surrounds and sustains you no matter what your circumstances hold. This is wealth no economy can measure — unconditional love as your truest inheritance.

Real abundance is not measured in accumulation. It is measured in alignment — with peace, with joy, with the unshakable rhythm of love. And HOPE anchors it all. HOPE is a silent prayer for tomorrow — that life will be just as good tomorrow as it was today, if not better. HOPE is the pulse of trust that keeps us moving forward, planting seeds of stability at the root, blossoms of love in the heart, and awakening through every center until we remember ourselves as whole.

This is why we now turn to the energy centers — the seven chakras. Not as abstract symbols, but as living maps of your healing. Each chakra carries both the wound of survival and the possibility of awakening. And here, the HOPE Method offers a path unlike the traditional ones you may have seen before.

Most healing models begin at the Root. But when survival itself has been wounded, to begin there is to risk being overwhelmed. Instead, HOPE begins where your soul is still whole — at the Crown.

At the Crown, you awaken Wisdom. This is not only mystical awareness but the re-education of the mind. Here, you begin to untangle the old scripts, reframe the inherited beliefs, and create new scaffolding for your inner world. What once kept you small becomes the soil for a renewed mindset. A sense of emotional intelligence is born when HOPE begins at the top — because when the mind is clear, you can discern between fear and intuition, between reaction and response.

From wisdom, the path flows downward: serenity through the Third Eye, compassion and repair through the Heart, reclamation of fire at the Solar Plexus, expression and truth at the Throat, and acceptance that softens the whole system. Finally, you arrive at the Root, where healing settles into unconditional Love.

This reversed journey is the rhythm of WiSH-to-HEAL through HOPE: reclaiming the mind, reweaving the heart, restoring the body, and remembering the soul. And from this place — with your centers restored from Crown to Root — the kundalini can rise safely, carrying your healing back upward into awakening.

This chapter is your invitation into that awakening. To let your energy centers become not just points of survival, but pathways of transformation. To see abundance not only as material wealth, but as joy, peace, and love woven into every layer of your being. And to know, without question, that HOPE is not low vibration. It is the foundation. It is the portal. It is the flame that leads you home.

Before we begin the journey through the centers, pause and notice: you are already changing. Simply by naming your fragments, choosing resonance, and practicing HOPE, you've been re-educating the mind, softening the heart, and restoring the body. Now, we turn to the subtle layers — the energy centers that carry both wound and wisdom. Each one will speak in its own language, and together they will reweave your wholeness. We begin, as HOPE always begins, at the top — with wisdom.

Yet even as change begins to take root, a shadow lingers — a misunderstanding of HOPE itself. Before we can open the language of the soul, we must pause to uncover it.

Forgotten Voices of the Feminine

ACROSS HISTORY, THE sacred feminine has spoken through many voices — some celebrated, many forgotten. To remember HOPE is also to remember them.

Sophia – In Gnostic tradition, she is divine wisdom itself, the spark of clarity that reminds us we were never separate from the light. She carries the vibration of remembrance and truth.

Oshun – In Yoruba tradition, she is the goddess of sweet waters, sensuality, and abundance. She teaches that joy and tenderness are not luxuries, but medicine.

Hecate – In Greek tradition, she is the guide at the crossroads, keeper of thresholds and shadows. She reminds us that even in darkness, the way forward can be lit.

Tara - The compassionate liberator; known as the "mother of all Buddhas," she guides souls through fear and suffering.

And these are only a few. The feminine has worn many names — Hildegard, Magdalene, Isis, Inanna — each carrying her own current of wisdom. They are not separate stories, but different expressions of the same truth: that love, intuition, and resilience have always been sacred.

Voices of the Masculine

JUST AS THE SACRED feminine has spoken through rivers, crossroads, and silence, the sacred masculine has carried wisdom through strength, clarity, and guardianship. Together they balance — not as opposites, but as complements.

Apollo – Greek god of light, healing, and order, reminding us that structure and creativity can exist side by side.

Odin – Norse seeker of wisdom, who sacrificed for knowledge and taught that true power lies in vision and sacrifice.

Krishna – In Hindu tradition, the divine play of love and protection, showing that joy itself can be holy.

Christ – Beyond religion, the archetype of unconditional love, surrender, and resurrection.

Shiva – The destroyer and transformer in Hindu tradition, who clears what no longer serves so new life can rise.

And like the feminine, these are only glimpses. The masculine has appeared through kings and sages, warriors and poets — each one carrying not domination, but devotion: to protect, to provide, to anchor, and to serve love.

For too long, we've been told a lie about HOPE — that it is fragile, naïve, or powerless. That to hope is to settle, to wait, to lack faith. This distortion has kept many from its true strength. Because HOPE is not weakness — it is endurance. It is the spark at the root of every transformation, the vibration that carries you when nothing else can. To uncover the truth of HOPE is to see it not as the opposite of manifestation, but as its foundation. HOPE is not the illusion; the illusion was ever believing you could live without it. And this is why we must finally name the distortion — the lie about HOPE — before we can reclaim our sovereignty.

By naming the lie, HOPE is restored to its rightful place: not weakness, but foundation. It is the current beneath every act of healing, the spark that steadies you when nothing else can. And it is from this foundation that the WiSH-to-HEAL path unfolds — guiding you deeper into the body, the soul, and the energy centers that carry both wound and wisdom.

WiSH-to-HEAL: Walking the Path of the Energy Centers

THE SOUL HAS ITS OWN vocabulary, spoken in signs, sensations, and subtle currents of energy. To understand it, we turn to the body's centers — each one a doorway carrying both the memory of wounding and the promise of healing. Unlike many traditions that begin at the root, the HOPE Method begins at the crown, where wisdom opens the way to the WiSH-to-HEAL cadence:

Crown/Wisdom (Journal it) – Re-educating the Mind / I Connect: Wisdom, in the HOPE Method, is where healing begins. Not in the chaos of survival, but in the clarity of vision. The Crown reminds us that we are more than our wounds, more than our fragments. It opens the space above the noise, where a wider perspective waits.

Here, wisdom is not lofty or out of reach — it is practical. It is the ability to see patterns, name distortions, and re-educate the mind so it no longer repeats the scripts of fragmentation. Old voices may still echo, but wisdom gives you the choice to question them. To ask: Is this true? Or is it only familiar?

Beginning at the Crown cultivates a kind of emotional intelligence. You learn to notice the difference between fear and intuition, between reaction and response. Wisdom doesn't erase the past; it reframes it, so your energy is no longer trapped in old cycles or triggers.

Through HOPE, wisdom becomes the first thread in WiSH-to-HEAL. It steadies your mind, clears your perception, and prepares you to move gently into serenity, heart, and healing.

Soul Scribbles: Naming the Noise: Set a timer for 5 minutes. Take a pen and paper — or open the notes app on your phone — and write down every word, phrase, or thought that floats into your mind. Don't analyze. Don't edit. Just let it pour out like a stream.

If you feel stuck, use this fragment question to stir your memory: What are the voices, rules, or beliefs that still echo inside me — the ones that make me feel scattered, small, or split from myself?

Remember: this isn't clean, legible journaling. It's mind-dumping. If "electric bill due Tuesday" comes up, write it down. If "I'm tired" repeats itself, let it fill the page. It all counts. These are the things weighing on your mind and body. Messy is progress.

When the timer ends, look back at what you wrote. Circle anything that feels heavy, familiar, or tied to old wounds. These are fragments — pieces of story that no longer get to define you.

You don't need to solve them today. The act of naming them is wisdom at work. It's the first step in gathering your scattered energy, reclaiming your mind, and beginning the HOPE journey from the top down.

Soul Seed to Take With You: Messy words are not mistakes. They are fragments finding light. Each time you name what weighs on you, you loosen its grip — and you gather yourself back, piece by piece. Through HOPE, this is the "Wi" in WiSH-to-HEAL. With the noise named, the mind can soften. Serenity now teaches you how to see without strain.

Third Eye / Serenity (Meditation) – Learning the Soul's Language / I See: The soul doesn't speak in sentences — it speaks in sensations. In symbols, synchronicities, and subtle nudges. In dreams that linger like smoke in the morning. In goosebumps that rise when truth brushes against your skin. In music that makes you cry without warning.

To live with HOPE is to become fluent in this soul-language. It may arrive as a feather on the ground after a prayer, a song lyric that lands like a personal message, a child's laughter that melts your resistance, or a full body yes you can't explain. These are not coincidences. They are clues of fragments that serenity is breaking through the noise.

The Third Eye is the seat of vision, the center that helps us see beyond illusion and rest into clarity. When fragmentation clouds our perception, we mistake fear for intuition and confusion for truth. But when serenity opens here, the fog begins to lift. We see not with frantic striving, but with calm awareness.

Through the HOPE Method, serenity is not escape. It is the steadying of the mind so that you can trust what you see, sense, and know. It's the moment you realize you don't have to chase answers because they are already arriving if you're willing to listen.

Soul Scribbles: Seeing Beyond the Noise - Set a timer for 5 minutes. Close your eyes, take three slow breaths, and recall a moment when your body whispered something you couldn't explain — a gut feeling, a dream, a sign, a synchronicity.

Open your eyes and begin writing. Let the memories spill out, even if they seem small or silly. Maybe it was the sudden urge to call a friend, a song that arrived at the exact right moment, or a choice you made without logic but with absolute certainty.

If you need a prompt, try: What are the moments when life spoke to me in symbols instead of words — and how did I respond?

Don't worry about neatness or meaning. This isn't about proving you're intuitive — it's about noticing the quiet ways serenity has already been guiding you. Trust whatever flows out.

Soul Seed to Take With You: Clarity is not a shout — it is a whisper. Serenity opens the space where your soul can speak. Through HOPE, this is the "S" in WiSH-to-HEAL. When sight steadies, the heart feels safe to open.

Heart / Healing (Feel it) – Returning to Compassion / I Love: The heart is more than a muscle. It is a frequency. It carries the rhythm of connection, the pulse of belonging, the resonance of love that asks for nothing in return.

But when life fragments us, the heart is often where the ache settles. Betrayal, grief, rejection, or loss can leave behind imprints that whisper: love is dangerous, joy is temporary, trust is not safe. In response, we armor up. We learn to silence our longings, to downplay our needs, to give without receiving.

Yet the heart remembers how to heal. Healing here does not mean erasing the ache. It means softening enough for compassion to return. It means allowing joy to take up space again — even if it feels fragile. It means remembering that love is not earned by perfection but received in presence.

Modern science affirms this. The HeartMath Institute has shown that the heart generates the strongest electromagnetic field in the body — measurable several feet outside the skin. Your heart is not only pumping blood; it is broadcasting information to every cell, and even to those around you. When you cultivate gratitude, compassion, or forgiveness, your heart's rhythm shifts into coherence — a state of harmony that calms the nervous system, improves brain function, and supports healing at every level. What poets and mystics have said for centuries — that the heart is wisdom — science now confirms.

Through the HOPE Method, healing at the heart is about reweaving connection: with yourself, with others, and with the greater whole. Each act of forgiveness, each moment of gratitude, each breath of tenderness becomes a thread that stitches together what once was torn.

Soul Scribbles: Listening to the Heart's Fragments - Set a timer for 7 minutes. Place your hand over your heart and breathe into its rhythm. Close your eyes and imagine a soft light glowing in your chest — expanding with each inhale, softening with each exhale. Let that light fill your ribcage, then spill outward like warmth into your shoulders, arms, and hands.

When you feel settled, pick up your pen and ask yourself: Where have I armored my heart out of protection? What moments of love or joy still feel too dangerous to trust?

Write without censoring. Let the fragments surface. Perhaps it's an old heartbreak, a friendship that fractured, or even the way you've withheld love from yourself. Allow every story, every pang, every flicker of memory to spill onto the page.

This is not clean or polished writing. It is release. It is permission. If what surfaces is as simple as "the bill due Tuesday," let it come. Messy is progress. Each word is a key that loosens the armor.

Soul Seed to Take With You: Your heart was never meant to be a fortress. It was meant to be a garden. Every breath of compassion waters it. Every act of forgiveness plants new seed. Every laugh, every tear, becomes proof that healing has begun.

Through HOPE, this is the "H" in WiSH-to-HEAL — Healing that mends the torn places with compassion and makes space for joy to return waters it. From softening comes strength; healing descends into the will and becomes action.

Solar Plexus / Healing Fire (Accountability) – Reclaiming Sovereignty / I Act: The solar plexus is the hearth of your being — the flame of sovereignty, self-trust, and inner direction. It is here that so many fragments hide: the shame you swallowed when you were silenced, the anger you buried to keep the peace, the fear you carried when you were told you were "too much" or "not enough." When this fire dims, you may feel powerless, uncertain, or disconnected from your own will. When it steadies, you move through life with quiet strength — not domination, but sovereignty.

But when fragmentation leaves its mark here, the fire flickers. It may burn too hot — showing up as anger, control, or the need to dominate — or too low, leaving you in cycles of shame, doubt, and hesitation. You may second-guess your worth or silence your "no" until resentment builds. These are not failures of character; they are signs that your fire has been starved of safe tending.

The gift of the solar plexus is this: the flame never fully goes out. Even if it is buried under years of doubt, it waits for breath, attention, and space to rise again.

Modern science affirms what ancient traditions have always taught: your center matters. The solar plexus lies in the gut region, which researchers call the enteric nervous system or the "second brain." This network contains over 100 million neurons — more than the spinal cord — and it constantly communicates with the brain through the vagus nerve.

When your gut is inflamed, your mood, confidence, and clarity suffer. Cortisol levels spike, decision-making falters, and anxiety may cloud your fire. But when your gut is balanced — nourished with whole foods, supported by a healthy microbiome, and given rest from over-processed fuel — your nervous system steadies. Your flame brightens. You feel calm, decisive, and able to trust yourself.

This is why healing the solar plexus is not just metaphor. It is physiology. It is the intimate dance between microbes and mood, hormones and willpower, digestion and direction.

When tending the solar plexus, remember: the flame is fed by more than breath and awareness. It is also fed by what you place into and onto your body. If your gut is inflamed or your body overburdened, the fire cannot burn steady.

We explored this deeply in Nourishing the Vessel — how food, minerals, hydration, and self-care either weigh us down or lift us up. Return there when you need guidance and let those practices support your solar plexus fire. Because sovereignty is not just emotional; it is physical. To stand tall in your choices, your body must feel safe, steady, and supported.

Healing the solar plexus is not about forcing confidence or puffing yourself up. It is about clearing the smoke so your flame can shine naturally. It is about reclaiming your fire, not to burn yourself out, but to light your way.

Through the HOPE Method, the solar plexus is where Healing deepens. It is where fragments of anger, fear, and shame are sifted into fuel — a steady flame that whispers: I am allowed to choose my own life.

Soul Scribbles & Embodied Practice: Tending the First - Set a timer for 7 minutes. Sit upright with your hands resting gently over your solar plexus (just above the navel). Breathe deeply, imagining a golden flame flickering under your palms. With each inhale, see it grow brighter; with each exhale, see it steady.

When you feel connected, pick up your pen and write to the flame:

Where have I given away my fire?

Where have I dimmed myself to avoid conflict or rejection?

What choices am I longing to make, but have delayed out of fear?

Let the answers tumble out, messy and raw. Don't worry if they don't make sense. Each word is kindling, each truth oxygen for your inner fire.

To tend the solar plexus is to feed the fire wisely. Return to the practices of Nourishing the Vessel and let them steady your flame. Choose foods that feel alive in your hands, not sealed in wrappers that promise more than they give. Be gentle with salt and processed additives that stir static into your system. Drink water as though it were a conductor, carrying clarity through every cell. Keep a journal of what you eat, when you eat, and how you feel when you rise in the morning — patterns will begin to whisper what your body already knows. Notice how late-night eating may leave you heavy or restless and honor your fire by closing the kitchen before sleep. These are not rules but invitations, ways of remembering that your gut is not only digestion — it is your second brain, the hearth of your sovereignty. When you care for it, your fire steadies.

Modern science affirms what the ancients always knew: the gut is a second brain. Within it lives the microbiome, trillions of organisms that influence mood, immunity, even the way we think. When it is inflamed or imbalanced, the solar plexus flame wavers — stress feels sharper, decisions feel heavier, and shame echoes louder. But when you nourish it with kindness, hydrate it with clarity, and give it rhythms of rest, the body responds with steadiness. Cortisol softens, energy steadies, and the nervous system remembers safety. This is not just food; it is frequency repair. It is the subtle yet powerful art of feeding your fire in every sense.

Feed the Fire: Choose living foods; hydrate generously; favor natural over ultra-processed; give digestion nightly rest. Track what you eat and how you feel on waking; let patterns teach you. Not rules — rhythms.

Soul Seed to Take With You: Your fire is not for burning yourself out; it's for lighting your way. Through HOPE, this is the deepening of "H" in WiSH-to-HEAL. A steadied fire rises looking for a voice.

Throat /Expression (Breathe) – Breathing and Speaking Your Truth / I Speak: When your solar plexus steadies, your fire rises — no longer hidden, no longer smothered. And as it climbs, it seeks a voice. What was once trapped in silence now longs to be spoken, to be sung, to be named.

The throat is the bridge between your inner truth and your outer life. It is where fragments find language, where needs are declared, where boundaries take sound. To heal here is to remember that your voice is not a weapon or a liability — it is a lifeline. Every word you speak carries frequency, shaping the energy between you and the world.

For many of us, the throat has been the most fragile place. Maybe you were silenced as a child, told you were "too loud" or "too much." Maybe you learned to stay quiet in order to stay safe. Maybe you swallowed truth after truth until it hardened in your body as tight jaws, sore throats, or shallow breath. Expression is not just about speaking — it is about unfreezing the places that silence carved.

Soul Scribbles & Embodied Practice: Giving Sound to Silence - Set a timer for 5–7 minutes. Place one hand on your throat and the other on your heart. Close your eyes and breathe deeply. On each exhale, let a simple sound escape — a hum, a sigh, or even a whisper. Don't force it. Just notice how your body feels when sound moves through you.

Then, pick up your pen. Without censoring, finish this sentence again and again: "The words I never said are..."

Let them tumble out — messy, raw, contradictory. They don't have to be shared. They don't have to make sense. What matters is that they are no longer trapped.

Why Expression Matters: Modern science shows that when we vocalize — whether through speaking, humming, chanting, or singing — we stimulate the vagus nerve, which activates the parasympathetic nervous system. This shifts the body from stress into safety. Ancient traditions knew this long before neuroscience gave it language. Mantras, prayers, storytelling, and song have always been ways of clearing stuck energy and weaving community.

In the HOPE Method, Expression is not about shouting louder or convincing others. It is about aligning your outer voice with your inner truth. Through WiSH-to-HEAL, the throat carries Expression as its gift: turning silence into sound, fear into freedom, and fragments into wholeness.

Soul Seed to Take With You: Your voice is not too much. It is the frequency of your freedom. Each word you speak in truth is a step toward healing. Your voice is the frequency of your freedom. Let your sound rise — not to prove, but to be. Once truth is spoken, it needs somewhere to land: acceptance.

Sacral / Acceptance (Walk with it) – Letting Feelings Flow / I Feel: When the throat opens, truth begins to move through sound and story. But expression is not the end of the journey. Words must land somewhere — and the first place they must be received is within yourself. This is why the next step is Acceptance.

It may seem unusual that we arrive here after the throat, rather than before, but the HOPE Method walks a reversed path. We began at the Crown with Wisdom, re-educating the mind and gathering the scattered pieces of self. We softened into Serenity at the Third Eye, restoring vision. We repaired the Heart, reweaving compassion. We healed the Solar Plexus, reclaiming our fire. We opened the Throat to Expression, giving voice to what had long been silenced. And now we arrive at the Sacral — the seat of Acceptance.

The sacral chakra is the water within you — the tides of emotion, the rivers of creativity, the ebb and flow of desire and pleasure. When fragmented, these waters can feel dammed or flooded: emotions too tightly held, or overwhelming waves that leave you gasping. But when balanced, the sacral becomes a lake of stillness that can both ripple and rest.

Acceptance here means allowing yourself to feel without judgment. To let sadness be sadness. To let joy be joy. To let grief, longing, desire, and delight all have a place at your table. In HOPE, Acceptance is not about resigning to "this is all there is." It is about creating enough space for every fragment of your experience to belong without shame.

When you accept your emotions as valid, you stop wasting energy resisting them. You stop fighting the tides and instead learn how to swim with them. This is where pleasure is no longer punished, where creativity becomes medicine, and where you remember that you were designed to feel deeply.

Through **WiSH-to-HEAL**, Acceptance at the Sacral teaches: **Wisdom** to know your emotions are not flaws but messengers. **Serenity** to let them rise and fall without drowning in them. **Heart** to welcome both pain and joy with compassion. **Healing** to dissolve shame that once silenced your desires. **Expression** to name your feelings honestly, without fear. And finally, **Love** — the current that holds it all together.

Acceptance matters because without it, every other step unravels. Wisdom without acceptance becomes judgment. Expression without acceptance becomes shame. Even love without acceptance becomes conditional. But when you allow what moves within you to rise and release, you return to wholeness — body, mind, and soul moving together like tide and moon.

Why Acceptance Matters in the Body: Modern neuroscience shows that emotions are not abstract — they are biochemical messengers. When you suppress them, the body stores the unprocessed stress response, often showing up as tension, digestive distress, or fatigue. But when you acknowledge and allow emotions, even briefly, the body metabolizes them — literally shifting hormones, neurotransmitters, and nervous system activity.

Neuroanatomist Dr. Jill Bolte Taylor has observed that an emotion in its pure physiological form lasts about 90 seconds if it is allowed to move through without resistance. After that, what keeps it lingering is the story we attach.

This is why acceptance is so powerful. When you stop resisting your feelings, the body stops looping the stress response and begins to reset, creating space for calm and clarity.

In the HOPE Method, Acceptance at the sacral chakra is this very reset: the willingness to let feelings move like rivers, rather than damming them into stagnation. It's not indulgence. It's regulation. It's permission for your body to complete what it already knows how to do — release. This is the blood that remembers your strength and the water that carries you back to yourself.

Soul Scribbles & Embodied Practice: Flowing with Acceptance: Find a quiet place where you won't be interrupted. Set a timer for 7–10 minutes. Take a few deep breaths and place one hand just below your navel — the seat of your sacral energy. Feel the rise and fall of your belly as you breathe.

Then, begin to write without pausing to edit or censor. Let it be messy, raw, even illogical. This is not for the world — it is for you. Start with the phrase:

"If I let myself feel what I've been avoiding…"

"If I allowed myself to want without shame..."

"The emotions I keep dammed behind walls are..."

Write as fast as your pen will move. If all that comes out is "I don't know" or even a grocery list, keep going. Sometimes acceptance begins with clearing the noise before the deeper truth surfaces. This is not about clean handwriting or polished reflections. This is about letting what stirs in you move — like current, like memory.

When the timer ends, close your eyes again. Place both hands on your belly. Whisper: "I accept what I feel. I allow my body to remember."

Soul Seed to Take With You: Your emotions are rivers carving truth. Acceptance is the shoreline that holds them. And when both water and blood are honored in their movement, love can root and hold everything you've reclaimed.

Root / Love (Feel it) – HOPE & Self-Love / I Am: The Root begins where life itself begins — at the threshold of the body, in the tissues and organs that anchor us to earth and give us form. In ancient wisdom, this center is called Muladhara — "root support." In the HOPE Method, we understand it as the ground of Love.

This is not romantic love or fleeting affection. This is unconditional love — the kind that says, "You are safe. You belong. You are worthy, simply because you are."

The Root lives in the base of the body — in the perineum, the sex organs, the lower spine. It is primal, physical, undeniable. It governs survival, stability, and embodiment. When fragmented, this is where fear coils, where shame hides, where belonging feels fragile. It may show up as money anxiety, insecurity, difficulty trusting your body, or even disconnection from sexuality. But when healed, the Root becomes the anchor of love that steadies every other part of your being.

In many traditions, healing begins here. But in the HOPE Method, we arrive here last — not in fear, but in fullness. By descending from crown to root, you have already gathered wisdom, serenity, compassion, healing, expression, and acceptance. Now, all of that learning flows downward, rooting into Love.

Love at the Root is not an idea. It is embodied presence. It is your soul remembering: "I belong in this body. I belong in this life. I am rooted, and I am loved." When this center is strong, you walk the world with grounded confidence. You trust the earth to hold you. You trust your body as a home. You trust love as your birthright.

Soul Scribbles & Embodied Practice: Rooting into Love

Find a quiet place where your body feels supported — perhaps sitting with your back against a wall, feet flat on the ground, or lying down with a blanket across your hips. Close your eyes and breathe deeply into the base of your spine. Imagine roots extending from your body into the earth, weaving you into stability.

Then, with a journal in hand, set a timer for 7–10 minutes and let the words spill without judgment. Use one or more of these invitations to guide your writing:

Where do I feel most at home in my body — and where do I feel like a stranger?

What fears or shames have tried to tell me I don't belong?

When have I felt most rooted, most loved, most safe?

If love could speak from the base of my being, what would it say?

Don't edit. Don't organize. This is not polished journaling. It's mind-dumping, body-speaking, soul-scribbling. Even if what comes out is messy or mundane ("I need to pay the credit card bill"), it matters — because it clears the clutter and makes space for the deeper voice beneath.

Soul Seed to Take With You: Love is not earned.

It is the ground beneath your feet, the pulse within your bones, the quiet truth that steadies you when all else shakes.

Carry this reminder with you: I am rooted. I am loved. I belong here — fully, freely, and forever. Love as the Root of All Healing

As we arrive at the Root, we find not only grounding but also the quiet truth that holds every practice together: love. It is the thread that has been weaving through each center, the pulse beneath every return, the current that steadies every rise. And it is here, at the foundation, that we remember — all healing begins and ends in love.

Love is not just an emotion; it is a frequency, the deepest current that runs through every cell, every breath, every bond. At the Root, love shows itself as unconditional belonging — not because of what you do, but because of who you are. This is where self-love takes root. To stand in love is to say: I deserve to be here, to take up space, to be nourished, to be safe. Without this foundation, every other practice wobbles. With it, every step of the HOPE Method steadies.

Love wears many faces, yet at its core each expression carries the same frequency of belonging. The Greeks named them: Agape — unconditional, divine love. Philia — the bond of friendship and shared trust. Storge — the tenderness of family and familiarity. Eros — passion and desire that awakens vitality. Pragma — enduring love that weathers time and trial.

Love is not one note but a spectrum. It whispers as friendship, steadies as family, burns as passion, endures as commitment, and expands as the unconditional pulse of the divine. However, it arrives — through words, touch, presence, or service — love is always the same frequency, reminding us that we belong.

Modern psychology echoes this in the language of how we give and receive love — through words of affirmation, acts of service, gifts, quality time, or touch. None is greater than another; all are channels of the same current. What matters is not the form, but the flow — that love is offered, received, and allowed to circulate freely.

When love is honored in all its expressions, it steadies the ground beneath you. This foundation prepares you for the final weaving of HOPE: Sovereignty.

Sovereignty Reclaimed – The Crown of HOPE

WISH-TO-HEAL IS NOT only about softening into wisdom, serenity, heart, healing, expression, acceptance, and love. It is about what all of these threads weave together: sovereignty reclaimed. True sovereignty is not dominance over others, but mastery within yourself. It is the state of no longer being ruled by fragmentation, fear, or borrowed stories. Instead, you live aligned with your soul's frequency — clear, grounded, and free. From this place, your choices ripple outward as integrity, your presence carries peace, and your energy radiates with resonance.

This is the undercurrent of HOPE: to return you to sovereignty, so that you can walk as both human and divine, rooted and radiant. And from sovereignty, the path opens wider — into the mysteries of awakening. For some, that path may be Kundalini. For others, it may be prayer, breath, or silence. Many doors, one light.

Paths to Awakening — Many Doors, One Light

SOVEREIGNTY IS THE quiet crown of wholeness — the moment when your fragments no longer define you, and you walk as a soul in alignment. But how do we reach this state of awakened resonance? Across history, cultures have described many paths, each unique, yet all leading toward the same horizon: the remembrance of who we truly are.

Across cultures, these practices look different — breathwork in Tibetan Buddhism, prayer and fasting in Christianity and Islam, chanting in Hindu and Sikh traditions, deep meditation in Taoist alchemy, even modern brainwave research in neuroscience. Yet they all point to the same truth: there is more to you than what meets the eye.

Each path is like a doorway. Some are gentle, some are fiery, some are hidden until life itself cracks them open. You do not need to walk them all. You need only find the one that resonates, the one that meets you where you are, the one that feels like homecoming in your bones.

For me, that doorway was Kundalini. I did not plan it, nor force it. It rose when the time was ripe — a current of fire and electricity, a dream of golden doors and soul contracts, a remembering I could not un-know. Kundalini is not the only path, but it is the one that met me, carried me, and showed me what it means to let energy awaken.

Across history, cultures have described many ways of awakening — unique in practice, but united in essence. Each path is a doorway, and though the doors differ, they all open toward the same light: the remembrance of who we truly are.

Kundalini (Yogic/Tantric traditions): A coiled energy at the base of the spine that rises like a serpent of light. When awakened, it clears blockages, stirs dormant potential, and ignites consciousness. For me, this was the doorway that opened — not by force, but by grace. Kundalini rose when the time was ripe, a current of fire and remembrance that changed me forever.

Buddhist Meditation: In the sutras, awakening is described as polishing awareness until it shines clear. Mindfulness and deep meditation cultivate presence, and modern neuroscience shows these practices literally rewire the brain toward peace and clarity.

Christian Mysticism: Saints like Teresa of Ávila and Julian of Norwich spoke of union with God through prayer, contemplation, and surrender. Their visions remind us that the Divine is not distant but alive within.

Sufism (Islamic Mysticism): Through whirling dances, poetry, and dhikr (remembrance of God), the heart is awakened. Rumi's words echo this truth: "The wound is the place where the Light enters you."

Vedic Yogas: Bhakti (devotion), Jnana (wisdom), Karma (selfless service) — each is a thread leading to union. Bhakti softens the heart, Jnana clears illusion, Karma transforms service into freedom. Together, they reveal that awakening has many doorways, but one destination.

Indigenous & Shamanic Traditions: Communion with nature, ancestors, and spirit guides opens the soul to connection and remembrance. Plant medicine and ceremony are seen as teachers, reconnecting us to Earth and community.

Modern Science & Somatic Pathways: Breathwork, trauma healing, and neurobiology now echo ancient truths. Conscious breathing can reset the vagus nerve, regulate the nervous system, and awaken presence in the body. Science is catching up to spirit, affirming that awakening is embodied.

Each path is valid. Some are fiery, some are gentle, some appear only when life cracks us open. You do not need to walk them all — only the one that resonates, the one that feels like home in your bones. For me, that was Kundalini. For you, it may be prayer, meditation, breathwork, or the whisper of wind in the trees. Many doors, one light.

Finding Sovereignty Through Awakening

AWAKENING IS NOT ABOUT fireworks or visions. It is about balance — the moment when body, mind, and soul return to rhythm. Sovereignty is the crown of this balance: no longer being ruled by fear, fragmentation, or borrowed stories, but walking in alignment with your own essence.

Each path of awakening offers its own way into sovereignty:

Through **meditation**, you train the mind to pause, and in that pause, you discover freedom from old reactions.

Through **prayer**, you surrender what you cannot carry and open to guidance beyond the self.

Through **Kundalini**, energy awakens through the body, burning away illusions until only clarity remains.

Through **devotion**, love itself becomes the anchor that steadies you.

Through **breath and somatic** healing, the nervous system resets, and you realize sovereignty is not abstract — it is felt safety in your own skin.

Sovereignty is not about dominance or control. It is about belonging fully to yourself, so that your choices flow from clarity, your presence carries peace, and your energy radiates integrity. Whether through stillness, movement, ritual, or breath, every path of awakening is pointing you back to this: the quiet power of being whole.

HOPEfully Human Moment

WHEN I FIRST ENCOUNTERED Kundalini, it wasn't in some mountaintop monastery or after years of meditation. It was right after finishing my trauma-informed yoga training. I had signed up for a Kundalini yoga class out of curiosity, not expectation.

The energy didn't rise during the practice itself. It came later — in the quiet of an ordinary day, when my mind wasn't trying to force anything. Suddenly, it felt like a current of electricity firing through my spine, alive and undeniable. That night, I dreamed of golden doors and soul contracts, as if my inner world had opened to a dimension I hadn't known was waiting.

I share this not as a roadmap, but as a reminder: Kundalini is personal. It will arrive in its own timing, in its own way. For some, it is fire. For others, it is gentle warmth. For many, it unfolds slowly, like the turning of a season. Your experience will be uniquely yours — and that is exactly as it should be.

Spirit Guides, Ancestors & the Unseen Allies

YOU ARE NEVER HEALING alone. Even when the room is silent. Even when it feels like no one understands. All around you, there are unseen allies — rooting for your return, guiding you toward your mission, carrying prayers you didn't even know how to form.

Call them angels. Call them ancestors. Call them Spirit Guides, Higher Self, inner light, God, Holy Spirit, or Source. Whatever name you choose, the essence is the same: you are held. You are accompanied. You are loved.

Some people feel them in dreams. Others in synchronicities — the sudden appearance of repeating numbers, the way a feather falls in their path after prayer, or the uncanny song that plays when they need it most. Science has even brushed against the mystical: modern medicine has documented a visible spark of light when a sperm penetrates an egg — the literal ignition of life, a flash so radiant it reminds us that energy, divinity, and creation are inseparable.

We live in a world that often labels these moments as coincidence, imagination, or superstition. But when you step back, you realize that every culture has spoken of the unseen. Native traditions teach of ancestors walking beside us. Christian mystics write of guardian angels. Eastern texts describe devas and bodhisattvas, guides who aid us on our path. These aren't fringe beliefs — they are echoes of a universal truth: we are guided.

And still, so much has been lost. Human knowledge moves in cycles. Every thousand years or so, entire bodies of wisdom slip away. The burning of the Library of Alexandria was not just the destruction of scrolls; it was the silencing of generations of science, astronomy, medicine, and spiritual maps. Civilizations rise, knowledge is gained, then catastrophe strikes, and much of it must be relearned from fragments. But here is the mystery: the knowledge never truly dies. It lingers in the collective unconscious, in the symbols of our dreams, in the whispers of our guides, in the sudden inner knowing that cannot be explained.

The Schumann resonance — the Earth's electromagnetic heartbeat — is one such reminder. Sensitive souls often feel its fluctuations like waves in their own bodies: sudden exhaustion, bursts of creativity, or moments of inner stillness. Science measures it. Mystics experience it. Both agree that we are woven into something far larger than ourselves, and its rhythms affect us whether we acknowledge them or not.

So, what does this mean for healing? It means that you are not only repairing your nervous system or reframing your mind — you are rejoining a conversation that has been happening since the dawn of humanity. A conversation between the seen and the unseen. Between your wounds and your wisdom. Between your ancestors and your becoming.

In the HOPE Method, this truth matters deeply. Because healing is not only about repairing the past — it is about awakening to the greater whole. Each of us carries a soul mission. Each of us was born with a purpose that extends beyond survival. To walk in that mission, we must learn to listen — not only to the body and the mind, but also to the unseen.

You don't need blind faith to begin. You only need openness. HOPE teaches that it is safe to commune with what can't be seen, as long as it aligns with your inner peace. And when you dare to open, you may discover that the ancestors, the guides, the divine itself has been whispering all along: Keep going. You are not alone. The mission is still alive within you.

The mysteries were never destroyed. They are waiting for us to remember. And just as civilizations recover wisdom after centuries of loss, you, too, can recover the fragments of your soul. That is the heart of HOPE — not just Harnessing Optimal Positive Energy for today, but remembering that you were never truly alone, never truly severed, never truly lost.

Rejoining the Greater Whole

SPIRITUAL HEALING is not escape. It is not about floating above the mess of life or silencing the ache of being human. It is the art of integration — the sacred weaving of body, mind, and soul into one luminous fabric of wholeness.

You are not here to ascend away from this world. You are here to descend more fully into it — to feel the soil beneath your feet and the stars above your head, to live both grounded and infinite, rooted and radiant, divinely human. The ancients called this the "as above, so below" principle: the truth that heaven and earth are not opposites, but reflections, and we are the bridge between them.

To walk with HOPE is to walk in both worlds: the tangible and the unseen, the present moment and the eternal. It is to breathe here and now while remembering you belong to something vast and ancient, pulsing beneath the chaos.

Why does belonging matter? Because belonging shapes the field around you. Science calls it emotional contagion — the way nervous systems mirror one another. Walk into a room frowning and you'll see shoulders tighten, brows furrow. Walk in smiling, and the atmosphere shifts. Laughter rises. Hearts soften. This isn't just psychology; it's physics. The heart radiates the strongest electromagnetic field in the body, extending several feet beyond your skin. Others don't only see your presence — they feel it.

This is why authenticity matters. A forced smile without the heart behind it falls flat; the room feels the dissonance. But when your smile flows from a heart at peace, it carries coherence — the resonance of safety, kindness, and connection. Belonging is not performance. It is frequency. And the more attuned you are to your own truth, the more others can relax into theirs.

We are born belonging. Before any title. Before any milestone. Before we proved a single thing, we were already claimed — by breath, by body, by the great heartbeat of creation itself. But the fractures of living — rejection, abandonment, cultural disconnection — can make us forget. We begin to believe belonging is something we must earn. Something fragile. Something that can be given and taken away.

The HOPE Method whispers otherwise: belonging is not a prize; it is a presence. You don't have to chase it; you tune to it. Each time you soften into your breath, each time you smile with sincerity, each time you remember that your soul cannot be fractured — you return to resonance. You rejoin the greater whole.

HOPE in Practice: Tuning to Belonging

PLACE YOUR HANDS GENTLY over your heart. Feel its steady rhythm — the first home you have ever known. Whisper softly to yourself: "I belong here. In this breath. In this moment. In this skin."

Say it again, until the words sink beneath thought and into your body. Say it until your nervous system begins to soften, until your chest loosens, until you remember what has always been true: you belong.

But belonging does not always begin where you came from. For some, home was loud. Unsafe. Violating. The very walls that were meant to protect became places of fracture. And so, part of the healing journey is to redefine home. Not as a house or a zip code, but as a felt sense that cannot be taken from you.

Home is a frequency. It is the quiet safety that floods you when you pause long enough to hear your breath. It is the softness that rises when your soul feels seen. It is the resonance in your bones that whispers: Here, I can exhale.

This is the radical reclamation of sacred self-belonging. It is the unlearning of performance, the shedding of masks, the releasing of old roles that told you to be smaller than you are. Belonging is not about fitting in. It is about returning — again and again — to yourself.

Wisdom Through the Ages

MAYA ANGELOU — POET, activist, truth-teller — carried a voice that refused to be silenced. Across her life she lived through fragmentation, injustice, and exile, yet her words became a compass for generations. She once wrote: "You only are free when you realize you belong no place — you belong every place — no place at all. The price is high. The reward is great."

Angelou's wisdom reminds us that belonging isn't about fitting neatly into the molds the world offers us. It is not about being welcomed everywhere, nor about earning acceptance through performance. Real belonging is paradoxical — it is belonging nowhere in particular, and everywhere at once.

To belong is to claim yourself. To anchor in your truth. To remember that you are woven into the great web of life, inseparable from the breath of the trees, the rhythm of the oceans, the pulse of humanity. You were never truly outside of belonging — only taught to forget.

This is the kind of belonging HOPE calls you back to. Not borrowed from culture, family, or approval, but rooted in the soul's knowing: I was always part of the whole. Through HOPE, belonging is not granted by others but remembered within yourself — a frequency you return to each time you honor your energy, choose your truth, and speak to yourself with love.

The Neuroscience of Belonging

THE HUMAN BRAIN IS wired for connection. To our ancestors, belonging wasn't a luxury — it was survival. To be cast out from the tribe was to be exposed to predators, hunger, and death. Even now, thousands of years later, our nervous system hasn't forgotten. When we feel excluded or rejected, the brain registers it as pain — the same neural pathways that light up with physical injury will also glow with the ache of disconnection.

And yet, the opposite is also true. When we are seen, when we are welcomed, when we feel the warmth of belonging, our brain floods us with oxytocin — the bonding hormone. Our heart rate steadies. Our stress hormones ease. Our nervous system whispers: safe. This is why even a single moment of true belonging — a hug that lingers, a laugh shared in sync, a glance of understanding — can feel like medicine.

Belonging is not abstract. It is embodied. It rewires us to receive love, to soften into trust, to remember that connection is possible. This is why community, practice, and affirmation matter in the HOPE Method. They are not just "feel-good extras." They are tools of repair.

Each ritual of reflection, each affirmation spoken into the mirror, each circle of safe community creates a new imprint in the nervous system: I belong. I am safe. I am connected.

Through HOPE, belonging becomes more than an idea. It becomes a lived frequency — one that steadies the body, softens the mind, and restores the soul to its place in the greater whole.

HOPEfully Human Moment

THERE WAS A SEASON where I felt like I belonged nowhere — not to family, not to religion, not even to my own reflection. I would look back at photographs and barely recognize the woman staring back at me. She seemed like a stranger wearing my skin.

One afternoon, while planting flowers in the quiet of my garden, a hummingbird hovered right in front of my face. For a breathless moment, the world stilled. The tiny creature didn't judge me. It didn't need me to explain myself or earn its presence. It simply saw me — and it stayed.

And in that fragile, winged pause, I remembered: belonging doesn't always come from people. Sometimes it comes from the earth, from a sky that holds you without condition, from a bird that greets you as if you've always been part of its world. Nature has always welcomed me.

That counts. And sometimes, it's enough to begin again.

Where in your life has nature reminded you that you belong?

HOPE in Practice: Build a Belonging Altar

CREATE A SPACE THAT whispers you home. It doesn't need to be ornate or elaborate — just a corner that feels like refuge. Place there a photograph, a feather, a stone, a line of poetry, or anything that reminds you of where your soul feels safe.

This is your belonging space. A place to return when the world feels loud, when disconnection presses in, when you forget who you are. Sit near it when you feel lost. Let its presence remind you: you are never as alone as you think. Every object you place here is not just decoration — it is a witness, a symbol of the threads that tie you back to yourself.

Soul Seed to Take With You

YOU ARE NOT A MISFIT. You are a map. And every time you honor your truth, you call yourself home. And this is the essence of WiSH-to-HEAL through HOPE: wisdom that clears the mind, serenity that steadies the vision, heart that softens the fractures, healing that restores the fire, expression that gives voice, acceptance that roots you, and love that anchors you in wholeness. When these threads are woven together, the energy of kundalini begins to rise — not through force, but through alignment.

From Crown to Root, you have gathered your fragments. From Root to Crown, your soul now awakens. This is not the end of your journey. It is the opening of a new one. Through HOPE, you have remembered: you are whole, you are home, you are here. But what happens when life trembles again — when loss rips open what felt sealed, when love collides with absence, when guilt whispers its unfinished stories?

This is where the path bends toward grief. Where sorrow and grace become companions, and where HOPE must prove it can carry you even through death's shadow. That is where we now turn.

Chapter Nineteen

Grief, Guilt & Grace – Coping with Loss, Death & Soul Sorrow

Grief has no timeline. No script. No proper shape. It arrives when it wants to, lingers longer than we expect, and morphs into something new the moment we think we understand it.

But grief is not the enemy. It is the proof that something mattered. Love left an imprint, and grief is the echo of that love still reverberating in your bones.

This chapter honors the raw terrain of loss — not only of life, but of identity, dreams, relationships, innocence, and even the versions of ourselves we had to shed in order to survive. We grieve friendships that faded without closure. We grieve children we couldn't protect. We grieve parents who never became who we needed. We grieve homes we left, faiths we released, and younger selves who never got to be fully held.

Grief is layered. It is sacred. It is not linear. It is not polite. It is a holy dismantling — and a holy rebuilding.

Yet grief rarely comes alone. It is often accompanied by guilt, its tangled twin. Guilt creeps in with whispered questions: Could I have done more? Why wasn't I there? Did I love them well enough? Was it somehow my fault?

These questions are not flaws in you. They are the brain's desperate attempt to find control in a world that does not guarantee fairness or certainty. Guilt is the mind trying to reassemble a shattered story. HOPE doesn't silence guilt; it listens to it. It asks gently: Is this guilt mine to keep, or is it asking to be released?

Sometimes grace is simply learning to forgive yourself for being human.

In the language of spirit, we often speak of cords — invisible threads that connect us to people, places, and experiences. Some cords are sacred; others are sorrowful. When someone passes, or when a chapter closes, the love remains. The cord of pain, however, can be loosened. Rituals — lighting candles, writing letters, planting flowers, or speaking their name at sunrise — help shift grief into reverence. Death does not end a relationship; it changes the way we love.

Grace is the hand that reaches for you when no one else knows you are drowning. It is the laughter that erupts in the middle of tears. It is the moment you rise — not because grief is over, but because something sacred still calls you forward. Grace does not erase the ache. It changes the way it lives inside you.

And woven through it all is joy. Joy is not a luxury or a prize for "getting through" sorrow. Joy is medicine. It is the nervous system remembering safety. It is the rebellion of your inner child who still knows how to play. It is the soul whispering: I remember how to live.

In the HOPE Method, joy and play are not frivolous extras — they are frequency repair. They are how we Harness the body's wisdom, choose the Optimal path of presence, reclaim the Positive in its authentic form, and re-align our Energy with life.

Every time you laugh, sing, dance, doodle, or plant a garden, you are not escaping your grief — you are transmuting it. You are raising your vibration. You are reclaiming aliveness.

This is grief. This is guilt. This is grace. This is HOPE.

The Seasons of Healing

HEALING IS NOT LINEAR. It is seasonal — it moves like the earth, in rhythms and in cycles. There are moments of bloom, of fullness, of fading, and of stillness. Each season has its own teaching. Each one carries its own medicine. And grief — like winter — arrives with both quiet and command.

Spring – The Season of Bloom: Spring is the season of tender beginnings. Here, even in the shadow of sorrow, tiny shoots of hope push through the soil of your soul. A laugh escapes in the middle of tears. A memory warms instead of wounds. Spring reminds you that your grief is not only about endings — it also clears the ground for something new to emerge.

Summer – The Season of Fullness: Summer is the season of aliveness. The heart, though bruised, begins to remember joy. This is the time when you feel the warmth of connection again — laughter with friends, the sweetness of a song, the way sunlight brushes your skin. Summer is not a denial of grief but a reminder that life, too, insists on being lived. That joy is not a betrayal of loss — it is a part of healing.

Autumn – The Season of Release: Autumn is the season of letting go. Just as trees surrender their leaves, we too must release what no longer belongs: the weight of guilt, the illusion of control, the fragments of "what if." Autumn reminds us that release is not failure — it is wisdom. It is the grace to allow what was sacred to remain so, without carrying the burden of trying to keep it unchanged.

Winter – The Season of Stillness: Winter is the season of deep grief. It is the silence after the goodbye, the hollow ache where someone once stood. Winter does not ask you to move on. It asks you to sit in the stillness, to feel the marrow-deep truth that something mattered. It is the most difficult season, but also the most sacred. For in the long dark, seeds are buried. Roots deepen. Something unseen prepares to rise again.

I know these seasons intimately. I have lost my daughter — a pain that rooted itself in my bones. I have mourned the futures I once imagined for my children, grieved miscarriages, carried sorrow for friends and family lost to suicide, and wept over identities and homes that no longer fit. Grief, I've learned, is not a single event. It is a constant cycling — and a holy remembering.

In the HOPE Method, these seasons are not interruptions. They are the path itself. Healing is not about racing through spring to avoid winter or clinging to summer, so autumn never comes. Healing is learning to honor each season as it arrives, to let it teach you, to let it move through you. HOPE is the reminder that no season is wasted. Each one carries you closer to wholeness.

When Sorrow Takes Root

THERE COMES A TIME when sorrow stops visiting… and begins to take root. It no longer comes and goes like weather. It settles into us, lingering in our posture, in our words, in our silence.

This is what we call a sorrow bond. It is not love itself, but grief woven so tightly into the fabric of our being that it begins to masquerade as identity. We wrap it around ourselves not because we want to, but because we fear that if we loosen our grip, we will lose the memory of what mattered most. We believe that letting go of sorrow means letting go of love.

But love and sorrow are not the same. Love is expansive, eternal, unconditional. Sorrow is the shadow love casts when something precious is taken away. When sorrow takes root, it can distort our relationship with memory, keeping us bound to pain instead of allowing us to live in reverence.

There is no shame in this. It is a natural response to unbearable loss. But when grief becomes the lens through which you see everything, when it steals your capacity for joy, belonging, or rest — that is when it asks for more than time. It asks for help.

This is the moment to reach out — to a therapist, grief counselor, spiritual director, or other trusted guide. Professional support is not a sign of weakness; it is a sign of love. Love for yourself. Love for the one you lost. Love for the life still calling you forward.

Because your story is not meant to end in sorrow. Grief will always be part of you, but it does not have to become all of you. With support, you can learn to release the bond of sorrow while holding onto the bond of love. You can learn to let the memory remain without the weight becoming your home.

Neuroscience now confirms what the ancients always knew: grief is not only an emotion of the heart, but a full-body event. Functional MRI studies reveal that grief activates the same neural pathways as physical pain, particularly in the anterior cingulate cortex. This is why your chest aches, why your stomach knots, why loss feels like being torn apart from within.

When grief lingers without integration, it can evolve into what psychiatrists such as Dr. M. Katherine Shear call prolonged grief disorder — the medical description of what we here name a sorrow bond. In this state, the nervous system gets trapped in loops of longing, avoidance, and despair. The body remains in survival mode, while the mind keeps replaying what was lost.

Neuroanatomist Dr. Jill Bolte Taylor offers us hope she observed that an emotion in its pure physiological form lasts only about ninety seconds if it is allowed to move through the body. It is the stories we attach — the "what ifs," the "I should have," the "if only" — that cause sorrow to take root and remain.

Long before brain scans proved it, our ancestors-built rituals to protect against sorrow bonds. They understood that grief must move.

The Egyptians practiced ritual mourning, sometimes with loud public wailing, to carry sorrow out of the body. Celtic women keened — singing grief into the air so it would not stay lodged in the chest. Indigenous communities danced their mourning into the earth, trusting that movement would transmute ache into belonging. In Jewish tradition, families sit shiva, surrounding the bereaved with presence so silence does not turn into isolation.

Candles have been lit for centuries to carry prayers into light. Trees have been planted in honor of the departed, reminding the living that love can still grow. These were not superstitions. They were medicine. They helped the grieving remember: sorrow belongs, but it does not have to bury you.

Guilt, Shame, and the Ache of What Could Have Been

GRIEF RARELY TRAVELS alone. More often than not, it drags companions behind it — guilt, shame, and longing.

Shame whispers of what we should have said or done — the apology never spoken, the goodbye missed, the kindness withheld because we thought there would be more time. Guilt points to what we didn't do but could have — the call we postponed, the visit we avoided, the moment we mishandled. And then there is longing, grief's most tender twin: not just for the person themselves, but for what could have been. The birthdays never celebrated. The milestones never reached. The promises that will never be fulfilled.

Researcher Brené Brown reminds us that shame is not just about our actions — it attacks our sense of self. Guilt says, "I did something wrong." Shame says, "I am wrong." When loss intersects with shame, the pain deepens. We stop grieving only what happened and start questioning our own worth within it.

And then comes longing — a quieter ache, but no less sharp. We don't only grieve what was. We grieve futures that will never arrive. We mourn the imagined lives we thought we'd share, the laughter that will never echo in our kitchens, the ordinary days that will never unfold. These unrealized tomorrows can tether us to sorrow as much as memory does, holding us captive to the ache of what might have been.

Yet HOPE offers a different path. To honor grief is to name these companions honestly, but not to mistake them for truth. You are not guilty for being human. You are not shameful for surviving. You are not broken because a future dissolved. You are simply tender. And tenderness itself is a sacred form of love.

The Fear of Forgetting

BENEATH ALL GRIEF LIES a quieter ache — the fear of forgetting. Not just the person, but the essence of them. The cadence of their laugh. The way their scent lingered in a room. The warmth of their hand in yours. The particular light that followed them like a shadow of the soul.

And so, often without realizing it, we clutch our sorrow like a talisman. We wear grief like a cloak, believing it is the final thread binding us to them. We think: If I let this go, I might lose them all over again.

But memory is not preserved by pain. Memory is preserved by presence.

Their spirit does not ask you to stay broken in order to remember. It asks you to let joy rise when you speak their name. To laugh at the stories that once brought light. To light a candle not only in mourning, but in gratitude.

Each time you allow love to expand instead of collapse, you weave them deeper into the fabric of your being. You do not forget by living — you remember differently. Less as ache. More as essence.

HOPE reminds us: forgetting is not the risk. The risk is letting sorrow be the only language we speak of them. True remembrance is love made visible — in stories, in practices or rituals of grace, in the way your life continues to bear their imprint in joy as much as in tears.

From Grief to Grace

HEALING BEGINS WITH the remembering that sorrow is not proof of love. Love does not require our suffering to validate it. Love stands on its own — steady, eternal, and whole.

You can release the sorrow and still hold them close. You can smile without betrayal. You can laugh without erasing them. You can dance again — not because you've forgotten, but because you've remembered how brightly they live within you.

I no longer visit my daughter's grave in search of connection. I do not need to. She is with me in ways the stone cannot hold. When I miss her, I light a candle and let its flame remind me that her light has not gone out. I plant flowers or trees and watch something grow in her absence, knowing each bloom carries her essence forward. These small acts are my devotion — not to grief, but to love.

Because grief was never meant to build a permanent home inside of us. It was meant to move through — to wash us in reverence, to soften us with humility, to remind us how much someone mattered. But it was not meant to imprison us.

Grace is what rises when sorrow has done its teaching. It is the soft hand that says, you may carry love without carrying the weight. It is the candle lit, the flower planted, the joy dared again — all proof that love does not end with loss.

In the HOPE Method, sorrow bonds matter because they keep our energy trapped in fragmentation. They bind us to the shadow of love instead of its light. Healing does not mean forgetting. It means learning how to release the bond of sorrow while holding on to the bond of love.

This is why HOPE invites us to remember that we are never healing alone. Spirit guides, ancestors, unseen allies — and even the very earth itself — walk with us. Grief will always be part of us, but it does not have to become us.

Your story is not meant to end in sorrow. You are not broken for grieving. You are human. And humanity, at its most sacred, is love learning how to live with loss.

Gratitude: The Bridge to Peace

IN THE TENDER LIGHT of healing, gratitude arrives like dawn — quiet at first, then steady, then undeniable. It does not erase grief, but it transforms it. Gratitude takes the sharp edges of sorrow and smooths them into remembrance, teaching us that love is not honored through pain, but through presence.

We begin to whisper thank you into the silence. Thank you for loving me. Thank you for existing. Thank you for your laughter, your light, your lessons.

Gratitude becomes a bridge — carrying us from ache into peace, from absence into memory alive. Each breath of thanks is a thread, weaving the departed back into our lives not as weight, but as warmth.

When sorrow floods in, try meeting it with gratitude: If you find yourself missing their voice, pause and say, Thank you for the sound of your words, which still echo in me. If an anniversary or holiday feels heavy, light a candle and whisper, Thank you for the years we had, and for how your love still guides me now.

Gratitude is not denial. It is reverence. It shifts the tether from pain to love, from loss to legacy. This is the path forward: not in forgetting, but in remembering with joy. Not in clinging, but in cherishing. Not in suffering, but in living as a continuation of their light.

HOPE in Practice: Joy Scavenger Hunt

GRIEF AND GRATITUDE often walk hand in hand, and between them hides a quieter companion: joy. Not the grand, sweeping joy of mountain-top moments, but the small sparks that flicker in the everyday — waiting for you to notice.

Today, make it your practice to seek them out. Call it a scavenger hunt for the soul. Look for five things that make you smile, even a little. A squirrel tumbling across a fence like a tightrope walker. A flower blooming sideways through a crack in the pavement. A silly typo that makes you laugh. These are not accidents — they are reminders that life still wants to delight you.

When you train your eyes to look for joy, you begin to rewire your brain. That's neuroplasticity in motion: creating new pathways where light can travel. Most of us were taught that play was frivolous, that laughter was childish, that being "too much" — too expressive, too alive, too free — would make us unlovable. But what if the very parts you silenced are the ones that know how to heal you?

Each time you catch joy hiding in plain sight, you are reclaiming a fragment of yourself. You are proving to your nervous system that delight is not gone — it is here, waiting, abundant, woven into the fabric of ordinary days.

Joy is your birthright.

IT IS WHAT YOUR NERVOUS system was designed for — not merely to survive, but to expand. To delight. To create. To connect. Grief may visit, guilt may linger, but joy is the homecoming. It is the thread that repairs what sorrow frayed, the spark that tells your body: it is safe to feel again.

Joy is not frivolous. It is not a bonus emotion for when the hard work is done. It is the healing — the restoration of your frequency, the rebellion of your inner child, the soul's way of remembering: I was made for life.

The Neuroscience of Joy

JOY IS NOT FRIVOLOUS. It is biology. When you laugh, dance, or let wonder catch you off guard, your brain lights up its dopaminergic system, releasing dopamine and serotonin — the very chemicals that lift mood, sharpen memory, and strengthen immune function. These are not fleeting "feel-good" moments. They are structural shifts in the brain's wiring.

Neuroscientists call this neuroplasticity: the brain's ability to adapt and rewire. Each time you choose play, delight, or creativity, you are strengthening pathways of resilience. Fragmentation narrows the nervous system into survival mode — but joy re-opens it, teaching your body what safety feels like.

And it doesn't stop there. Movement, laughter, and play also release endorphins, the body's natural pain relievers, which soothe stress and invite ease. Shared joy — a meal with friends, a belly laugh, a hug — releases oxytocin, the bonding hormone that roots us in belonging. Joy is not only personal; it is communal. It reminds us that healing deepens in connection.

In fragmentation recovery, this practice is sometimes called counterbalancing: purposefully introducing moments of lightness, connection, and play to tip the scales back toward wholeness. It's why painting a rock, skipping down a sidewalk, or dancing barefoot in your kitchen is not childish — it's regenerative.

Joy is how the nervous system remembers that life is not only about enduring. It is about expanding.

Wisdom Through the Ages

CENTURIES AGO, IN 13TH-century Persia, a mystic and poet named Jalāl al-Dīn Rūmī began weaving words that still ripple across cultures and centuries. Rumi was not just a poet; he was a Sufi mystic, a seeker who believed the soul was meant to dance with the Divine. His verses carried the wisdom of ecstatic love, the ache of longing, and the truth that joy is not frivolous but holy.

Rumi wrote: "When you do things from your soul, you feel a river moving in you, a joy."

For Rumi, joy was evidence of alignment. It was not shallow or fleeting. It was the current of spirit moving through human form — proof that the soul is awake. His whirling dances and ecstatic poetry taught that joy is not a distraction from God or from healing — it is a doorway into both.

In the HOPE Method, we remember this same truth. Play is not the opposite of depth — it is the proof of it. The deepest souls are often the most whimsical. They laugh, they dance, they notice the squirrel leaping sideways or the child's lopsided drawing on the fridge — because they have learned that life is too sacred to carry seriously all the time.

Joy is not only allowed. It is essential. It is the river inside you, carrying you back to wholeness.

HOPEfully Human Moment

ONCE, IN THE STILLNESS of a somber yoga class — the kind where even your breath feels too loud — my phone betrayed me. Out of nowhere, it played a clip of a goat yelling like a man. The room froze in stunned silence... and then cracked wide open with laughter. Students doubled over on their mats. I turned beet red, apologizing as if that would gather the giggles back up, but my own laughter betrayed me too.

Someone leaned over and whispered, "Thank you. I needed that."

And in that moment, I realized I did too. Sometimes the medicine isn't in perfect posture or silent meditation. Sometimes it's in the absurdity that breaks the heaviness wide open. Laughter doesn't just lighten the air — it shifts the energy in our bodies, softening the places grief and tension have lodged. I'm convinced it realigns chakras better than any chant.

Because joy especially the unexpected kind is holy work too.

HOPE in Practice: Creative Joy Map

TAKE A BLANK SHEET of paper and draw a circle in the center. Inside, write the words: "I feel alive when I..."

From that circle, let your hand wander. Sketch lines outward like rays of light, and on each one, write or doodle whatever stirs your aliveness. Maybe it's singing at the top of your lungs. Maybe it's hiking until your lungs burn with mountain air. Maybe it's the simple act of jumping in puddles, dancing barefoot in the kitchen, or letting color spill across a canvas. There is no wrong answer here — only truth.

Your joy map is not frivolous. It is sacred. It is a mirror of the soul's freedom and a trail back to your essence. Follow it gently, and you will find your way home to the part of you that grief or fragmentation could never extinguish.

Soul Seed to Take With You

JOY IS NOT A DETOUR on the healing path. It is the path itself. Every laugh, every spark of play, every burst of wonder is the soul remembering its freedom. This is the Positive in HOPE — not forced smiles, but the vibration of aliveness returning to your bones. Create anyway. Laugh anyway. Love anyway. Live as though light is your native tongue — because it is.

Grief changes us. It carves valleys where once there were plains. It softens what once was rigid, and it humbles what once was certain. Yet even in the weight of loss, the current of HOPE does not disappear, it waits. Through guilt, sorrow, and the aching silence of absence, we discover that love does not end. It shifts. It asks us to live differently, to carry memory in one hand and possibility in the other. Grief deepens us, but it does not have to define us. The question, then, is this: after we've walked with sorrow, how do we begin to walk again in rhythm with life? How do we repattern ourselves so that HOPE is not just a lantern in crisis, but a lifestyle we embody every day?

Chapter Twenty

Practices, Rhythm & Repatterning – Living HOPE As a Lifestyle

Healing is not a single breakthrough. It is the quiet accumulation of a thousand small beginnings. You light a candle. You take a breath. You pause instead of panic. You begin again — and again — and again. This is the essence of living with HOPE: not a rigid program, but a rhythmic invitation to keep coming home to yourself.

HOPE becomes a lifestyle the moment it moves from idea into practice. And practice does not mean perfection. It means participation. It means showing up in the small, daily ways that tell your nervous system: it is safe to be here, it is sacred to be here, it is good to be here.

Daily practices are not reserved for temples or ceremonies. They are the micro-moments that bring meaning to your day. Stirring intention into your morning tea. Whispering affirmations into the mirror. Touching the earth before you speak. Saying thank you before you sleep. These acts may look small, but they carry a magnetic charge. They build trust with your body. They teach your soul a rhythm of return.

Life, like nature, is cyclical. Seasons shift. Tides move. Emotions rise and fall. When you try to live by someone else's pace, you burn out. But when you honor your own rhythm — slow, steady, sacred — you begin to repattern your nervous system. You reawaken your intuitive pulse.

Your rhythm may be found in morning walks with no agenda, in eating a meal without distraction, in noticing how your body responds to the moon's cycles, or in moving your body when words won't come. The HOPE lifestyle asks only this: what restores you? And then it whispers: do that often.

Neuroscientists like Bessel van der Kolk and Bruce Perry remind us that the body carries our history in its cells and circuits. Fragmentation lays tracks in the brain, keeping us rehearsing pain. But repetition lays new ones. Psychologists call this neuroplasticity — the miracle that our brains can rewire, heal, and adapt. Each time you choose silence over reactivity, joy as a priority instead of a reward, pausing before people-pleasing, or breathing instead of fleeing, you are literally reshaping your inner pathways. These choices are not trivial. They are revolutions of the nervous system.

Even modern contemplative science echoes what ancient traditions knew: ritual and rhythm regulate. The practice of returning — to breath, to grounding, to self-kindness — signals safety to the nervous system and strengthens the vagus nerve (the very channel that calms us). Over time, these small acts teach your body what your soul has always known: peace is possible.

This way of living does not ask you to be enlightened. It asks you to remember — again and again — that your life is yours to shape. To shape it with HOPE is to speak to yourself with love, to move your body like it belongs to you, to ground before you give, to rest without guilt, to seek meaning instead of milestones.

HOPE isn't just what you feel when life is easy. It is what you practice when life is hard. And with enough practice, it becomes who you are.

Spirituality is not only in mantras or mountaintops. It is not hidden in temples or texts. It is here, in the dishes. In the detours. In the breath you just took. The sacred is not something we visit — it is something we remember.

In the HOPE Method, spiritual integration is about embodying your connection to Source, soul, and self — not just in the silence of practice, but in the middle of real life. Healing becomes whole when it is woven into the ordinary.

HOPE in Practice: Spiritual Pause

BEFORE RUSHING INTO your next task, pause. Place one hand on your heart, the other on your belly. Whisper softly: "I am here. This moment matters. The divine lives here, too." Let your breath sanctify the space. Let the ordinary become holy simply because you chose to be present in it.

There is a difference between bypassing and integration. Spiritual bypassing uses sacred words to avoid the ache of being human. It polishes pain instead of sitting with it. But spiritual integration is the opposite. It welcomes the tears onto the altar. It makes no distinction between the sacred and the messy. It whispers: God is not waiting for you to be perfect — only to be present.

Whether you name this presence Spirit, Source, God, the Divine Feminine, Higher Self, or the Great Mystery, the name is less important than the relationship. What matters is not the label, but the way you let it move through you. Integration means remembering that there is no corner of your life untouched by the sacred.

Wisdom Through the Ages

THICH NHAT HANH, THE gentle Vietnamese monk often called the father of modern mindfulness, once wrote: "Drink your tea slowly and reverently, as if it is the axis on which the whole earth revolves." He wasn't speaking about tea alone — he was offering a way of living. A reminder that presence is not a lofty practice reserved for temples and retreats. It is found in the ordinary moments we usually rush past.

Spiritual integration is not performance — it is presence. It is the art of letting breath, beauty, and being braid themselves into even the smallest gestures. Washing a dish becomes prayer. Folding laundry becomes meditation. Sipping tea becomes communion with the whole of creation.

Thich Nhat Hanh taught that peace is not something to chase; it is something to touch in every step, in every inhale, in every act of reverence for the now. His wisdom echoes across centuries of spiritual teachers who have said the same in different words: the sacred is not somewhere else. It is here, woven into the fabric of your daily life.

This is the heart of HOPE. To live as though every gesture, every pause, every sip of tea is an axis — a turning point where you remember: life is happening now, and now, and now again.

And so, we practice. Not by adding more to our to-do list, but by bringing reverence into what is already here. By choosing to pause, to breathe, to let even a single moment remind us: the divine lives in the ordinary.

The Science of the Sacred

SCIENCE NOW AFFIRMS what wisdom traditions have always whispered: the sacred heals. Researchers like Andrew Newberg, studying the brain under prayer and meditation, have shown how the default mode network lights up during moments of reflection and reverence. These regions are tied to empathy, meaning making, and the sense of connection that dissolves isolation. When you sit in silence, when you breathe a prayer or whisper gratitude, your brain is not imagining healing — it is rehearsing it.

Medical journals echo the same truth. Studies in Psychoneuroendocrinology — the field that explores how the mind (psycho), the brain and nervous system (neuro), and our hormones (endocrine) all dance together as well as Frontiers in Psychology reveal that contemplative practices lower cortisol, strengthen immune function, and increase resilience. In other words, pausing to pray, meditate, or give thanks isn't escapism — it is biology aligning with grace. Your cells know the difference between chaos and calm, and they respond.

Yet this knowing is not new. Across centuries and cultures, the ancients practiced what we now measure. Indigenous peoples danced prayers into the earth. Monks counted beads with devotion. Mystics sat in silence until the veil grew thin. Their authority is endurance: practice carried across generations because it worked, because it healed, because it reminded us, we belonged to something greater.

And then there is the authority of lived experience — perhaps the most undeniable of all. Survivors of loss, wanderers through trauma, seekers in exile — they tell the same story: when they turned toward the sacred, something in them steadied. The rituals did not erase pain, but they carried it. They rewove what fragmentation had torn.

The sacred, then, is not abstract. It is embodied. It is written into our neurology, echoed in our ancestors, and proven in our own survival. To pause, to pray, to breathe with reverence — this is not indulgence. This is medicine.

HOPEfully Human Moment

I DON'T ALWAYS CRY when life cracks me open. More often, I pick up a paintbrush or a hammer. I've painted entire rooms after heartbreak. I've built sheds after loss. My hands move before my tears do. It's not avoidance — it's how I remind myself I can still create, still shape, still bring order to what feels broken.

And sometimes, in the rhythm of painting strokes or the steady swing of a hammer, I hear the same whisper I once found on the bathroom floor: "Okay, God... I'm still here." That, too, is enough. That, too, is church.

HOPE in Practice: Sacred in the Mundane

EVERYDAY LIFE IS FILLED with hidden altars. The sink, the mirror, the grocery bag — each holds a quiet invitation. When you light a candle while washing dishes, you remind yourself that even cleansing can be holy. When you bless your body as you moisturize, you teach your skin it is worthy of reverence. When you pause to offer gratitude for each grocery item as you unpack it, you weave thankfulness into the rhythm of your day. The sacred isn't far or reserved for mountaintops and temples. It lives here, in the ordinary — hiding in plain sight, waiting for your noticing.

Soul Seed to Take With You

YOU DO NOT HAVE TO ascend to touch the divine. You only have to arrive. Each breath you take is already a prayer. Each heartbeat is already a hymn. Your body itself is a temple, and this moment — right here, as it is — is your altar.

Chapter Twenty-One

Legacy & Light – The Ongoing Journey of HOPE

You made it here. Not to an ending, but to a threshold. You have peeled back layers, sat with sorrow, honored your truth, and planted seeds of light. What rises now is not a conclusion — it is a continuation. The work of living it forward.

The HOPE Method was never meant to be a tool you put away when the wounds fade. It is a way of being. A rhythm. A remembrance. A frequency you can return to, again and again, until it becomes the pulse of your days.

Legacy is not only measured in monuments or milestones. It is carried in the imprint of your presence — in how you soften a room, in the way you speak to yourself out loud, in the boundaries you honor with clarity and kindness. It is the gentle ripple of your light moving outward, touching lives you may never even know.

Healing is not linear. It is cyclical. Some days you will surge forward, other days you will circle back, and sometimes you will simply pause. But now you have a compass. You have language. You have rituals that remind you: breath is a return, softness is strength, choosing what's optimal is not selfish — it is soul-honoring.

HOPE is not a finish line. It is a frequency. And you have tuned to it. You have transmuted pain into wisdom. You have learned not just to survive, but to radiate. And now you are called to share it — not through perfection, but through authenticity. Whether as a guide, a lighthouse, or simply as a gentler friend to yourself, your light is part of what keeps this world turning toward healing.

You will change. Your needs will shift. Your understanding of HOPE will deepen. That is the beauty of it — this method was never meant to be static. It was written to evolve with you. As you grow, return to these pages. Revisit the practices. Rewrite the affirmations. And when they no longer fit, create your own. That is what legacy truly is: not preserving what was but building what comes next.

Through this journey, you've walked the path of WiSH-to-HEAL. You've gathered Wisdom, learning that your mind is not your enemy but your ally. You've touched Serenity, finding that stillness can hold you even when the world shakes. You've opened your Heart, remembering compassion for yourself and for those who could not love you well. You've stepped into Healing, dissolving shame and reclaiming pieces of your soul once thought lost. You've given yourself Expression, a voice that no longer whispers but speaks in truth. And you've chosen Acceptance, allowing your feelings to flow like water without drowning in them. Finally, you have remembered Love — the current that runs beneath it all.

This is what it means to HEAL through HOPE: not erasing your past but weaving it into a greater wholeness. Not chasing perfection but remembering you already belong. Not finishing but continuing. Always continuing.

You are not here by accident. You are here because something in you remembered. You are a vessel of HOPE. A carrier of healing. A torchbearer for times that can feel unbearably dark.

So go softly. Go boldly. Go honestly. But go — knowing your light was never meant to stay hidden. HOPE lives on in the way you love, in the way you live, in the way you lead.

There is no final arrival in healing. Only the next breath. The next brave choice. The next moment you decide to rise, return, and remember: You are the one you've been waiting.

Revealing the Light Frequency

YOU ARE NOT ONLY A body — you are frequency. Every thought, heartbeat, and breath carries an electrical signal that radiates beyond your skin. Yet we live in a modern world saturated with signals that do not honor this natural rhythm. From 5G towers to Wi-Fi routers, from constant phone notifications to fluorescent lights, we are bathed in frequencies that pull us away from the Schumann resonance — the natural heartbeat of the earth.

Science affirms what ancient traditions always knew: when we live disconnected from the earth's field, our nervous system loses coherence. Sleep cycles become erratic. Mood and energy plummet. Inflammation rises. We call it burnout or anxiety, but at its root, it is often static — misaligned frequency.

But technology is not only an energetic weight — it is also a fragile net we've been taught to depend on. What happens if the grid falters? If the cloud collapses? If the signal disappears and the photos, voices, and memories you trusted it to hold vanish with it?

This is not fear-mongering. It is wisdom — the same kind that kept our ancestors alive when storms came, when fires swept through, when libraries burned and knowledge was scattered. They preserved stories in stone, songs in ceremony, memory in ritual and relationship. They built redundancies, safety plans, and sacred practices that could survive collapse.

The HOPE Method asks you to do the same. Not out of panic, but out of love. To keep backups not only of your data, but of your spirit. To tend to your nervous system so that when the world wobbles, you are not pulled into chaos. To create a plan: Grounding tools: Sheets, mats, and daily barefoot contact with the earth to restore your frequency. Tech hygiene: Keep routers, phones, and devices out of your sleeping space. Create unplugged hours so your nervous system remembers stillness. Backup practices: Print a few precious photos. Write letters to your children. Keep a journal. Make tangible what you don't want lost. Sacred redundancy: Create altars, rituals, or practices that carry memory without electricity. Light candles. Plant trees. Share stories aloud. Resonant spaces: Carve out places in your home and life where no device intrudes, so you can listen to your own pulse without interference.

Because in truth, you are not fragile. You are frequency itself. And when you return to alignment — with earth, with breath, with spirit — you carry stability wherever you go.

The spark of life has always been there — the same spark seen in the moment a sperm enters an egg, the same spark that countless ancestors tended when they lit fires to keep watch through the night. It is the spark that reminds us: even if the world goes offline, the soul never does.

Wisdom Through the Ages: History reminds us how easily knowledge can vanish. When the great Library of Alexandria burned, thousands of years of wisdom — science, medicine, philosophy, and spiritual teachings — were lost in a matter of days.

Entire civilizations have risen and fallen, carrying their discoveries with them into silence. Every thousand years or so, humanity seems to forget and then relearn what once was known.

But the truth is, wisdom never dies. It lives in story, in practice, in the human heart. And when we ground ourselves — barefoot to the earth, voice to the song, breath to the moment — we keep that current alive. HOPE is part of that remembering.

HOPE in Practice: The Gentle Recommitment

EACH MORNING, OR AFTER any stumble, pause long enough to place a hand over your heart and whisper: "I return to HOPE. I return to me."

These words are not about beginning again. They are about remembering that you never left. Healing is not a straight path with a single finish line — it is a circle, a spiral, a rhythm that mirrors the earth itself.

Spring brings the tender shoots of new growth, the first green of possibility. Summer lets your light expand, unapologetic and full. Autumn invites you to release what has run its course, to let the leaves fall without shame. Winter teaches you to rest in silence, to honor stillness as sacred ground.

A HOPE-filled life does not cling to one season or resist another. It allows them all. It welcomes joy and sorrow as companions, both proof that you are alive. It learns to see setbacks not as failures, but as invitations to soften back into rhythm.

Recommitment is not punishment. It is grace. It is the soul's quiet way of saying: You are still here. You are still whole. And you are still walking home.

Wisdom Through the Ages

THE PSYCHIATRIST VIKTOR Frankl, a survivor of the Nazi concentration camps, wrote: "When we are no longer able to change a situation, we are challenged to change ourselves."

Frankl knew grief, despair, and dehumanization on a scale most of us will never face. Yet even in the camps, stripped of freedom and dignity, he discovered something unshakable: the freedom to choose one's response. Out of this revelation, he created logotherapy — a school of thought built on the belief that meaning is the core of human survival.

Those who could not find meaning often lost hope. Those who did — even in unspeakable conditions — found the strength to endure.

This is the work of HOPE. Not to control everything around us, but to alchemize within. To remember that while we cannot always prevent loss, injustice, or fragmentation, we can choose how we carry them. We can choose how we turn suffering into story, despair into devotion, pain into purpose.

Frankl reminds us that the inner life is never fully imprisoned. And the HOPE Method invites us to live in that truth daily — to harness, choose, release, and rise.

HOPE as a Neurological Pattern

HEALING IS NOT ONLY spiritual — it is biological. Every time you return to the practices of HOPE, your brain responds. Neuroscientists call this neuroplasticity — the ability of the brain to rewire itself, forming new connections that align with how we think, feel, and act.

When trauma or chronic stress shapes us, the brain often learns patterns of hypervigilance, self-doubt, or shutdown. But by practicing the HOPE Method daily — even in the smallest moments — you've begun to carve new pathways. Each breath that steadies you, each pause before reacting, each choice to speak kindly or rest intentionally sends a signal: it is safe to be here.

Over time, those signals build into structure. The nervous system relaxes. The body begins to metabolize stress instead of storing it. The mind learns to expect love, trust, and possibility instead of only bracing for threat. This is not lofty theory — it is lived neuroscience.

A HOPE-Filled Life is not about perfection. It is about patterning resilience into your very neurons. It is about ritualizing self-trust until your body believes it. It is about teaching your mind that love is not a rare exception, but the default frequency you were designed for.

This is the great secret: HOPE is not just a feeling. It is a pattern. And the more you practice, the more your whole being learns to rest in its rhythm.

HOPEfully Human Moment

THERE ARE STILL DAYS when I forget everything I teach. Days when dinner is nothing more than crackers, and the shower becomes a sanctuary for tears. But now, I leave a towel waiting —

a small kindness to my future self. Now, I light a candle —

a flicker against the heaviness. Now, I whisper to my reflection

as though she is my oldest friend. And somehow, that is enough.

This is what a HOPE-Filled Life really looks like: not glossy, not linear, but tender, imperfect, and alive.

HOPE in Practice: Your Living Legacy

PAUSE AND ASK YOURSELF: What am I planting with the energy I carry today? What seeds of love, presence, or peace will take root in the wake of my being? What one small act, offered now, could ripple farther than I can see?

Remember, your life is not only measured in milestones. It is whispered through gestures, sung through kindness, etched in the courage to keep showing up. Your life is your message. Let it speak in compassion, in beauty, in breath.

Soul Seed to Take With You

A HOPE-FILLED LIFE is not the absence of hardship. It is the lamp you learn to carry into the dark. It is the courage to soften when the world grows sharp. The wisdom to laugh when sorrow lingers. The grace to begin again — and again — as many times as it takes.

Claiming Your New Identity Through HOPE

YOU ARE NO LONGER THE one searching the shelves for answers, circling back to the same tools that only scratch the surface. You are no longer simply a reader of healing books, gathering quotes but feeling unchanged.

Through HOPE, you have crossed a threshold. You are now the authority of your own energy. You are the one who can sense when your breath grows shallow and choose to soften it. You are the one who can catch the whisper of self-betrayal and answer with compassion instead. You are the one who remembers that joy is not frivolous — it is frequency.

This is your new identity: not seeker, but sovereign. Not survivor, but alchemist. Not fractured, but whole. Traditional models often told you to wait months, even years, for healing to take hold. They asked you to defer to experts, to keep working the same cycle until someone else declared you ready. The HOPE Method is different. It insists that wholeness is not outside you — it was always yours to reclaim.

You carry a living compass inside you. Harness. Optimal. Positive. Energy. When you live in this rhythm, you do not just do the HOPE Method — you become it.

The truth is, your life has already shifted. You notice it in the way you pause before saying yes. In the way you laugh more freely. In the way you allow your nervous system to rest without shame. These are not small things — they are revolutions. And they reveal the authority you now hold: the authority to live your own light. If HOPE has reshaped your identity, what happens when that identity steps beyond the private self — and into community?

Becoming Part of the Movement of HOPE

EVERY TRANSFORMATION ripples outward. A healed breath becomes a softer word. A reclaimed boundary becomes a freer child. A single act of compassion becomes the seed of a legacy. You are not meant to carry HOPE alone. Movements are born when ordinary people remember extraordinary truths together.

The HOPE Method is not a program or a fad — it is a rhythm of living that belongs to empaths, survivors, truth-tellers, cycle-breakers, and soul-seekers. It belongs to those who are tired of performing healing and ready to embody it. It belongs to those who refuse to bypass the pain yet still choose to carry light. You are one of them.

This is your invitation:

To speak the language of HOPE in your home, your work, your friendships.

To live as a carrier of wisdom, serenity, heart, healing, expression, acceptance, and love.

To join the circle of others who have chosen to transmute trauma into power, sorrow into song, and fragmentation into wholeness.

The invitation is not to a club, but to a way of being. And when you say yes, you become part of a lineage — ancient in wisdom, modern in expression, eternal in light.

The next words you read will not only close this book but open a vow — a vow between your soul and the greater whole. In the Epilogue, we step fully into that light together.

Epilogue: The Laws of HOPE

Our healing does not erase our fragmentations or wounds. It transforms them.

Because if memory is energy, and energy is eternal, then every fragment you carry has a vibration. Pain hums. Grief echoes. Sorrow binds. Trauma, left untouched, can loop endlessly — repeating its discord through your body, your breath, and even your lineage.

But when you choose to heal, the story changes. The wound does not disappear as if it never happened. Instead, it is transmuted. The sharpness softens into wisdom. The heaviness reshapes into compassion. The fracture becomes a thread that binds you closer to wholeness. The wound becomes memory, and the memory becomes energy.

This is the Archive Effect: healed energy is never lost. It enters the eternal field, strengthening not only your own soul but others who will one day face similar shadows. Every private victory becomes a public gift.

And this is why you do not need to exile your fragments. They are not proof of brokenness — they are proof of becoming. You can walk alongside them and still live at a higher vibration. In fact, integration is what lifts you.

This is what the Laws of HOPE reveal: that Harnessing, choosing the Optimal, living in the Positive, and embodying Energy are not only steps in a method — they are eternal laws woven into the very fabric of the universe.

The Law of Attraction - Harness

LIKE ENERGY ATTRACTS like. Energy calls energy. What you carry within becomes the frequency you broadcast — and life responds.

Every time you choose compassion over bitterness, or stillness over chaos, you shift your magnetic field. HOPE begins with this inner harnessing, and the world notices.

Hope is like a lantern. Hold it close, and it draws warmth and light toward you. But carry despair, fear, or resentment, and the same magnetism calls back shadows.

The Law of Attraction whispers that what you nurture within becomes the resonance you live in. To Harness your energy with intention is to tend your inner flame — trusting that the outer world adjusts itself to the light you allow yourself to carry.

And remember: there is no comparison when it comes to attraction. Your lantern does not need to shine like anyone else's. Some flames glow steady, others flicker, others blaze. What matters is that you honor your own flame. The world responds not to perfection, but to authenticity.

The Law of Cause & Effect - Optimal

WHEN A PEBBLE FALLS into water, the ripples do not ask permission. They simply expand.

The Law of Cause & Effect teaches that every thought, word, and action sends waves outward into the fabric of life. Nothing you choose exists in isolation. Even what feels small, or unseen has consequences that echo far beyond the moment.

To live in the Optimal is to awaken to this truth. It is to recognize that your soul-honoring choices are not just about survival or self-improvement — they are about creation. Every time you choose forgiveness over resentment, stillness over reaction, or courage over avoidance, you set into motion effects that ripple through families, friendships, communities, and even generations.

Healing is not passive. Every private victory is a cause. Every act of courage, every moment of choosing your truth, is an effect already in motion — one you may never see in full, but one the universe records completely.

HOPE teaches that your optimal choices matter more than you realize. They are not just about shaping your path but about nourishing the lives of all who touch your ripples.

The Law of Detachment - Positive

A FLOWER NEVER CLINGS to the bee, nor does the river cling to the stone. Both give. Both flow. Both allow what is meant to move freely.

The Law of Detachment reminds us that grasping creates resistance. Control is the enemy of peace. Positivity, in its truest form, blossoms not from force but from surrender.

To live in the Positive is not to deny pain or decorate sorrow with false smiles. It is to open your hands, release what cannot be held, and trust that what is truly yours will never pass you by. Detachment is not indifference — it is confidence in divine timing, in the flow of life, in the gentle truth that you do not need to chase what is already meant for you.

True positivity is not forced light. It is the quiet courage to stop clutching at what drains you and trust that joy will find you when you make space for it to land.

HOPE reminds us that surrender is not weakness — it is strength, because it takes greater faith to release than to control.

The Law of Polarity - Energy

SHADOW AND LIGHT ARE not enemies but partners. Energy is refined when both are honored and integrated.

Everything has its opposite. Grief and joy, shadow and light, silence and song. Healing is not about erasing the dark but about learning to see it as the contrast that reveals the light.

Night teaches us to cherish the morning. Winter sharpens our hunger for spring. Grief carves the hollow where joy can one day sit.

The Law of Polarity reveals that everything has its opposite. Light and dark, joy and sorrow, silence and song, fracture and wholeness. To embody Energy is to allow polarity to refine you.

Shadow and light are not enemies; they are partners. Together, they create contrast — the backdrop that allows you to see truth clearly. Without shadow, you would never know light. Without loss, joy would have no depth. Without fragmentation, wholeness would carry no meaning.

Your private victories often arise not from escaping darkness, but from walking courageously through it. HOPE lives in this sacred middle — the space where brokenness transforms into wholeness, where polarities are honored and integrated, where your energy becomes steady, resilient, and whole.

The Law of Vibration – the Song of HOPE

EVERYTHING HUMS. STONES sing low, stars sing high, and even silence carries a tone. Your body has its own melody—the steady rhythm of your heartbeat, the rise and fall of your breath, the quiet current of your thoughts. Nothing in creation is ever still. All is vibration.

The ancients knew this truth. They felt the song of the earth beneath their feet, the chant of water over stone, the drumbeat of their pulse in prayer. To them, healing was not merely about mending the body or calming the mind; it was about tuning the soul. They understood that wholeness comes when one is being is raised into resonance with truth, love, and freedom.

This is the Law of Vibration: what you are, you resonate—and what you resonate, you broadcast into the archive of eternity. HOPE itself is a vibration practice. To harness is to listen to the note you are currently humming. To choose what is optimal is to refine that note, releasing what is off-key. To live in the positive is to raise your pitch into trust, joy, and peace. To embody energy is to send your resonance outward as a gift to the whole.

Yet a compass of vibration still asks for practice. How do you shift your frequency in daily life? This is where WiSH-to-HEAL becomes the pathway. Each of its seven steps serves as a tuning process, raising or refining your vibration until your scattered pieces hum as one. Wisdom lifts you from confusion into clarity, altering the frequency of thought. Serenity stills the static, harmonizing your inner rhythm with peace. Heart opens and amplifies, radiating love that draws matching frequencies back. Healing integrates what was fractured, turning chaos into steady strength. Expression releases your truth outward, broadcasting clarity into the world. Acceptance ends resistance, restoring a natural flow of energy. And Love, embodied at the root, anchors your resonance so that it becomes steady, safe, and enduring.

Like strings on an instrument, each energy center is tuned one by one until the whole being resonates in harmony. WiSH-to-HEAL is not separate from the Law of Vibration; it is its daily embodiment—the act of raising, refining, and broadcasting your soul's frequency.

The Law of Vibration reminds you that you are not static, not broken, not silent. You are a living frequency, an instrument forever capable of tuning. Every choice you make draws you either closer to love or deeper into dissonance. And always, the invitation remains: through the HOPE Method you reclaim authenticity, self-love, and sovereignty — and in raising your own vibration, you help lift the world.

Closing Reflection

The ancients taught these truths long before we gave them names. They knew that what is remembered, lived, and loved becomes eternal.

Healing does not erase your wounds or fragmentations — it transforms them. The scar remains, but the vibration shifts. The broken pieces are gathered into wholeness, and what once weighed you down becomes part of the energy that lifts you higher. You do not need a shelf of supplements to heal your soul. (Though your body may benefit from nourishment, and we will honor that in the supplemental guide.) What you truly need is the courage to live in harmony with the laws of the universe. Because when you do, your frequency rises — and when your frequency rises, you not only change your life, but you also change the entire world.

There is no comparison on this path. Your healing will never look like anyone else's, and it is not meant to. Each soul hums in its own tone. Each lantern shines with its own glow. And every time you lift your own frequency, you contribute a note to the great song of humanity. Your private victories are public gifts.

Your frequency is your offering. And your HOPE is the vibration the world has been waiting for. So let it begin — with you.

Author's Note

Writing this book was never about handing out answers. It was about remembering. About gathering the fragments of my own story and laying them here in case they might spark a remembering in you too.

The HOPE Method was not born out of perfection — it was born out of necessity. It became my compass when life felt unlivable, my lantern when everything went dark. It taught me that even the smallest flicker of light is enough to guide us forward.

This is not a doctrine. It is a devotion. A love letter to the resilience of the human soul.

If even one sentence here helped you pause, breathe, or remember who you are beneath the ache. Then this book has done its work.

We are all just walking each other home. Sometimes barefoot. Sometimes messy. Sometimes radiant. Always human.

Acknowledgements

To the ones who walked beside me in the dark — thank you for your steady hands, your open hearts, and the way you reminded me that I was never truly alone.

To the healers, mentors, therapists, and sacred strangers who showed up at just the right time — your presence lit lanterns along my path, and your wisdom still echoes in my soul.

To my children — you are my greatest teachers, the living proof of unconditional love. And to the soul of my daughter, who now dances in light — every word in these pages carries your heartbeat.

To every reader, seeker, and survivor who dared to open this book — thank you. You are the reason HOPE keeps rising.

And to the Divine, the Mystery, the Great Source of Light — may this offering ripple outward in ways I cannot see, touching the world with love.

About the Author

Sharon Lea is an empathic, intuitive, clairvoyant healer who once struggled to understand the very gifts that now define her work. For years, she carried grief, trauma, and questions about why her sensitivity felt like both a burden and a calling. Out of that struggle, the HOPE Method — Harness Optimal Positive Energy — was born. First created as a survival map for herself, it has grown into a transformative system that helps others reclaim energy, embody sovereignty, and walk in vibrational resonance.

Born and raised in the mountains of Montana, Sharon grew up with grit, wonder, and a love for wide-open skies. She often jokes that she knows a little bit about a lot of things — just enough to be dangerous — but the truth is, curiosity has always been her compass. It keeps her exploring, experimenting, and creating new ways to weave healing into everyday life.

She is the founder of WiSH-to-HEAL, a company devoted to trauma-informed, soul-centered healing. Through her books, workshops, SoulHOPE™ app, and HOPE & Honey™ apothecary line, Sharon offers tools that blend nervous system awareness, ancient wisdom, and spiritual practices into accessible, practical guidance. Her WiSH-to-HEAL framework teaches others to recognize their shadows and walk alongside them with compassion, turning fear into a guide instead of an enemy.

A lifelong learner, Sharon delights in geeking out on philosophy and ancient teachings. She believes the manuals of the ancients were never meant to be forgotten but applied to the challenges of our time. Every day she learns something new, and she steps into the world with a curious mind and an adventurous heart. She loves with her whole being; unconditionally and fully, until given a reason not to, and even then, she chooses grace as often as she can.

Outside of her work and stoic demeanor, Sharon is a wild soul at heart. She journals among wildflower dreams, stirs apothecary blends in her kitchen, laughs with ease alongside her children and grandchildren, and rests in the encouragement of her greatest love shines through kindness, attention, and protection that keep her steadfast on the path she was born to walk.

Her life is proof that joy and hope can bloom even in unexpected places. And her work is an invitation: not just to heal, but to remember who you are, and to live in resonance with both your light and your shadow.

Final Blessing

May your breath be your anchor. May your heart stay tender, even when the world feels sharp. May you find meaning in the mess and music in the silence. May your healing be yours alone — not rushed, not compared. Remember: you are not broken. You are becoming. You are remembering. You are light.

Walk with it. Dance with it. Rest with it. Share it. And when the world grows heavy, may HOPE rise to meet you — in your bones, in your belly, and in your beautiful becoming. Trust that healing is not a finish line, but a rhythm. Your light is not something to search for, but something to free.

You are not behind. You are blooming. You are not too late. You are right on time. Carry this HOPE into every space you enter, every silence you keep, and every soul you touch — especially your own. And when the world grows loud, come home here: to yourself, to this page, to your power, to HOPE.

Resources & Sources

Suggested Readings, Tools & Teachings

The following resources reflect the blend that shaped this book — ancient wisdom, modern science, trauma-informed healing, and holistic living. They are not prescriptions, but invitations. Explore them as steppingstones. Question them. Follow the ones that light you up and leave the rest behind.

This book does not attempt to provide an exhaustive list of every healing practice, therapy, or tradition. There are countless paths that support trauma and grief recovery. I chose to highlight those most relevant to the HOPE Method — practices that align with its rhythm of Harnessing, Optimal choice, Positive energy, and embodied Energy. My hope is that these examples serve as doorways of exploration while honoring that no single book could contain the full breadth of human healing wisdom.

Trauma & Somatic Healing

BESSEL VAN DER KOLK – The Body Keeps the Score

Peter Levine – Waking the Tiger, Healing Trauma

Resmaa Menakem – My Grandmother's Hands

Francis Weller – The Wild Edge of Sorrow

Megan Devine – It's OK That You're Not OK

Tara Brach – Radical Acceptance

Richard Schwartz – Internal Family Systems (IFS) (parts work and trauma integration)

Polyvagal-informed therapy resources (Deb Dana, The Polyvagal Theory in Therapy)

Neuroscience, Psychology & Healing the Mind

NORMAN DOIDGE – THE Brain That Changes Itself, The Brain's Way of Healing

Jill Bolte Taylor – My Stroke of Insight, Whole Brain Living

Stephen Porges – The Polyvagal Theory

Gabor Maté – When the Body Says No, The Myth of Normal

Imposter Phenomenon Research – Clance & Imes (1978); Parkman (2016); Sakulku & Alexander (2011)

Viktor Frankl – Man's Search for Meaning (logotherapy and meaning in suffering)

Positive Psychology research – Martin Seligman (Flourish, Learned Optimism)

Positivity, Gratitude & Laughter

BARBARA FREDRICKSON – Positivity

Research on Positive Affect & Health – Moskowitz et al. (2012)

Gratitude Studies – Emmons & McCullough (2003); Wood, Froh & Geraghty (2010)

Laughter & Healing – Berk et al. (1989); Mora-Ripoll (2010)

Swearing & Pain Relief – Stephens, Atkins & Kingston (2009); Stephens, Robertson & Allsop (2020)

Energy, Frequency & Spiritual Science

JOE DISPENZA – BECOMING Supernatural

Bruce Lipton – The Biology of Belief

Candace Pert – Molecules of Emotion

HeartMath Institute – Heart coherence research

Frequency & Sound Healing – Tuning forks, binaural beats, sound baths, music as medicine

Breathwork Studies – Hajek et al. (1987, 1989); Gerritsen & Band (2018)

Rupert Sheldrake – Morphic Resonance (fields and collective memory)

Masaru Emoto – The Hidden Messages in Water (vibration and intention in water molecules)

Anodea Judith – Eastern Body, Western Mind

Spirituality, Archetypes & the Soul

CAROLINE MYSS – ANATOMY of the Spirit, Sacred Contracts

Clarissa Pinkola Estés – Women Who Run With the Wolves

Thich Nhat Hanh – The Miracle of Mindfulness, Peace Is Every Step

Rumi & Hafiz – Sufi poetry

Maya Angelou – Writings on belonging, resilience, and spirit

Carl Jung – Archetypes, shadow, collective unconscious

Joseph Campbell – The Hero with a Thousand Faces

Feminine archetypes (Sophia, Oshun, Hecate, Tara, Magdalene, Hildegard, Isis, Inanna)

Masculine archetypes (Christ, Krishna, Shiva, Odin, Apollo)

Holistic Practices & Daily Living

AYURVEDA & HOLISTIC Nutrition

Chinese Medicine & Meridian Theory

Reiki & Energy Healing

EFT (Emotional Freedom Technique)

Breathwork & Meditation Traditions – Pranayama, mindfulness, contemplative prayer, mantra

Journaling – free writing, guided prompts, trauma-informed reflection

Somatic Movement – yoga, dance, walking meditations, nature immersion

Creative Expression – art, music, writing

Community Healing Circles

Akashic Record Reading

Conscious Clothing & Vibrational Fabrics (Soul-Aligned Fabric Field Guide)

HOPE Nourishment tools (14-Day Plan, Soul & Vessel Reset)

Clinical Supports & Recommended Therapies

WHILE THE HOPE METHOD is designed as a self-guided rhythm for recovery, it can be deeply complemented by clinical and therapeutic supports. These evidence-based approaches are widely recognized for their effectiveness in trauma and stress recovery:

Eye Movement Desensitization & Reprocessing (EMDR): Evidence-based therapy that helps reprocess traumatic memories through guided eye movements, reducing their impact on the nervous system.

Somatic Experiencing (SE): A body-based approach that aligns with the somatic practices mentioned in this book — restoring safety, presence, and balance to the nervous system.

Cognitive Behavioral Therapy (CBT) / Cognitive Self-Change: A structured method of noticing, questioning, and reframing thought patterns, similar to the cognitive self-change principles explored here.

Mindfulness-Based Stress Reduction (MBSR): A proven program of meditation, breath, and mindful awareness that complements HOPE's emphasis on nervous system resets and energy regulation.

Contemplative Science & Modern Research

MARCUS AURELIUS – MEDITATIONS

Epictetus – The Enchiridion

Seneca – Letters from a Stoic

Davidson et al. (2003) – Meditation, neuroplasticity, immune function

McEwen (2007) – Stress, cortisol, long-term health

Toussaint et al. (2015) – Forgiveness and stress

Pennebaker (1997) – Journaling and immune health

APA (2021) – Social media & mental health

Pew Research Center (2020) – Teens, Social Media & Technology

Inspirations & Guiding Voices

MARY OLIVER – POETRY as prayer

Hildegard of Bingen – Mystic visions

Rumi & Hafiz – Sufi poets

Maya Angelou – Truth and belonging

Marcus Aurelius, Seneca, Epictetus – Stoic guides

Clarissa Pinkola Estés – Myth and story as medicine

Viktor Frankl (logotherapy and meaning)

Teresa of Ávila & Julian of Norwich (Christian mysticism, union with God)

Rumi's The wound is where the Light enters as reminder of HOPE

Supplemental Nourishment

SUPPLEMENTAL NOURISHMENT Guide — a trauma-aware companion for vitamins, minerals, and vibrational foods.

APPENDIX

The HOPE Method Foundational Tools

Full Guide with Pillars and Chakras

The **HOPE** Method is a trauma-informed, spiritually aligned framework for Harnessing Optimal Positive Energy. It is designed to guide individuals through the process of reclaiming their energy, making soul-aligned choices, redefining positivity, and embodying their highest vibrational self.

The Four Pillars of the HOPE Method

SELF-AWARENESS — The ability to recognize your own energy state, emotional patterns, and thought cycles.

Self-Regulation — Tools and practices to bring your nervous system and energy into balance.

Self-Honoring Choices — Consistently choosing what aligns with your highest well-being.

Soul Connection — Living in alignment with your inner truth, spiritual purpose, and highest frequency.

H – Harness · Acknowledge · Reclaim · Direct

HARNESSING IS THE CONSCIOUS act of gathering, containing, and reclaiming your scattered energy after trauma, grief, or depletion. It means becoming aware of where your energy is leaking and taking steps to bring it back into alignment. Harnessing involves nervous system regulation, breathwork, grounding practices, and setting firm boundaries to stop energetic leaks. It is the first step in regaining control over your life force.

Harnessing is awareness turned into action. It is reclaiming what was lost and directing it toward your healing. **Affirmation**: "I call back my energy from every place I have left it. I am safe to hold my own light." **Chakra**: Root (Muladhara) — grounding, safety, nervous system regulation. **Crystal Companion**: Black Tourmaline — protection and anchoring. **Food/Beverage**: Root vegetables, earthy soups, mineral-rich broths. **Essential Oil/Herb**: Cedarwood or vetiver for grounding; nettle tea for stability. **Movement Practice:** Grounding breathwork or pressing feet firmly into the earth. **Harness** = safety + stability → reclaiming your ground and personal fire.

O – Optimal · Align · Choose · Evolve

OPTIMAL IS CHOOSING what is best for your soul, not simply what is familiar. It is a conscious shift toward habits, environments, and relationships that nourish rather than drain. This includes soul-aligned decision-making, saying no to what harms your nervous system, and restructuring life to allow optimal healing conditions.

Optimal living is not perfection; it is alignment. Each choice becomes a declaration: I am worthy of what sustains me, not just what I've survived. **Affirmation**: "I choose what serves my highest good, even when it feels unfamiliar." **Chakra**: Solar Plexus (Manipura) — clarity, willpower, soul-aligned decisions. **Crystal Companion**: Citrine — willpower, clarity, and confidence. Food/Beverage: Ginger tea, turmeric golden milk, or warming spices to fuel courage. **Essential Oil/Herb**: Rosemary or lemon for clarity and activation. **Movement Practice**: Journaling choices (two columns: drains/nourishes) or strong core postures. **Optimal** = clarity + willpower → aligning choices with inner vision and voice.

P – Positive · Honor · Cultivate · Uplift

POSITIVE IN THE HOPE Method is not about forced happiness or toxic positivity, but about cultivating authentic moments of joy, gratitude, and connection even in the presence of grief or challenge. This means creating space for creativity, laughter, pleasure, and community while honoring emotional truth.

Positivity here is not about denying the shadow — it's about letting light and shadow dance together, creating balance instead of bypass. **Affirmation**: "I allow joy to coexist with my healing." **Chakra**: Heart (Anahata) — joy, gratitude, compassion. **Crystal Companion**: Rose Quartz — softening and expanding love. **Food/Beverage**: Fresh fruits, green vegetables, or cacao for heart-opening. **Essential Oil/Herb**: Rose or bergamot; hawthorn tea for heart vitality. **Movement Practice**: Dance, laughter yoga, or creative expression like painting or singing. **Positive** = heart expansion + creative flow → joy that coexists with truth.

E – Energy · Protect · Refine · Elevate

ENERGY IS THE FREQUENCY and vibration that flows through and around you. Healing means raising and refining this frequency, so it supports your mental, emotional, physical, and spiritual well-being. Practices include energy hygiene, breathwork, grounding, nourishment, movement, and intentional rest.

Energy is not something you "have" — it is something you are. Every thought, word, and action shapes the current you live in. When you learn to protect what drains you and elevate what restores you, you step into coherence — a state where body, mind, and spirit hum in harmony. **Affirmation**: "I am a vibrant being of light. My energy flows in harmony with my soul." **Chakra**: Crown (Sahasrara) — connection to source and divine flow. **Crystal Companion**: Clear Quartz — amplification and harmonizing. **Food/Beverage**: Clean water, herbal infusions, hydrating fruits. **Essential Oil/Herb**: Frankincense or peppermint; ginseng tea for vitality. **Movement Practice**: Somatic shaking, sun salutations, or restorative yoga to reset vibration. **Energy** = flow + frequency → living as a vibrant being of light, grounded yet elevated.

HOPE in Practice: The Four-Minute Flow

JUST AS WISH-TO-HEAL offers a seven-minute rhythm, HOPE can be practiced daily in four simple steps — one minute for each pillar:

Harness: Place your hands on your belly, take one deep grounding breath, whisper: "I call my energy home."

Optimal: Write down one aligned choice for today and say it aloud.

Positive: Smile, even softly. Name one thing you are grateful for.

Energy: Stand tall, inhale with arms overhead, exhale and release. Whisper: "I am light."

Four minutes. Four steps. The compass of HOPE, alive in your day.

The HOPE Method offers the compass: Harnessing your energy, choosing what is Optimal, releasing into the Positive, and embodying Energy as your gift to the world. It is the orientation, the true north that shows you what alignment feels like. But a compass alone is not enough—you must walk with it. That is where WiSH-to-HEAL comes in.

WiSH-to-HEAL is the second layer of the HOPE Method, the steady rhythm that turns insight into embodiment. If HOPE tells you where to go, WiSH-to-HEAL shows you how to get there. It takes the philosophy of HOPE and breathes it into your body, weaving soul awareness into your every step.

Through Wisdom, Serenity, and Heart, you anchor yourself in awareness and presence—learning to pause, breathe, and soften into compassion. Through Healing, Expression, Acceptance, and Love, you turn that awareness into transformation—shedding old patterns, releasing what you carry, and opening yourself to wholeness.

HOPE points the way. WiSH-to-HEAL is how you live it. Moment by moment. Breath by breath. Center by center. Until your whole being hums in alignment and you remember what it feels like to come home to yourself.

WiSH-to-HEAL

The Daily Rhythm

WiSH-to-HEAL is the daily rhythm within the HOPE Method. If HOPE is the compass, WiSH-to-HEAL is the steady walk beneath your feet—the gentle cadence that carries you home. It is a soul-song of seven notes, guiding you through awareness, balance, and embodied love, aligning crown to root until your whole being hums in resonance.

Each step is both tender and transformative. Wisdom opens the page, inviting you to listen as your soul writes itself back into being. Serenity arrives like a still breath, settling the storms within. Heart whispers, "Feel—don't flee," teaching compassion for yourself and others. Heal asks you to stand honest and accountable, knowing your story is the soil where new roots grow. Expression is the exhale, the dance, the release that frees what no longer belongs. Acceptance softens your edges, allowing you to walk with what is, without resistance. And Love—the final note—is where the whole song resolves, where you embody the HOPE Method: Harness Optimal Positive Energy. Here, pain becomes strength, fear becomes faith, and heaviness lifts into healing.

Together, these steps form not just a path, but a rhythmic pulse you can return to again and again—restoring harmony to your mind, your body, and your soul.

W – Wisdom · See · Know · Discern

WISDOM IS THE CROWN of healing — the capacity to see clearly and to remember that you are more than your pain. It opens you to divine awareness and reconnects you with your higher self.

Affirmation: "I connect."

Chakra: Crown (Sahasrara).

Crystal Companion: Amethyst — clarity, vision, spiritual connection.

Food/Beverage: Warm water, lavender tea, or holy basil — clearing and calming the mind.

Essential Oil/Herb: Frankincense or sandalwood for focus and attunement.

Movement Practice: Journaling for 2–5 minutes, a self-inquiry mind-dump, or silent meditation.

Wisdom Through the Ages: Mirrors the alchemists' Separation — the courage to see truth and name it.

Wisdom = awareness + discernment → remembering you are more than your pain.

S – Serenity · Still · Calm · Trust

SERENITY IS THE QUIET strength that comes when you allow your nervous system to settle and your mind to still. It is the practice of trusting the flow of life rather than resisting it. Serenity does not mean life is without storms; it means you carry calm in the middle of them. Serenity is trust, breath, and stillness flowing together.

Affirmation: "I see."

Chakra: Third Eye (Ajna).

Crystal Companion: Lapis Lazuli — calm focus, intuition, inner sight.

Food/Beverage: Chamomile or peppermint tea — soothing and cooling.

Essential Oil/Herb: Lavender or clary sage — settling restless energy.

Movement Practice: 2–3 minutes of deep breathing or guided meditation.

Wisdom Through the Ages: Echoes the alchemists' Dissolution — softening what is rigid, allowing flow to return.

Serenity = stillness + trust → carrying peace through life's storms.

H – Heart · Open · Feel · Connect

THE HEART IS THE CENTER of healing. Here, compassion, forgiveness, and connection take root. To feel is to heal. To return to the heart is to return to connection — with yourself, with others, and with the divine. Healing requires heart, because love is the frequency that restores wholeness.

Affirmation: "I love."

Chakra: Heart (Anahata).

Crystal Companion: Rose Quartz — compassion, forgiveness, tenderness.

Food/Beverage: Green tea or leafy greens — nourishing vitality.

Essential Oil/Herb: Rose or hawthorn — opening the heart and softening grief.

Movement Practice: Hand-to-heart meditation, or a simple act of feeling presence without fleeing.

Wisdom Through the Ages: The alchemists called this Conjunction — the sacred union of soul and emotion.

Heart = openness + compassion → the center where healing begins.

H – Heal · Integrate · Strengthen · Renew

HEALING IS INTEGRATION — gathering scattered pieces back into wholeness. It is accountability, honesty, and the fire of renewal. Healing does not mean erasing the wound; it means stabilizing your willpower and transforming chaos into steady strength.

Affirmation: "I act."

Chakra: Solar Plexus (Manipura).

Crystal Companion: Citrine — strength, confidence, renewal.

Food/Beverage: Ginger or golden milk with turmeric — warming and strengthening.

Essential Oil/Herb: Rosemary or eucalyptus — clearing stagnation and fueling inner fire.

Movement Practice: Journaling about accountability or core-strengthening postures.

Wisdom Through the Ages: Reflects the alchemists' Calcination — burning away what no longer serves.

Heal = integration + renewal → strength made steady through wholeness.

E – Express · Speak · Create · Release

EXPRESSION IS HOW YOUR truth takes form in the world. When you voice your feelings, share your art, or live authentically, you broadcast your frequency with clarity. Expression is the exhale — breath, voice, creativity, truth taking shape in the world. It frees trapped energy and makes the unseen visible.

Affirmation: "I speak."

Chakra: Throat (Vishuddha).

Crystal Companion: Aquamarine — courage in communication, fluid expression.

Food/Beverage: Herbal teas with honey, or cooling fruits like pear or apple.

Essential Oil/Herb: Peppermint or blue chamomile — opening breath and voice.

Movement Practice: Breathwork, singing, humming, or simple free movement.

Wisdom Through the Ages: Parallels the alchemists' Fermentation — awakening new life through breath and spirit.

Express = truth + creation → energy released as authentic voice.

A – Accept · Allow · Flow · Belong

ACCEPTANCE IS THE GENTLE art of ending resistance. It does not mean approval of harm, but rather a willingness to let life move freely through you. Acceptance restores flow, helping you reconnect with your body, emotions, and sense of belonging. Acceptance is surrender without collapse.

Affirmation: "I feel."

Chakra: Sacral (Svadhisthana).

Crystal Companion: Carnelian — creativity, vitality, safe belonging.

Food/Beverage: Orange fruits, coconut water, or teas that restore flow.

Essential Oil/Herb: Ylang-ylang or jasmine — sensuality, joy, release.

Movement Practice: Hip-opening stretches, gentle swaying, or walking meditation.

Wisdom Through the Ages: Aligns with the alchemists' Distillation — refining shadow into clarity.

Acceptance = allowance + flow → restoring rhythm and belonging.

L – Love · Ground · Embody · Radiate

LOVE IS THE FOUNDATION and culmination — grounding you in safety and radiating through every center. It is sovereignty, authenticity, and divine alignment. Embodied love makes you unshakable. It is both your anchor and your offering.

Affirmation: "I am."

Chakra: Root (Muladhara).

Crystal Companion: Black Tourmaline — grounding, protection, stability.

Food/Beverage: Root vegetables, warm soups, herbal infusions.

Essential Oil/Herb: Cedarwood or patchouli — anchoring and earthy.

Movement Practice: Standing strong, feet pressed into the earth, visualizing roots of light.

Wisdom Through the Ages: The alchemists called this Coagulation — the embodied gold of transformation, wholeness realized.

Love = grounding + radiance → embodied love as your foundation and gift.

HOPE in Practice: The Seven-Minute Flow

HEALING is not only found in deep sessions or long reflections. It is also in the simple rhythms of return. This flow touches each step of WiSH-to-HEAL daily — one minute per step, seven minutes to come home to yourself.

Wisdom: One-minute mind-dump journaling.

Serenity: One minute of slow breath (inhale 4, exhale 6).

Heart: Hand-to-heart, whisper: "I forgive myself."

Heal: Speak one accountability truth: "I choose growth in…"

Express: Exhale with sound — a sigh, a hum, a word. Move your shoulders.

Accept: Whisper: "I allow what is." Release your jaw, soften your belly.

Love: Press feet into the ground. Whisper: "I am safe. I am love."

Seven minutes. Seven steps. A daily rhythm of remembrance.

The HOPE Method gives you the compass: Harness your energy, choose what is Optimal, live in the Positive, and embody your Energy. WiSH-to-HEAL gives you the rhythm: Wisdom, Serenity, Heart, Healing, Expression, Acceptance, and Love. One is direction, the other is cadence. Together they form a complete map — universal law paired with daily practice — guiding you from knowing into becoming, from fragmentation into wholeness.

These hidden rhythms remind us that healing is not just doing but attuning — aligning with patterns of flow that are ancient and always within reach. And beneath it all, there are deeper patterns still.

Hidden Rhythms of Frequency

NOT ALL HEALING IS visible. Across mystic traditions and modern science, we glimpse hidden rhythms — spirals, vortices, torus fields — the same geometry that shapes galaxies, atoms, rivers, and the human heart. These patterns remind us: energy is not linear but circular, forever renewing.

The torus offers one such image — energy rising up through the body, arcing outward, then returning through the center. Breath mirrors this rhythm: inhale expands, exhale returns. Light and life move in the same way.

Whether you hold this as metaphor or metaphysics, it offers an invitation: to feel yourself as part of the ancient flow. Healing is not only doing but attuning — aligning your daily rhythm with the greater pulse that has always held you.

So, as you practice HOPE, as you walk the steps of WiSH-to-HEAL, imagine yourself within this living current. Breath rising. Energy circling. Love returning. A loop of grounding and expansion — a hidden rhythm made visible through your own embodied light.

Somatic Wheel Practices

The Body's Language of Stress

Your body speaks in sensations long before the mind finds words. Use this quick-reference guide to notice what your body is saying — and how to respond through WiSH-to-HEAL.

Mental fog, headaches, or overthinking → Often scattered thoughts or stress overload. Practice: Quick journaling to release the mind's clutter, or a brief pause in silence.

HOPE Step: Wisdom — I connect.

Eye strain, racing thoughts, or insomnia → Often overstimulation. Practice: Gentle eye covering, three slow breaths, or brief stillness with eyes closed.

HOPE Step: Serenity — I see.

Chest tightness or heaviness → Often grief, anxiety, or sadness. Practice: Gentle heart-opening stretches, hands over the chest, or slow deep breaths.

HOPE Step: Heart — I love.

Knotted stomach, nausea, digestive upset → Often fear or disempowerment. Practice: Belly breathing, gentle abdominal massage, or placing warm hands on the belly.

HOPE Step: Healing — I act.

Jaw clenching or tight shoulders → Often unspoken anger or held tension. Practice: Neck rolls, mindful yawns, or humming to release vibration.

HOPE Step: Expression — I speak.

Heavy back or slumped posture → Often shame, burden, or feeling unsupported. Practice: Stand tall, roll shoulders back, or take a mindful walk to reset posture.

HOPE Step: Acceptance — I feel.

Numbness or dissociation → Often overwhelm or emotional shutdown. Practice: Ground by pressing feet into the floor, tapping arms/legs, or naming objects around you.

HOPE Step: Love — I am.

Group Application Guide

The HOPE Method is designed to be practiced both individually and in community. Healing multiplies when we are witnessed in safe, supportive spaces. If you are a facilitator, therapist, or practitioner, consider the following adaptations:

Opening

BEGIN WITH A GROUNDING practice (deep breath, short silence, or shared affirmation) to create safety. Set agreements around confidentiality, respect, and self-care.

Sharing

INVITE PARTICIPANTS to reflect on the HOPE prompts. Remember and remind them that listening is as valuable as speaking, and that silence can be part of healing. Participation is always optional.

Practice

CHOOSE ONE "HOPE IN Practice" exercise to experience together — a guided journaling pause, gentle breathwork, mindful movement, or collective gratitude practice.

Integration

ENCOURAGE EACH PERSON to carry one small action home for the week — such as reflection, breath practice, or new boundaries and revisit it at the next gathering.

Closing

END WITH GRATITUDE, affirmation, or acknowledgment of the courage it takes to heal in community. Optionally, invite a brief ritual (lighting a candle, sharing a word of hope, or a group breath) to mark completion.

Additional Notes

Always emphasize safety: participants are free to step out, journal privately, or pass on sharing. Adapt the method for different needs — age, culture, and accessibility all shape how groups connect. Healing in community is not about perfection but presence.

For those who wish to go deeper: SoulHOPE offers guided practices, journaling spaces, and meditations that make it easy for groups to stay connected between sessions.

The HOPE Practitioner Certification Program provides advanced training and tools for those ready to integrate the HOPE Method professionally, with structure, community, and support.

Quick Start Guide

The HOPE Method

Step 1: Harness

Notice where your energy is leaking (through thoughts, relationships, environment). Reclaim your energy with grounding, breath, or a single centering practice.

Step 2: Optimal

ASK: IS THIS CHOICE optimal for my soul, or just familiar? Choose what nourishes and restores, even if it feels new or uncomfortable.

Step 3: Positive

REDEFINE POSITIVITY as authenticity. Allow joy, creativity, forgiveness, and grief to co-exist. Practice daily gratitude or expression that feels real, not forced.

Step 4: Energy

TREAT YOURSELF AS FREQUENCY. Align your body, mind, and spirit through nourishment, movement, stillness, and space. Remember: energy is not endless — it requires tending.

Practice Rhythm:

REPEAT THESE FOUR STEPS daily in any situation. Return to them whenever you feel fragmented, drained, or disconnected.

Healing Rhythms

A 14-Day Reset: Soul & Vessel Reset

A 14-day energetic clearing plan designed to support your body, nervous system, and soul. This is not a diet — it's a gentle invitation to rest, release, and realign with your natural vitality. Through intentional nourishment, hydration, and soul practices, you create space for your healing light to rise.

Phase 1: Ground & Release (Days 1–4)

FOCUS: Calm the system, reconnect with the body, create a foundation of safety.

Day 1 – Arrival

MORNING: WARM LEMON water.

Movement: 10 minutes of stretching or yoga.

Soul Practice: Write one line: "Today I honor my body's pace."

Affirmation: "I am safe to begin again."

Day 2 – Rooting In

MEALS: STEAMED VEGETABLES, root-based soups.

Movement: Gentle walk outside, notice your breath with each step

Evening: Light a candle before bed.

Prompt: "Where does my body already feel safe?"

Day 3 – Letting Go

ADD GROUNDING FOOT soak with Epsom salt.

15 minutes of slow movement (tai chi, restorative yoga).

Journaling: Write what you're ready to release this week.

Affirmation: "I let go of what is heavy."

Day 4 – Steady Presence

KEEP FOODS SIMPLE (smoothies, soups, teas).

Try dry brushing or gentle lymph massage.

Evening breathwork: 4-7-8 breathing.

Prompt: "When I slow down, what wisdom rises?"

Phase 2: Clear & Cleanse (Days 5–10)

FOCUS: Gently detox, reduce inflammatory triggers, create space for renewal.

Day 5 – Clearing Space

ELIMINATE sugar, dairy, processed oils.

Add leafy greens + healing proteins.

Journaling: "What clutter — physical or emotional — am I ready to clear?"

Affirmation: "My body knows how to renew."

Day 6 – Release Through Breath

BREATHWORK: BOX BREATHING (4-4-4-4).

Meals: Broths + herbal teas.

Evening: Write down worries, then symbolically "release" (tear, burn, or bury).

Day 7 – Flow

ADD FERMENTED FOOD (sauerkraut, kimchi) to support gut health.

20 minutes walking meditation — notice rhythm of steps.

Affirmation: "I move with the flow of life."

Day 8 – Softening

KEEP MEALS LIGHT, COLORFUL vegetables.

Practice silence for 30 minutes.

Prompt: "What do I most need to forgive myself for?"

Day 9 – Nourish the Lymph

GENTLE REBOUNDING (mini trampoline or bouncing).

Warm herbal tea (ginger, peppermint, or chamomile).

Evening: Salt bath with intention to cleanse.

Affirmation: "I am cleansed. I am clear."

Day 10 – Trusting the Rhythm

CONTINUE WHOLE-FOOD meals.

15 minutes of intuitive movement (dance, shake, sway).

Journaling: "Where in my life can I trust the process more?"

Phase 3: Realign & Radiate (Days 11–14)

FOCUS: Rebuild energy, invite joy, cultivate vibrancy.

Day 11 – Inviting Radiance

ADD FRESH FRUIT + SPROUTED grains.

Movement: Dance to one joyful song.

Affirmation: "I invite light into my body."

Day 12 – Joyful Nourishment

MEALS: AVOCADO, OLIVE oil, bright vegetables.

Practice: Sunlight exposure (10–15 min).

Prompt: "What joy am I willing to claim today?"

Day 13 – Creative Energy

TRY A PLAYFUL ACT: doodle, collage, sing.

Movement: Rebounding or a walk in nature.

Affirmation: "Creativity flows freely through me."

Day 14 – Celebration & Integration

COOK A COLORFUL, SOUL-nourishing meal.

Reflection: Review journal from Day 1. Note what has shifted.

Evening practice: Write a gratitude letter to your body.

Affirmation: "I am radiant. I am whole. I am aligned."

Closing Note: This is not about perfection or strict rules. It's about rhythm, renewal, and remembering that your vessel is sacred. Every choice — each sip of water, each intentional breath, each gentle release — is a vote for life.

Vibrational Nourishment

A Soulful Beginning

True nourishment isn't just about calories or macros — it's about energy. Every food, every activity, and every intention we carry holds a vibration. That vibration either supports your healing or disrupts your harmony.

Vibrational nourishment means choosing what makes your soul feel light, your cells feel alive, and your spirit feel supported.

Foods that grow from the earth, bask in the sun, or carry life force in their color and texture tend to vibrate higher. Likewise, movement that feels like joy, rest that feels like love, and rituals that invite presence all feed your frequency.

This is not a diet — it's a reunion with your body's intuition. Start where you are. Listen. Choose what uplifts. Leave what depletes. And remember: Your vessel is not a project. It is a temple.

Vibrational Foods to Favor

THESE FOODS CARRY A living frequency that supports clarity, grounding, and cellular vitality. Choose what resonates with your season of healing.

Fresh, organic fruits (especially berries, pears, apples, mango, melon, citrus)

Leafy greens and herbs (spinach, arugula, parsley, cilantro, nettle)

Root vegetables (sweet potato, carrots, beets, jicama)

Whole ancient grains (quinoa, millet, amaranth, wild rice)

Plant-based proteins (lentils, mung beans, soaked nuts/seeds)

Clean animal proteins (pasture-raised eggs, wild fish, organic poultry)

Healing fats (avocado, coconut, cold-pressed olive oil)

Fermented foods (if tolerated: sauerkraut, coconut yogurt, kefir)

Vibrational Activities

SUPPORT YOUR FREQUENCY with movement, stillness, and intentional engagement:

Morning sunlight on your face

Barefoot walking on natural ground

Dance, stretch, sway, simply move like no one is watching

Breathwork and slow exhales

Restorative baths or warm showers

8+ hours of healing sleep

Journaling or intuitive doodling

Time in nature — trees, rivers, dirt, sky

HOPE in Practice: Nourishment as Reverence

EACH TIME YOU PREPARE or eat something, pause to ask: "Does this nourish my light?" "Am I choosing this to love myself or to punish myself?" Let your food be a prayer. Let your rest be an offering. You're not healing to become someone new. You're healing to remember who you are.

Gentle Foods Energy Card

THESE FOODS TEND TO be more calming and body-safe for those sensitive or prone to inflammation:

Peeled pears

Peeled apples (golden or pink)

White rice or jasmine rice

Carrots (cooked)

Zucchini (peeled)

Cucumber (peeled)

Organic turkey or chicken

Coconut milk (plain)

Chamomile or rooibos tea

Peaceful Cup Morning Practice

THIS GENTLE, GROUNDING drink is a sacred start to your day – made with carob, coconut milk, and love. It's designed for those with sensitivities, and it's safe, soul-soothing, and delicious.

Ingredients

1 cup brewed coffee or chicory root coffee

1/2 cup unsweetened coconut milk (or oat milk if tolerated)

1 tsp carob powder (optional or to your taste less is more)

Optional: pinch of vanilla bean, dash of sea salt, or ground flax

Optional: 1 scoop of collagen or protein powder, dash of cinnamon or vanilla extract Stir with intention. Inhale deeply. Sip slowly. Let your body guide you into the day.

Preparation: Brew your base: coffee or a caffeine-free herbal alternative like roasted chicory root. In a small pan or milk frother, warm your coconut milk with the carob powder, vanilla, and salt. Whisk gently. Combine the milk mixture with your brewed base in your favorite mug. Whisper a blessing: "May this potion fill me with peace, ground my mind, and remind me I am safe in this moment." Sip slowly and soulfully. Let it become a practice of presence and nourishment.

Optional Morning Mantras: "I sip serenity. I exhale doubt." "My body is a friend to my healing." "This moment is enough. I am enough."

Mini Food & Energy Tracker

TRY USING THIS SIMPLE tracker to reflect on how food feels — not just how it tastes.

Meal/Snack: Energy After (1–10):

Mood or Emotion Noticed:

Body Reaction (Swelling? Calm? Tingling?):

Would I eat this again? Why or why not?

HOPE Insight Quote

"SOMETIMES THE WEIGHT we carry isn't just on our bodies, it's in the rules we followed that were never made for us."

Daily HOPE Tracker

USE THIS TRACKER DAILY or weekly to gently check in with yourself. This is not about perfection; it is about awareness and intention. Return to it often and let it evolve with you.

Date: _____ Energy Level: Low / Medium / High

Emotional Climate: _____

Physical Sensations: _____

What I Need Today: _____

Frequency Support (Sound/Oil/Movement): _____

One HOPE Practice I Committed to Today: _____

Self-Speak or Affirmation of the Day: _____

Closing Thought or Blessing: _____

Vibrational Living

A Guide to Plastic-Free & Soul-Aligned Swaps

A HOPEful Replacement List for Elevated Living

As you raise your vibration, you'll begin to notice what supports your frequency... and what subtly drags it down.

This guide offers soul-aligned swaps that help you replace energetically stagnant items (like plastic or Teflon) with materials that honor the Earth, your body, and your evolving consciousness.

These aren't rules — they're invitations. Choose what resonates and begin, one breath at a time.

Kitchen & Food Storage

INSTEAD OF PLASTIC baggies - Choose beeswax wraps, cloth covers, or glass containers. These options breathe with your food, keep it safe without suffocating it, and invite you into a rhythm of reuse instead of waste.

Instead of plastic water bottles - Carry stainless steel or glass bottles. Your water tastes purer, free of chemical leaching, and every sip becomes a small act of care for both your body and the earth.

Instead of Teflon cookware - Cook with cast iron, stainless steel, or ceramic. These elemental tools are timeless, non-toxic, and durable — vessels that connect your meals to generations of nourishment.

Instead of plastic straws - Sip through stainless steel, glass, or bamboo. Each use feels intentional, reusable, and earth-honoring, reminding you that even the smallest daily choices ripple outward.

Instead of plastic cutting boards - Chop and prepare food on bamboo or wood boards. Natural fibers hold memory and grounding energy, turning the simple act of slicing vegetables into an ancient rhythm of preparation.

Self-Care & Body

INSTEAD OF PLASTIC razors - Choose safety razors with solid metal handles. They last for years, reduce waste, and carry the grounding weight of durability in your hand.

Instead of plastic toothbrushes - Brush with bamboo. These biodegradable tools return gracefully to the earth and carry a simplicity that feels elegant in its honesty.

Instead of plastic lotion bottles- Opt for glass jars or refillable aluminum pumps. Natural containers preserve the energy of what they hold and invite you into a cycle of reuse rather than discard.

Instead of synthetic loofahs - Cleanse with a natural sea sponge or a sisal brush. Earth-grown and compostable, they gently polish the skin while reconnecting you with the textures of nature.

Instead of plastic combs and brushes - Use wooden combs or boar bristle brushes. Natural fibers soothe the scalp, reduce static, and harmonize with your body's energetic field.

Home & Energy Field

INSTEAD OF SCENTED plastic plug-ins - Choose essential oil diffusers made of ceramic or glass. They carry cleaner energy, infuse your space with plant-based aroma, and turn scent into a subtle ritual of renewal.

Instead of polyester cleaning cloths - Wipe with cotton, hemp, or bamboo. Plant-based fibers are biodegradable, gentle on the earth, and feel softer against both skin and spirit.

Instead of plastic organizers - Store with woven baskets, reclaimed wood boxes, or glass containers. Natural materials harmonize your home's energy, reminding you that order can feel alive, not sterile.

Instead of disposable lighters - Use rechargeable electric lighters or simple matches. Both reduce waste and transform a spark into a mindful moment — a flame that feels ceremonial rather than disposable.

Instead of plastic trash bags - Choose compostable bags or paper liners. They break down naturally, offering a gentler option for both the earth and your own energetic field.

Energy & Clarity

Soul-Aligned Fabric Field Guide

A Conscious Closet Companion from Wild Soul HOPE™

What you wear is more than fashion — it's frequency. The fabrics that touch your skin daily influence your energy field, your nervous system, and even your sense of self. This guide was created to help you make vibrationally aligned clothing choices that feel modern, grounded, and soul-nourishing.

This isn't about becoming perfect or purist. It's about becoming aware.

The Energetic Vibe of Fabrics

COTTON - Grounding, breathable, and familiar. Cotton holds the comfort of earth and body, making it a staple for daily wear and restful bedding. It is steady and neutral, a fabric that feels like home.

Linen - Cooling and high-vibration, linen carries an ancient wisdom in its fibers. Strong yet softening with every wash, it whispers of endurance and lightness, like wind moving through wheat fields.

Wool - Protective, warm, and ancestral. Wool carries the memory of flocks and firelight, shielding the body with a primal strength. But energy teaches us this: wool and cotton cancel each other when worn together, one charged positive, the other negative. The blend dulls their natural gifts, muting their frequency. Wool is best honored alone, allowing its warmth and protection to shine fully.

Silk - Luxurious and sensual, silk hums at a high vibration. Smooth as water, it carries both elegance and intensity, often holding the imprints of emotion. To wear silk is to drape yourself in memory — so choose it for moments when you want your presence to be deeply felt.

Hemp - Earthy, strong, and resilient. Hemp resists bacteria and thrives with durability. It is a fabric that refuses fragility, grounding the wearer with stability and offering the body a protective layer of the earth's medicine.

Bamboo - Light, hypoallergenic, and soft. Bamboo feels like gentleness itself, cooling the skin while reminding you of nature's adaptability. Chosen organically or through closed-loop processing, it honors the earth as much as the body.

Spandex - Restrictive and synthetic. Designed for flexibility yet often constricting natural flow, spandex fuels performance but rarely nurtures presence. Worn too long, it can leave the body feeling cut off from its own frequency.

Polyester - Dense, static-prone, and low-vibration. Non-breathable and resistant to decay, polyester often holds the body in stagnation. It carries convenience, yes — but rarely connection.

Rayon / Viscose - Smooth and versatile, born from natural fibers yet altered by heavy processing. When responsibly sourced, it can offer balance between comfort and eco-consciousness, though its vibration is gentler than raw plant-based fabrics.

Conscious Clothing Swaps: Dressing with Energy in Mind

INSTEAD OF SYNTHETIC leggings - Slip into cotton or bamboo stretch leggings. Breathable and soft, they release static and let your body move with ease. Your skin sighs in relief when it can actually breathe.

Instead of poly sports bras - Choose natural-fiber support bras. Comfort becomes a quiet companion, holding you without harsh compression. Your chest expands, your breath deepens, your heart softens.

Instead of fast fashion tees - Reach for 100% cotton or hemp shirts. These fibers age with you, growing softer over time, offering not only natural feel but true longevity. They carry the patience of plants, not the rush of factories.

Instead of microfiber bedding - Curl into linen or cotton sheets. Breathable, cooling, and timeless, they invite the body to rest more deeply, allowing each night's sleep to become repair instead of battle.

Instead of cheap synthetics - Seek out thrifted natural-fiber pieces. Not only do you lighten your impact on the earth, but you also wrap yourself in energy that has already been softened by life, carrying stories yet ready for your own.

Caring for Fabric, Honoring Energy

YOUR CLOTHING HOLDS energy. Wash with natural detergents, dry in sunlight, or refresh with herbal smoke, salt soaks, or sound rituals. You don't need to replace everything overnight.

Start with: Replacing worn-out pieces with better fabric options

Noticing how you *feel* in certain clothesCreating a conscious closet that breathes with your spirit

You deserve to feel supported— skin to soul.

Nourishing The Vessel

A HOPEful Guide to Supplements

Vitamins and minerals are quiet guardians — unseen, yet essential to the harmony of your body. They are the catalysts of energy, the subtle sparks that keep your heart steady, your thoughts clear, and your immune defenses strong. In an ideal world, every need would be met through the rhythm of food, seasonal, whole, and nourishing. But modern soil is depleted, stress fragments digestion, and the pace of life leaves many bodies running on empty. This is where supplements can serve as bridges, not replacements, but companions chosen with wisdom.

The Case for Testing Before Guessing

SUPPLEMENTS ARE POWERFUL tools, yet without clarity, they can become costly guesses. Your body deserves more than trial and error. This is why full blood panels matter. Ask a trusted physician or practitioner to check your vitamin D, your B12, your iron, your magnesium, your thyroid and hormone markers, and your levels of inflammation.

These tests shine light on what is truly missing, guiding you toward precision instead of uncertainty. When you choose from knowledge rather than fear, your supplements become allies instead of burdens.

What to Look For in Quality Supplements

PURITY IS THE FIRST promise — supplements should be third-party tested, free from contaminants, and true to their label.

Transparency is essential — avoid vague "blends" that hide what you're really taking.

Bioavailability matters — choose active forms your body can receive, like methylated B vitamins or magnesium glycinate.

Simplicity is kindness — skip the dyes, the sweeteners, the fillers that do not serve you.

Consistency builds trust — look for companies that publish batch tests and show reliability across every product.

Forms That Work Best

LIQUIDS AND LIPOSOMALS — deeply absorbable, though often costly, best used for children or short-term needs.

Capsules and tablets — the most common but choose clean capsules free from coatings that burden digestion.

Powders — versatile for blending into food or drink, though always check for hidden sugars or flavors.

Whole food based — gentler on the system, drawn from herbs or concentrated foods, and often easier to integrate.

Supplements Worth Considering

VITAMIN D3 WITH K2 — for immune strength, bone health, and mood.

Magnesium (glycinate, malate, citrate) — for rest, sleep, and muscle relaxation.

B Complex (methylated) — for energy, nervous system balance, and clarity.

Omega-3 fatty acids (fish or algae oil) — for heart, brain, and cellular vitality.

Probiotics or fermented foods — for gut harmony and resilience.

Supplements to Be Cautious About

MEGA-DOSING — MORE is not always better; fat-soluble vitamins can be toxic in excess.

Cheap multivitamins — often poor quality and poorly absorbed.

Supplements from unknown sources — if transparency is absent, trust your intuition and avoid.

Trendy powders or miracle blends — often more marketing than medicine.

A Seasonal Approach to Supplementation

SUPPLEMENTS ARE NOT meant to replace whole food nourishment. Think of them as seasonal allies or as gentle support that helps your body flow with the rhythms of nature. Just as the earth shifts in light, temperature, and harvest, your body shifts in need. Listening to these cycles allows you to offer timely care.

Winter: With less sunlight, many people benefit from vitamin D to lift mood and support immunity. Omega-3s can help reduce inflammation and bring steadiness during colder, heavier months.

Spring: A season of renewal. Herbs like milk thistle or dandelion root support gentle liver detox and help the body release what it no longer needs, mirroring the fresh growth around you.

Summer: Heat and activity call for hydration and mineral balance. Electrolytes, magnesium, or trace minerals help steady your energy and prevent depletion when the sun is strongest.

Autumn: As the air cools and routines return, probiotics support gut health and resilience, while vitamin C bolsters the immune system for the seasonal shift.

Supplements are most powerful when paired with awareness. Notice how your body responds and choose what feels aligned with your current season of life — both in nature and within yourself.

Supplement Reference Guide

A sensitivity-aware resource for conscious healing.

These are the allies I've found most supportive in my own journey — companions that bridge gaps and help restore balance. They are not prescriptions, but possibilities. Each carry both gifts and cautions, and your body remains the wisest guide. Work with a trusted holistic practitioner, seek out proper testing, and let these words be a doorway for your own discernment.

Please remember supplements affect everyone differently. What nourishes one body may overwhelm another. This guide is an invitation to explore, not a directive. Before beginning any new regimen, speak with your physician, holistic practitioner, or trusted health guide. Ask for proper testing when possible and let research and discernment walk alongside you.

Phosphatidylserine (PS) is a gentle companion for the mind and nervous system. It supports clarity, helps soften the edges of cortisol spikes, and steadies emotional waves. I've found sunflower-derived forms to be clean and kind, though many capsule versions contain soy or fillers that may not serve sensitive systems.

Saffron extract carries the light of joy — a golden thread that can lift mood and soften anxious energy. For empaths, it can feel like a buffer when emotions run too high. Yet saffron is also a spice with a moderate salicylate load, so it must be met with mindfulness. Low doses, taken slowly, are often enough, and it's wise to pause if inflammation stirs.

Shilajit, especially in sun-dried tablet form, is mineral-rich and deeply grounding. It strengthens stamina, supports mitochondrial fire, and can bring a subtle focus. Dissolved in warm water, it becomes a nourishing tonic. For hypersensitive bodies, though, even small amounts may feel too stimulating — so I recommend beginning with micro-doses only a few times a week.

Magnesium glycinate is a balm for the body — easing muscles, quieting the nervous system, and opening the door to restful sleep. It is one of the most reliable allies for sensitive systems. Still, not all forms are equal. Chewables often hide flavors or sweeteners that irritate. Clean powders or simple capsules usually serve best.

Medicinal mushrooms — reishi, chaga, lion's mane, and others — have long been revered for their immune wisdom and longevity support. Yet for those with salicylate sensitivity, histamine issues, or aspirin allergy, they can trigger inflammation instead of easing it. They are powerful teachers, but not always gentle ones.

Trace mineral drops offer another way to replenish. Just a few drops in water can restore hydration at the cellular level and strengthen immunity. Their taste can be earthy, even sharp, but the effect is subtle strength. Go slow, one or two drops at first, and let your body adjust.

Iron with vitamin C may be needed when energy wanes, especially for those prone to deficiency. Gummies are convenient but often come with synthetic ascorbic acid or flavorings that burden sensitive bodies. I lean toward liquid forms, or Floravital: gentler and more easily absorbed.

Spirulina is like sunlight condensed into deep green powder: rich in protein, chlorophyll, and antioxidants. It nourishes cells, supports detox, and carries an almost electric vitality. Yet its intensity can be too much for some, stirring digestion or overwhelm. Begin with the smallest pinch, and honor what your body says in return.

Chlorella is a companion for cleansing — a binder of heavy metals, a purifier of inner waters. It supports cellular renewal and gives strength after depletion. Like spirulina, it is potent, and not every system receives it as a gift. Choose clean, lab-tested sources and introduce it slowly, as if meeting a new teacher.

Vibrational Sound & Frequency Guide

SOUND IS ONE OF THE oldest medicines we know. Every culture has used it — chants, drums, lullabies, bowls, bells — to shift energy and open space for healing. Modern science now confirms what ancient wisdom always held: that vibration in the form of sound changes our brain waves, calms our nervous system, and helps the body reorganize itself toward balance.

Listening to music at specific frequencies can shift your state:

Foundational Frequencies

174 → A FREQUENCY OF safety and stability, often associated with easing pain and tension.

285 → Cellular support; thought to encourage tissue repair and energetic realignment.

→ Releases fear and guilt; grounding for those carrying

heavy trauma.

→ Clears old patterns and supports new beginnings.

Relational Frequencies

528 → THE "MIRACLE TONE," linked with DNA repair, heart opening, and renewal.

639 Hz → Resonates with love, compassion, and harmonious relationships.

Expressive & Spiritual Frequencies

741 → BRINGS CLARITY, detoxification, and freedom of expression.

→ Awakens intuition and strengthens spiritual awareness.

963 Hz → Sometimes called the "Divine frequency," associated with unity consciousness and pineal activation.

Natural & Brainwave Frequencies

7.83 HZ → THE SCHUMANN resonance, also called the Earth's heartbeat: grounding and stabilizing.

Theta wave entrainment (4–8 Hz) → Encourages meditation, dreams, and creativity.

Alpha wave entrainment (8–12 Hz) → Calm focus and learning.

Gamma (30–40 Hz) → Linked with heightened states of awareness, compassion, and insight.

Practice in Daily Life

SOUND BATHS WITH GONGS, crystal bowls, or chimes help clear stagnant energy and restore harmony. But you don't need special equipment — even a simple playlist can become vibrational medicine when you listen with intention. What matters is choosing sound that restores you, not overwhelms you.

At its heart, sound reminds us: you are made of vibration, and you can be tuned back into resonance.

Crystals

Companions in Healing

Crystals are not magic tricks or quick fixes — they are companions. Each one carries a unique vibration, shaped by the earth over millions of years. When you hold them, wear them, or keep them nearby, you invite their steady frequency to remind your own energy of balance, clarity, or protection.

A crystal bracelet can rest against your pulse, harmonizing with your rhythm. A small satchel in your pocket or under your pillow can lend its energy through the day or night. What matters most is not perfection in ritual, but intention: the willingness to let these natural allies support your journey.

Crystals for the 12 Energy Touch Points

WISDOM (CROWN): CLEAR Quartz — amplifies clarity, connection, and divine wisdom.

Serenity (Third Eye): Amethyst — calms mental chatter, opens intuition, deepens stillness.

Heart: Rose Quartz — softens grief, awakens compassion, and invites unconditional love.

Healing (Solar Plexus): Citrine — rekindles inner fire, confidence, and vitality.

Expression (Throat): Blue Lace Agate — eases communication, dissolves fear of speaking.

Acceptance (Sacral): Carnelian — supports creativity, pleasure, and emotional flow.

Love (Root): Red Jasper — anchors safety, stability, and grounded strength.

Hands: Labradorite — shields from energy drains, strengthens creativity.

Feet: Hematite — grounds scattered energy, anchors you in belonging.

Hara (Lower Abdomen): Moonstone — soothes emotional cycles, nurtures feminine wisdom.

Back of the Heart: Rhodonite — heals betrayal and heartbreak, reopens trust.

Aura: Black Tourmaline — clears heaviness, protects boundaries, transmutes negativity.

Other Protective & Supportive Allies

OBSIDIAN: A MIRROR stone that reveals truth and protects from hidden shadows.

Selenite: Cleanses energy fields and charges other crystals with gentle light.

Smoky Quartz: Transmutes fear into clarity, anchors light in heavy times.

Labradorite: A shield for empaths, guarding against energy leaks.

Fluorite: Clears confusion, strengthens mental focus, supports energetic hygiene.

How to Care for Your Crystals: Crystals carry energy — yours, and what they absorb for you. Just as you tend your body, they too benefit from being refreshed.

Cleansing: Moonlight, selenite, smoke, or salt. Place them in moonlight (especially full moon), rest them on a bed of sea salt or selenite, or rinse them gently in clean running water (note: some crystals are water-sensitive — check first).

Charging: Sunlight (short), intention, or breath. Set them in sunlight for a short time or hold them in your palms and breathe intention into them. Imagine light filling the stone until it glows.

Intention: Hold and name your purpose — protection, grounding, peace. Whisper your purpose into the crystal. Name the support you are seeking — protection, grounding, courage, or peace. Intention is the bridge between you and the stone.

Closing Invitation: Crystals are not the healer. You are. But they are steady companions — reminders that the earth itself longs to hold you, protect you, and call you back into alignment. When you slip on a bracelet, tuck a satchel into your pocket, or place a stone under your pillow, let it be more than a ritual. Let it be a whisper: You are not alone. You are held. You are safe to heal.

Pineal Clarity

Sensitivity-Aware Resource – Conscious Seekers

The pineal gland — often called the third eye — is more than a tiny crystal in the brain. It is a rhythm keeper, a dream maker, a compass of intuition. Many traditions teach that calcification, stress, and toxins can dim its light. While science is still catching up, ancient wisdom and modern research agree on this: your choices — food, light, minerals, rest — can nourish the pineal back to resonance.

This guide was created not only to give you a starting point, but to place tips and tools directly at your fingertips. That way, when you sit down with your health advocates — whether a physician, a holistic practitioner, or a trusted mentor — you already have language, questions, and options in hand. Think of this as both a compass and a conversation starter: a way to align your daily choices with clarity, while also partnering more fully with those who support your healing.

Soul Seed to Take With You

THE PINEAL GLAND doesn't need fixing. It needs remembering. Supplements can help, but it is presence, rhythm, and light that polish the inner lens.

Vitamins & Nutrients

Vitamin K2

WHY: GUIDES CALCIUM into bones instead of soft tissues, helping prevent calcification. When to be cautious: Always pair with Vitamin D3. Not a substitute for balanced diet.

Vitamin D3

WHY: REGULATES CIRCADIAN rhythm and immune health, supports pineal function. When to be cautious: Fat-soluble — test your levels to avoid excess.

Magnesium (glycinate, malate, citrate)

WHY: BALANCES CALCIUM, calms the nervous system, aids deep rest. When to be cautious: High doses can cause loose stools — start gently.

Iodine

WHY: DISPLACES FLUORIDE, supports thyroid and metabolic balance. When to be cautious: Needs practitioner guidance; too much can disrupt thyroid health.

Methylated B-Complex (especially B12)

WHY: REPAIRS NERVES, clears brain fog, sharpens intuition. When to be cautious: Over-supplementing can overstimulate sensitive systems.

Plant Allies & Superfoods

Raw Cacao

WHY: ANTIOXIDANT-RICH, heart-opening, and dense in magnesium.

When to be cautious: Naturally stimulating — small amounts may be best.

Chlorella & Spirulina

WHY: BIND HEAVY METALS, support detox, enhance energy clarity.

When to be cautious: Choose clean, tested sources — some powders are contaminated.

Sea Vegetables (Kelp, Nori, Dulse, Wakame)

WHY: NATURAL IODINE sources help balance thyroid and pineal health.

When to be cautious: Can be high in sodium and iodine — don't overdo.

Turmeric / Curcumin

WHY: POTENT ANTI-INFLAMMATORY, brain-protective, may reduce micro-calcification.

When to be cautious: Can thin blood; check if on medications.

Cayenne Pepper

WHY: IMPROVES CIRCULATION and oxygen delivery, supporting pineal detox.

When to be cautious: May irritate sensitive stomachs.

Ginger

WHY: ANTI-INFLAMMATORY, supports digestion, enhances circulation.

When to be cautious: Can thin blood — use with care alongside medications.

Pineapple (especially core)

WHY: RICH IN BROMELAIN, supports circulation and reduces inflammation.

When to be cautious: Naturally high in sugar — balance with protein/fiber.

Gotu Kola

WHY: AYURVEDIC HERB for meditation, subtle awareness, and "third eye" clarity.

When to be cautious: Can be mildly sedating; avoid excess.

Raw Honey

WHY: ENZYMES AND TRACE minerals, supportive of immune and vibrational energy.

When to be cautious: Not for infants under 1 year.

Hazelnuts

WHY: VITAMIN E AND healthy fats for brain and nervous system support.

When to be cautious: Allergens for some; keep portions moderate.

Shilajit

WHY: MINERAL-RICH ADAPTOGEN, boosts energy, resilience, and longevity.

When to be cautious: Must be purified — choose reputable sources only.

Blueberries & Dark Berries

WHY: ANTIOXIDANTS FOR brain health, memory, and cellular repair.

When to be cautious: Best consumed fresh or frozen, not overly sweetened.

Beets

WHY: RICH IN NITRATES that increase oxygen and blood flow to the brain.

When to be cautious: Can temporarily tint urine/stool — harmless but surprising.

Coconut Oil / MCTs

WHY: PROVIDE CLEAN brain fuel and enhance ketone production.

When to be cautious: High calorie density — use as part of a balanced diet.

Lemon / Citrus

WHY: GENTLE DETOXIFIER, vitamin C-rich, enhances hydration.

When to be cautious: Can erode tooth enamel — rinse after drinking.

Apple Cider Vinegar

WHY: SUPPORTS DIGESTION, alkalizes body, enhances mineral absorption.

When to be cautious: Always dilute — can damage enamel if taken straight.

Optional Allies to Consider

Holy Basil (Tulsi)

WHY: ADAPTOGEN THAT calms stress, supports clarity, enhances meditation.

When to be cautious: May lower blood sugar — monitor if diabetic.

Rosemary

WHY: ANTIOXIDANT-RICH herb, historically used for memory and mental clarity.

When to be cautious: Concentrated oils can be too strong — stick to culinary use or teas.

Ginkgo Biloba

WHY: INCREASES CIRCULATION to the brain, enhances memory and focus.

When to be cautious: Can thin blood — avoid if on anticoagulants.

Mineral Support

Boron

WHY: COUNTERACTS FLUORIDE build-up, supports bone and hormone balance.

When to be cautious: Needs careful dosing; more is not better.

Trace Mineral Drops

WHY: REPLENISH ESSENTIAL minerals for cellular hydration and energy flow.

When to be cautious: Start with one or two drops; flavor can be strong.

Zeolite or Bentonite Clay

WHY: NATURAL BINDERS for heavy metals and toxins.

When to be cautious: Must be food-grade; hydrate well to avoid constipation.

Soul Seed to Take With You

SUPPLEMENTS ARE NOT shortcuts, but companions. They are bridges that carry you back toward balance — when chosen with care, and when your body's own wisdom leads the way.

Soul Practices That Matter More Than Pills

SLEEP IN DARKNESS to encourage melatonin and pineal repair.

Choose clean water — filter fluoride where possible.

Soak in sunlight every morning to reset circadian rhythm.

Meditate, hum, chant, or listen to healing tones — vibration nourishes the pineal.

Ground in nature — barefoot on soil, trees, rivers; the earth re-tunes your inner crystal.

HOPE in Practice: Food First, Supplement Second

WHENEVER POSSIBLE, choose food sources first:

Vitamin C → citrus, bell peppers, berries

Magnesium → leafy greens, nuts, seeds

Omega-3 → wild salmon, walnuts, flax, chia

Iron → lentils, spinach, grass-fed beef

B vitamins → eggs, whole grains, nutritional yeast

Then, if bloodwork or symptoms reveal a gap, use supplements as bridges.

Soul Seed to Take With You

SUPPLEMENTS ARE NOT shortcuts. They are reminders. Reminders to return to nature. Reminders to listen to your body's needs. Reminders that healing is not about chasing pills, but choosing nourishment — whether from the Earth, the sun, or the wisdom passed down through generations.

HOPE in Practice: Journals for Healing

HEALING INVITES US to become both witnesses and storytellers of our own lives. Writing is not about neat sentences — it is about listening. When pen touches paper, patterns emerge. The body begins to speak.

Keep two simple journals — nothing fancy, even a spiral from the corner store will do. Nothing must be perfect or polished — just real.

The Daily Awareness Journal is where you track the rhythm of your days: energy rising and falling, sleep that soothes or eludes you, foods that nourish or inflame, emotions that swell, symptoms that whisper, breathe that grounds. Over time, these messy pages become a map of your becoming. You begin to see what restores you, what depletes you, what your body has been trying to say all along.

The Wellness & Provider Journal is your bridge to care. Before appointments, carry forward notes from your daily pages: the patterns you've noticed, the questions you need answered, the places where clarity is still missing. Write down lab results, instructions, or shifts in treatment. Let this little book be your advocate — a reminder that your healing is a collaboration, not a guessing game.

Together, these journals become a dialogue: between your soul and your body, between your body and those entrusted to its care. Most importantly, they keep you connected to the truth: your body is always speaking, and you are learning how to listen.

Soul Seed to Take With You

YOUR JOURNALS ARE MORE than paper and ink. They are living proof that you are listening, learning, and leading your own healing.

Important Note

THE INFORMATION SHARED here is not medical advice. It is meant as a gentle starting point with a collection of practices and considerations you may explore as you begin again. Everybody is unique. Supplements, herbs, and even lifestyle shifts can affect people differently. Always consult with your physician, holistic provider, or trusted health guide before beginning any new regimen. Whenever possible, request proper blood work and testing so your path is guided by insight, not guesswork. Let discernment, research, and your own intuition walk beside you.

Companion Chapter Journal

Soul Scribbles: Reflections & Journal Prompts

Welcome to this space of reflection. A sanctuary for your thoughts, your healing, your truth. These are not just prompts, and this is not only a place for words. Think of it as a mirror for your inner landscape and a companion to your transformation. You have already walked through the HOPE Method in these chapters. Now, this section invites you to live it, breathe it, and embody it.

Here, your handwriting is holy. Your pauses are purposeful. Your honesty is honored. And so is your creativity. Healing is not only about what you can explain, but it is also about what you can color, sketch, whisper, dance, or scrawl across the page. Sometimes your soul speaks in sentences. Sometimes it speaks in symbols. Both belong here.

There is no wrong way to engage. You may move in order or jump to the chapter that calls your name. You may write long answers, or simply one word that carries weight. You may doodle, collage, scribble sideways, or tuck flowers and photographs between the lines. This is your sacred space for messy, alive, and utterly your own creativity.

The rhythm is simple

READ THE REFLECTION prompts. Let them stir what is already inside you. Write freely. Do not edit or censor because messy is progress. Even a grocery list can become the doorway to deeper truths.

Create beyond words. After writing, let yourself integrate what you have uncovered in color, symbol, or movement. Draw what pain looks like. Sketch your joy. Paint HOPE. Trace your hand like you did when you were five. Let expression be as wild or tender as you need. Healing is both language and art. Here is where the two meet.

Now that you know how to approach these pages, let the questions that follow be your companions. Each set of reflections is tied to a chapter from The HOPE Method. Not as homework, but as doorways. Some will invite you to look back. Others will nudge you to dream forward. All of them are here to help you weave the teachings of HOPE into the fabric of your own life.

Take them slowly. Return as often as you need. And remember there is no right way to answer, only your way.

Chapter One

Everything You Think You Know About HOPE Is Wrong

WHAT HAVE YOU been told about HOPE — that it is fragile, naïve, or unrealistic? Write down every definition you've inherited. Whose voices shaped those beliefs?

Now pause. If those were distortions, what might the truth be? Journal about moments when hope carried you through — when it was not weakness but endurance, not fantasy but fuel.

Consider how your body feels when you give yourself permission to hope. Does your breath change? Your posture? Your energy? Describe the difference.

Creative Invitation

DRAW THE WORD HOPE in the center of the page. Around it, write the lies you've been told. Then cross them out and replace them with truths you are ready to embody.

Soul Seed to Take With You

HOPE is not an illusion. The illusion is believing you could live without it.

Chapter Two

The Hidden Problem

WHAT IS THE STORY BENEATH your story — the one you rarely say out loud? Write it down without censoring. Notice how it feels to see it on the page instead of carrying it in silence.

Whose voice echoes in that story — a parent, a teacher, a partner, a culture? How long have you been carrying words that were never yours?

Now pause and ask: what if these fragments were never the whole truth of me? Write about the possibility of loosening their grip.

Reflect on how unspoken beliefs live in the body. Where do you feel the weight of shame, fear, or self-doubt? Where does hope or safety soften you? Trace the contrast between constriction and release.

Creative Invitation

SKETCH A MIRROR. ON one side, write the hidden messages you've absorbed. On the other, write the truths you are ready to claim. Let this be your first glimpse of a new reflection.

Soul Seed to Take With You

THE PROBLEM YOU CARRY in silence is not who you are. Naming it loosens it. And every time you choose truth over the old story, you remember yourself more clearly.

Chapter Three

Remembering the Pulse of Being

WHAT DOES IT MEAN TO simply be? Close your eyes for a moment, then open your journal and describe what "being" feels like in your body. Is it stillness, a pulse, a weight, a warmth? Let words rise without editing.

When was the last time you allowed yourself to rest without guilt? Write about that moment or write about why rest feels difficult. Imagine if your body could whisper its gratitude — what would it say?

How do you currently define healing? Has that definition shifted since beginning this journey? Write freely, then sketch a symbol for your healing as it feels right now — maybe a spiral, a flame, a seed, or a broken line mending.

This is not about perfection. It is about presence. Let your pen wander. Let your soul remember.

Creative Invitation

DIP INTO THE PRESENT moment. Trace your hand on the page, and inside its outline, write words or draw colors that capture how "being" feels right now. Each finger can hold a different quality — stillness, breath, warmth, weight, pulse. Let your body leave its imprint of presence.

Soul Seed to Take With You

BEING IS ENOUGH. YOUR breath is proof.

Chapter Four

The Energy Matrix

WHERE IN YOUR BODY do you feel your energy most often — alive and buzzing, or heavy and drained? Write about the patterns you notice.

Think of a recent time when stress took over. How did your body signal depletion? Now recall a moment of joy or safety. How did your body signal abundance? Compare the two maps.

What rhythms or practices help restore your current when it feels scattered? Write about what brings you back into flow.

Creative Invitation

SKETCH YOUR PERSONAL energy map. Mark the places in your body where stress collects, and where joy radiates. Use colors, shapes, or words to show the contrasts.

Soul Seed to Take With You

YOUR ENERGY IS THE quiet current beneath everything. Listen to it, and it will always guide you home.

Chapter Five

Inner Child, Soul Fracture & Reclamation

WHAT MEMORIES ARISE when you picture your inner child? Don't rush. Describe them as if you were telling their story to someone who has never met them. Capture their light, their laughter, even their loneliness. Have you ever betrayed your own innocence to survive? Write about a time when you silenced yourself, denied your needs, or hid who you were. Honor the strength it took but also notice what was lost.

Now, write a letter to your inner child. Tell them what they most need to hear. "You were never too much. You were never too little. You were always enough." If words don't come, draw and let shapes, colors, or doodles carry the message.

Your inner child does not need polished sentences. They need your presence. Give it to them here.

Creative Invitation

FIND OR SKETCH A PICTURE of yourself as a child. On the page, create a frame around it and decorate it with colors, symbols, or words that reflect how you now see them: cherished, magical, whole. Let your journal become a safe home where your inner child belongs.

Soul Seed to Take With You

YOUR INNER CHILD IS still listening. Speak love into them.

Chapter Six

The Four Directions of HOPE

HOPE IS NOT A SINGLE step but a compass. It points us in four directions — Harness, Optimal, Positive, Energy — each one guiding us back to wholeness. When you feel lost, this compass becomes a way to orient yourself again, no matter how stormy life feels.

To Harness is to gather what has been scattered, reclaiming the fragments of your attention, time, and spirit.

To choose the Optimal is to lean toward what strengthens rather than what depletes, even when old patterns tug you back.

To embrace the Positive is to honor joy, forgiveness, and creativity as medicine — not as a mask, but as authentic presence.

To remember Energy is to live as vibration, tending your frequency through breath, body, and awareness.

Which of the four directions feels most natural to me right now?

Which one feels like the hardest to embody? Why?

How can I use HOPE as a compass when I feel scattered or unsure?

Creative Invitation

DRAW A CIRCLE AND DIVIDE it into four quadrants. Label each with a direction of HOPE. In each space, write or sketch how you practice it today — and what you'd like it to grow into tomorrow.

Soul Seed to Take With You

HOPE IS YOUR COMPASS. No matter where you stand, one step in any of its directions leads you closer to yourself.

Chapter Seven

Harness and Reclaim Energy.

YOUR ENERGY IS YOUR lifeline. Every thought, word, and interaction either scatters it or strengthens it. To harness your energy is to call back what has been leaking into fear, people-pleasing, or old wounds — and to reclaim it for your healing, your joy, your life.

Begin by noticing: how do you currently use your voice? Do you use it to heal, to hide, to harmonize? Journal about the ways your words have both freed and silenced you.

When words fail, the body still speaks. Where do sensations arise — in your chest, your throat, your belly? Place your hand there and let it express itself through writing, drawing, or movement.

Reflect on the frequency of love in your life. Not only romantic love, but the love found in friendship, in community, or in the quiet ways you care for yourself.

What is one truth I've been holding in silence that my body longs to release? Where have I been leaking energy, and how can I reclaim it?

Creative Invitation

CREATE A "SOUND MAP" on the page — doodle the shapes of words you want to speak more of (kindness, truth, joy). Color them as vibration, visual reminders of your reclaimed energy.

Soul Seed to Take With You

YOUR VOICE IS MEDICINE. Every truth spoken is a frequency of freedom. Every boundary honored is energy reclaimed.

Chapter Eight

Optimal vs Familiar

FAMILIAR CAN FEEL SAFE simply because it's known — even when it drains you. Choosing what is optimal may feel uncertain at first, but it is the doorway to freedom. Every time you step toward optimal, you are teaching your soul that it is worthy of breathing fully.

Where in your life are you still choosing what's familiar over what's optimal? Be honest with yourself on the page.

What would it feel like to make the optimal choice — even if it feels uncomfortable at first?

Describe the shift you imagine. What patterns are you ready to outgrow? Write them as though you're packing them in a box, preparing to carry them out of your house.

Creative Invitation

DRAW A DOORWAY. ON one side, list what is familiar but draining. On the other, write what is optimal and life-giving. Let your hand decorate the threshold.

Soul Seed to Take With You

FAMILIAR IS NOT ALWAYS safe. Optimal is where your soul begins to breathe.

Chapter Nine

The Power of Positivity

TRUE POSITIVITY IS not about ignoring pain — it's about widening your vision. When you allow grief and joy to share the same table, you discover that joy becomes deeper, more grounded, and more real. Positivity is resilience, not performance.

What does authentic positivity mean to you — beyond forced smiles or toxic optimism?

How do you create space for both grief and joy? Write about how they coexist in your life. List three moments of unexpected beauty you've noticed recently.

What did they stir in you?

What is one small joy I can notice today without dismissing my sorrow?

Creative Invitation

SKETCH THE SUN. IN its rays, write words, colors, or memories that bring you genuine joy.

Soul Seed to Take With You

POSITIVITY IS NOT PRETENDING. It is remembering joy even in the shadow.

Chapter Ten

Energy Hygiene

ENERGY HYGIENE IS NOT indulgence — it is maintenance for your soul. Just as you wash your hands or sweep your floor, tending to your energetic space clears residue that doesn't belong to you and restores what does. This is how you protect your vitality and keep your light strong.

How do you currently cleanse your emotional and energetic space?

What practices help you feel grounded, clear, and aligned?

Where are you leaking energy — and how can you lovingly seal those leaks?

What is one simple act I can do today to clear my energy and call it back to myself?

Creative Invitation

DRAW A CIRCLE AROUND yourself on the page. Inside, write what nourishes you. Outside, write what drains you. Notice what needs to shift.

Soul Seed to Take With You

ENERGY IS SACRED CURRENCY. Spend it with care.

Chapter Eleven

Practices for Regulation

REGULATION IS NOT ABOUT forcing stillness — it is about creating safety so your body and spirit can remember what calm feels like. Even the smallest practices — a sip of water with presence, a deep breath before speaking — teach your nervous system that it is safe to rest and restore.

What daily practices help you feel rooted and calm?

How can you turn an ordinary moment into a sacred one?

What rhythm is your body asking for today?

What is one simple action I can repeat today that tells my body, "You are safe with me"?

Creative Invitation

DESIGN A "DAILY PRACTICE wheel" — draw a circle and fill it with grounding rituals you can rotate through each day.

Soul Seed to Take With You

REGULATION IS NOT CONTROL. It is communion with your rhythm.

Chapter Twelve

The Sacred Nervous System

YOUR NERVOUS SYSTEM is not your enemy; it is your oldest protector. Every racing heartbeat, every tight chest, every restless thought is your body whispering: "I am trying to keep you safe." When you pause to listen without judgment, survival begins to soften into sanctuary.

How does your body respond when it feels safe?

Describe what safety feels like in your skin.

What signals does your nervous system send when it feels overwhelmed?

How can you begin offering compassion to your body in these moments?

Creative Invitation

TRACE THE OUTLINE OF a body. Mark the places where you carry tension, and where you feel most at ease. Notice how your map shifts over time as you learn to listen with love.

Soul Seed to Take With You

YOUR BODY REMEMBERS what the mind forgets. Listen gently.

Chapter Thirteen

Nourishing the Vessel

TRUE NOURISHMENT IS more than food — it is the energy, relationships, and practices that sustain you. When you choose with love instead of shame, your body stops being a project to fix and becomes a sacred partner to cherish.

What does it mean to nourish your vessel with love, not punishment?

What are you ready to release from your body?

How can you create rhythms of nourishment this season?

What is one simple choice I can make today that says to my body, "I am on your side"?

Creative Invitation

ON ONE SIDE OF THE page, write "Fuel." On the other, "Drain." List what nourishes and what depletes you — food, habits, emotions, relationships.

Soul Seed to Take With You

YOUR BODY IS NOT A battleground. It is a garden. Feed it with care.

Chapter Fourteen

Community: Heal Together

HEALING WAS NEVER MEANT to be carried alone. For centuries, people leaned into family, neighbors, and circles of care. Today, we live in a culture of isolation, scrolling more than gathering, silencing struggles as if self-sufficiency were strength. Yet your soul remembers the web of care — to be held, seen, and supported. Community is not perfection but presence: circles where your light is welcomed, your tears honored, and your truth safe. True belonging is not fitting in but being received as you are — while learning to receive others the same.

What does "belonging" mean to you at this season of life?

Where do you feel most seen, most accepted?

How can you begin to build or find soul-aligned community?

What boundaries help you feel safe within community?

Creative Invitation

DRAW A CIRCLE AND PLACE yourself in the center. Around you, write the names of people, groups, or communities that bring you life. Then notice the empty spaces. Who or what kind of community would you like to invite into your circle?

Soul Seed to Take With You

COMMUNITY IS A MIRROR. It reflects back the truth that you were never meant to heal in isolation. Belonging multiplies hope.

Chapter Fifteen

Emotional Alchemy

EVERY EMOTION CARRIES a message. Grief asks us to honor love. Rage asks us to defend what matters. Tenderness asks us to soften and trust. When you listen instead of resisting, emotions become allies — raw energy that can be shaped into wisdom and strength.

Which emotion have you been resisting — and why?

How might you express grief, rage, or tenderness creatively?

What happens when you stop judging your emotions and begin listening to them?

If your emotion could speak one sentence to you right now, what would it say?

Creative Invitation

ON A BLANK PAGE, GIVE your avoided emotion a color and shape. Let your hand draw what it feels like.

Soul Seed to Take With You

YOUR EMOTIONS ARE NOT enemies. They are alchemists, turning pain into wisdom.

Chapter Sixteen

Somatic Healing & Frequency Repair

YOUR BODY IS AN INSTRUMENT, and every experience leaves an echo in its strings. Somatic healing is the process of gently retuning those strings, while frequency and sound act as vibrations that remind your body what harmony feels like.

Where in your body do you still carry old fragmentation?

What touch, movement, or sound practice brings you the most peace?

How does music, frequency, or sound shift your state of being?

What is one sound I can invite into my day — a hum, a chant, or a piece of music — to remind my body, it is safe?

Creative Invitation

CREATE A "SOUND DIARY." Write the names of songs, chants, or sounds that soothe you. Sketch how they feel in your body.

Soul Seed to Take With You

HEALING HUMS IN EVERY cell when you let vibration move through you.

Chapter Seventeen

Neuroplasticity & Self-Speak

EVERY THOUGHT YOU REPEAT is like water carving a groove in stone. Over time, those grooves become the paths your brain walks most easily. When you choose words of love and possibility, you are not lying to yourself — you are rewiring your brain to believe in your own worth.

What words do you most often repeat to yourself? Are they loving or limiting? Write a new internal dialogue rooted in love and possibility.

What would change if you spoke to yourself like someone you loved?

What is one phrase of love I can repeat today until it feels true in my body?

Creative Invitation

WRITE YOUR LIMITING beliefs in pencil, then cross them out in ink and rewrite them as affirmations.

Soul Seed to Take With You

EVERY WORD YOU REPEAT is a path in your brain. Choose words that lead you home.

Chapter Eighteen

Spirituality & Soul

SPIRITUALITY DOES NOT ask you to leave yourself behind — it invites you deeper in. Your soul is not somewhere "out there"; it is the quiet thread that has always been woven through your being. When you pause to listen, you find that home was never lost.

How do you define soul — in your own words?

What spiritual practices help you feel connected to something greater?

What does "coming home to yourself" feel like in your body and spirit?

When was the last time you felt awe — a moment that reminded you of something greater than yourself?

Creative Invitation

DRAW A SPIRAL. AT THE center, write "Soul." Around the spiral, add words, colors, or symbols that bring you closer to your essence.

Soul Seed to Take With You

YOUR SOUL is not lost. It has been waiting for you to remember.

Chapter Nineteen

Grief, Guilt & Grace

GRIEF IS LOVE WITH nowhere to land, and guilt is love turned inward with blame. Grace is the bridge that allows both to soften — giving you permission to keep loving, even as you learn to live without what was lost.

Who or what have you lost that still lives in your heart?

What guilt are you ready to release — even if just a little?

What does grace mean to you right now?

If your grief could speak as love, what would it want you to remember?

Creative Invitation

LIGHTLY SKETCH A CANDLE. Around its flame, write names, memories, or blessings of those you carry in love.

Soul Seed to Take With You

GRIEF IS NOT THE END of love. It is proof that it lived.

Chapter Twenty

Rhythm & Repatterning

PATTERNS ARE NOT PUNISHMENTS; they are pathways your body and spirit have learned to walk. When you choose new rhythms with awareness, you aren't just changing habits — you are teaching your nervous system what safety, joy, and alignment can feel like.

What outdated patterns are ready to be repatterned?

What new rhythms feel nourishing to your soul?

Describe a daily practice you'd like to begin and why it matters to you.

What is one rhythm I can begin today — even for five minutes — to remind myself that I am free to choose?

Creative Invitation

ON ONE SIDE, DRAW A winding path of old habits. On the other, a flowing river of new ones. Notice how you want to cross over.

Soul Seed to Take With You

REPETITION IS NOT PRISON. It is power when chosen with love.

Chapter Twenty-One

Legacy & Light

LEGACY IS NOT JUST what we leave when we are gone; it is what we practice in every interaction, every choice, every moment of courage. Your legacy is being written now, in the way you speak to yourself, in the love you extend to others, and in the light, you refuse to hide.

What legacy are you creating — not in status, but in spirit?

How do you wish to be remembered by those who witness your light?

What does "living with HOPE" look like in your daily life?

Creative Invitation

CREATE A PAGE TITLED My Legacy. Write or draw three ways you want your presence to ripple into others' lives – starting today.

Soul Seed to Take With You

YOUR LIGHT WAS NEVER meant to stay hidden. To live with HOPE is to become a living legacy.

Reflect & Create: An Invitation

HEALING IS NOT ONLY something you read about. It is something you touch, taste, write, move, and breathe into being. That is why these pages are here — not as homework, but as doorways. Each Reflect & Create section offers two invitations: Reflection, through guided Soul Scribbles, where words meet truth on the page. Creation, through playful prompts, where color, doodles, or symbols remind you that healing is not just cognitive, it is embodied.

There is no right way to do this. Some days you may write paragraphs. On other days you may only draw a single word, a shape, or a tear stain. All of it counts. All of it is sacred.

Science affirms what the ancients already knew: journaling, art, and creative expression literally rewire the brain. Neuroscientists call it neuroplasticity — the brain's ability to form new pathways. Each time you put pen to paper, you are training your nervous system to release old imprints and create new ones. Each time you sketch or scribble, you are metabolizing what once stayed stuck as fragmentation and allowing it to flow into integration.

Let these reflections meet you exactly where you are. Let the creative invitations stir something wordless inside you. And let the Soul Seeds anchor what matters most, so you can carry them forward like pocket prayers.

This is not an ending, but a practice — a rhythm of remembering that your life is the canvas, and your soul is the artist.

Moon Intention Practice

THE MOON TEACHES US the beauty of cycles — waxing, waning, never rushing, always returning. Use this practice during the new moon to call in intentions, or during the full moon to release what no longer serves.

Suggested Tools

A CANDLE, YOUR JOURNAL, crystals, and a quiet space.

Light a candle. Let its flame become your signal of presence. Reflect on your current cycle: Are you creating, releasing, pausing, or rising? Write an intention (if calling in) or a release statement (if letting go). Place your hands over the page and say aloud: As the moon changes, so do I. As I shift, I rise.

Optional

PLACE THE PAGE BENEATH your pillow or on an altar for seven days.

Reflections Under the Moon

WHAT AM I CALLING IN? What am I surrendering to the stars?

Mirror Work — Sacred Self-Speak

THE FIRST VOICE YOU hear each day is your own. Let it become a blessing.

Mirror work is not vanity — it is remembrance. It is a way of reprogramming old scripts with words that honor your soul. At first, it may feel uncomfortable. With practice, it becomes a ritual of truth: you are worthy of your own love.

Stand in front of a mirror. Gaze into your eyes. Speak slowly, with breath and belief. Let resistance come if it must — tears, laughter, doubt. All belong. Keep speaking anyway.

Try Saying

I AM SAFE IN MY BODY and strong in my spirit. I trust the wisdom of my soul. I am healing. I am whole. I am HOPE. I forgive myself for believing I had to earn love. I release the stories that no longer serve me. I am enough. Even now. Especially now.

Mirror Practice

WRITE ONE AFFIRMATION of your own. Speak it aloud for seven days.

HOPE in Practice: Release

THERE COMES A TIME when your body knows it cannot hold one more ounce of what has weighed you down. Release is not abandonment — it is reverence. A way of saying: this pain mattered, and now I set it free to become something else.

Light a single candle. Let its flame remind you of the light that never left. Write down what you are ready to release — a name, a memory, a weight, even a single word. Place it in water or burn it safely, watching it dissolve into something larger than you. Wash your hands or bathe your body, whispering I am not what I let go of. I am who I am becoming.

Optional Letter Practice

IF WORDS ARE YOUR MEDICINE, write a Letter of Release. Let your sorrow speak honestly on the page, then let the page go — into fire, water, or earth.

Affirmation

I AM NOT WHAT I LET go of. I am who I am becoming.

Soul Scribble Prompt

WHAT AM I MAKING SPACE for as I release?

HOPE in Practice: Self-Devotion

HEALING IS not only about letting go. It is about returning — again and again — to yourself with tenderness. Stand in front of a mirror and meet your own gaze. See not flaws, but the ancient spark that has carried you through every storm.

With oil or lotion, trace circles of care over your heart, your belly, your feet. Let your hands become prayers of touch. Speak aloud words your soul longs to hear I am worthy. I am whole. I am HOPE.

When you are ready, place your hand over your heart and write a few lines to yourself — a love note, a vow, a devotion. Whisper: I devote myself to my healing, to my becoming, to my joy.

Optional Letter Practice

WRITE A LETTER OF DEVOTION as a vow of reverence to yourself. Place it somewhere you will see on the days you forget.

Affirmation

I DEVOTE MYSELF TO my healing. I am worthy of my own love.

Soul Scribble Prompt

HOW CAN I SHOW UP FOR myself more tenderly in daily life?

HOPE in Practice: Grief & Grace

GRIEF DESERVES A PLACE at the table. Not to consume you, but to be witnessed. To name loss is to honor love, and to honor love is to make space for grace.

Light a candle. Place beside it a flower, a photo, or a keepsake — something that carries the essence of what has been lost. Write a letter, not to the person or thing itself, but to your grief. Speak to it directly: tell it how it feels, what it has taken, what it has taught. Read your words aloud, even if your voice trembles. Let tears come, if they need to. They are not weakness — they are holy water.

When you are ready, close by whispering: Even in sorrow, there is sacred space for grace.

Optional Letter Practice

WRITE A LETTER OF GRIEF & Grace. Let sorrow speak — but let grace have the final word.

Affirmation

EVEN IN SORROW, THERE is sacred space for grace.

Soul Scribble Prompt

WHAT HAS THIS GRIEF taught me about love? How can I carry grace alongside my sorrow, rather than against it?

HOPE in Practice: Intention Reset

THERE WILL BE SEASONS when you feel scattered, when the noise of life pulls you from your center. This space is your return. A pause to listen. A moment to realign.

Begin by noticing your energy as it is right now. Heavy or light, restless or calm — let it name itself without judgment. This is your starting point.

Then, gently ask yourself: What am I ready to release? Perhaps it is a story that has outlived its season, a habit that no longer serves, a weight that has hidden your joy. Write it here. Let it go.

Next, turn your heart toward receiving. What is waiting for you on the horizon? A softening? A spark? A new rhythm? Call it in with words, sketches, or symbols that remind you of its shape.

Now set an intention, not as a demand but as an offering. Something simple, soul-honoring, and true. It might be to live with more presence, to honor your body's pace, or to trust the unfolding. Let this intention become your compass for the days ahead.

And finally, leave yourself a reminder — a phrase, an affirmation, a truth that will steady you when doubt or fatigue tries to lead.

Optional Letter Practice

WRITE A LETTER OF INTENTION. Speak your future in the present tense — as though it is already alive within you. Keep it under your pillow, at your altar, or in your journal.

Affirmation

AS I SHIFT, I RISE. As I rise, I remember.

Soul Scribble Prompt

WHAT AM I READY TO release? What am I willing to receive?

Closing Reflection

Living in Resonance

Every swap you make is not just about sustainability — it's about resonance. These choices whisper to your nervous system: you are safe, you are sacred, you belong to something beautiful.

This is not about running out and replacing everything at once. That would only feed urgency, not healing. Instead, let it be a rhythm — a gentle unfolding. As you buy something new, choose differently. As you release what no longer serves, welcome what does. One item. One shift. One breath at a time.

Over weeks and years, these small, steady choices begin to transform your environment into a sanctuary. Your home becomes lighter. Your body feels clearer. Your spirit rests easier. And in these exchanges — plastic for glass, synthetic for natural, clutter for clarity — you begin to rewrite the frequency of your life.

Remember, this is not about perfection. It's about presence. It's about tuning your surroundings to support the healing already happening inside you. Each conscious choice becomes an act of HOPE — Harnessing Optimal Positive Energy — lived out in the tangible world. So, pause. Notice. Swap gently. Let each step remind you: you are not just creating a healthier space... you are creating a sanctuary for your soul.

Closing affirmation

I have carried my words as seeds, and now they are ready to bloom. I trust the timing, the flow, and the light that guides them. I am both the vessel and the legacy. I am enough, even in rest.

"Sometimes all we have left is HOPE" – Sharon Lea

Wild Soul HOPE, LLC

The HOPE Method - Harness Optimal Positive Energy

SoulHOPE

APP + Book + Community

When the Soul Remembers HOPE, Healing Begins.

HOPE & Honey

Empath-Aligned Product Line

Softness in Strength

www.ingramcontent.com/pod-product-compliance
Lightning Source LLC
Chambersburg PA
CBHW071310150426
43191CB00007B/565